SEX AND THE SPIRIT

SEX AND THE SPIRIT

THE ROMANCE OF HEAVEN AND EARTH

VERLEE A. COPELAND AND

DALE B. ROSENBERGER

The Pilgrim Press

Cleveland

I dedicate this volume to my beloved wife, my inspiration, Cecile.

Arise, my love, my fair one,
    and come away.
Let me see your face, let me hear your voice;
    for your voice is sweet,
    and your face is lovely. (Song of Solomon 2:13–14)

—Dale Rosenberger

With gratitude for the faith and generosity of my devoted husband, Ellis.

This is my beloved
    and this is my friend. (Song of Solomon 5:16b)

Set me as a seal upon your heart,
    as a seal upon your arm;
for love is strong as death,
    passion fierce as the grave. (Song of Solomon 8:6)

—Verlee Copeland

The Pilgrim Press, 700 Prospect Avenue, Cleveland, Ohio 44115
thepilgrimpress.com
© 2014 by Verlee A. Copeland and Dale B. Rosenberger

Printed in the United States of America on acid-free paper

17   16   15   14   13   5   4   3   2   1

ISBN: 978-0-8298-1957-1

CONTENTS

CONTENTS

Introduction

We invite you to join us for a frank and refreshing conversation about the relationship between faith and sexuality. People of faith seem to have a great deal of difficulty talking about sex. Perhaps our reluctance stems from the storm of criticism we face from all sides as soon as we hazard a conversation of any honesty or significance. Maybe we feel ill-equipped to speak at once from places transcendent and earthy, thinking they inherently clash, even though our holy scriptures do not. Perhaps we're reluctant to discuss our sexuality because over the centuries we have imposed upon ourselves a painful chasm between our spiritual and physical natures. We consequently segregate them, enforcing false boundaries that we don't really understand. Or could it be that we are simply poorly prepared and unrehearsed for an exchange about such intimate and personal matters? Most of us don't really know where to begin.

Whatever the reason, Christians can no longer afford to remain silent about sex. For today expanding technologies put sex "out there" in ways that alter our understanding of what we once called romance and courtship. The world reduces sex to a video game with special effects to be played with manic intensity. Devoid of soul, such thin and flat renderings of human sexuality reduce us from creatures fearfully, wonderfully, and mysteriously made to mechanical cogs in the transmission of pleasure. Treating the orgasm as our one shot at self-transcendence, sex gets transacted in ways as rote as they are shallow. Despair is the upshot. People become deadened to sex, to self, and to God. As long as Christians remain silent about God's alternatives, rooted in our divine origins and destiny, how can we find our way to passionate and faithful sexuality?

In *Sex and the Spirit* we intend to explore how to claim and affirm sexual intimacy in our increasingly isolated and alienated culture, addled by technology and unwilling to look each other in the eye. We aim to lift up passion—human and divine—to bridge this painful chasm persisting between our spiritual and sensual selves. Among others, theologian Soren Kierkegaard described faith as life's highest passion—our passion for God—placing our desire for a relationship with God above all other passions. We try to contain our passion for God, reducing faith to a set of rules, facts, doctrine or activism. We similarly reduce our momentous and transforming passion whenever we settle for sex merely as release, amusement, marketing or entertainment. God promises us so much more.

Sex and the Spirit is written for those who seek a sense of deeper sexuality than society's prevailing affirmation of sex as entertainment. This work is also written for those who glimpse the potential of sexuality to express life's mystery and complexity, and for those who feel there must be a better way than our current course even if no one is talking about it. We believe their number is legion, maybe even a silent majority, rooting for conversations like this one from the anonymity of the sidelines.

We approach faith and sexuality from the perspective of unifying God's passion for us with our passion for each other as women and men. We hope you will find this work an effective bridge to advance this conversation and to alleviate the sexual estrangement we so often experience with one another. We also be-

lieve the sexual union of hearts and minds, souls and spirits has
been sadly underrepresented over against the physical merging of
bodies in telling the story of our sexuality. So this discussion hopes
to help reconcile our spiritual and physical nature from a distinc-
tively Christian perspective.

Currently, as sex talk blares from radios and blazes across the
Internet, the conversation is remarkably shallow, driven by tech-
nical advice on how to have sex. In this spiritually barren landscape, people jump from casual hellos over cappuccino right into
bed. Instant gratification displaces the slow ritual of dating practiced by previous generations. Hooking up, "friends with benefits," and online encounters replace authentic spiritual friendship,
the context for healthy sexual intimacy.

The world prattles endlessly about sex, but contributes little to
authentic intimacy. At the same time, the church talks little about
sex, apart from our continuous elusive quests after ethical consensus
and our politically charged exchanges around same-sex relations.
Clearly the church has made significant strides with these important
sexual issues. Yet vital support for the sexuality of heterosexual men
and women remains elusive. We neglect one of the most essential of
human experiences and one of the sweetest of God's good gifts. As
things stand, many couples feel invisible and need help with issues
of personal and shared intimacy, but feel too awkward to ask directly for it.

What if we were to affirm our sexuality as spiritual beings without ponderous ethics and divisive politics always having the first and
last word? Having said that, we do affirm an implicit commitment
to Christian ethics throughout our work. We assume certain underlying ethical commitments such as just relationships between persons
as equal participants in God's gifts that uphold mutuality, love and
justice as witness to God's intention for human life on earth as in
heaven. We refer the reader to other fine works for a more fulsome
discussion on Christian sexual ethics, which is beyond the scope of
this conversation.

Here we invite the reader to suspend judgment or preconceived opinions about what the church teaches and what we may think the Bible has to say about sex. What if we were to linger over the mystery of our femaleness and maleness to appreciate its tender power in its own right rather than driven by outside agendas? What if Christians had the nerve to freely explore sexuality within the church on the church's own God-given terms just as Song of Solomon unabashedly describes and celebrates it within the canon of Scripture?

We lift up the Song of Solomon from the Old Testament as the touchstone for this essential conversation on sex and the spirit. Many Christians will discover Song of Solomon, also called Song of Songs, through this work for the first time. You're not alone if you are unfamiliar with it, nestled as it is near the center of our Bible.

You may wonder what to expect from these reflections that celebrate Song of Solomon sexuality. You can count on having a conversation cast more in the indicative than the imperative mood. That means our reflections will be more expressive and imaginative than commanding of how you should think and behave. We encourage you to engage this surprising conversation that begins with affirming sex as God's gift but not unaware of its power, both creative and destructive; a conversation unafraid of the connecting of bodies but unwilling to forget the union of souls; and a conversation marked by the pulls and tugs of real everyday attraction. This will be a conversation where the erotic is treasured rather than hidden and obscured; where we candidly enjoy how God has made and declared our sexuality good; where our desire leads us to discover our most intimate selves and points us beyond ourselves to our yearning for God. This alternative, countercultural approach to sex recalls a hymn written by Thomas Troeger:

> Holy and good is the gift of desire.
> God made our bodies for passion and fire.

Intending that love would draw from the flame.
Lives that would shine with God's image and name.[1]

In *Sex and the Spirit,* we initiate the conversation of what it looks like to live fully sexual and authentically Christian lives. We affirm that wholesome and passionate sexuality is God's gift to us. God created us such that our spirituality and sensuality naturally connect. What God has joined together, we have sadly torn asunder, and this brokenness is writ large against the backdrop of our living.

While having sex is easy, sustaining sexual intimacy in the context of a faithful relationship is difficult. The mystical union of body and soul requires a courageous and vulnerable conversation. We think the Church can do more to support and sustain intimate and fully sexual relationships that are faithful to God.

Our faith teaches us that we humans are created for deep and abiding relationships with one another and with God. Some geneticists claim we are hardwired for God. We yearn for meaningful relationships, for enduring connections. In like manner, we long for intimacy with God, to know more fully who we are and to whom we belong. We long for full expression of healthy sexuality at the core of our being, yet this hope is too often ignored in our Christian formation.

As pastors dedicated to parish ministry, living and serving in the trenches with our people's struggles and joys, we know the grass roots where they live. And yet as female and male, our perspectives also differ. With fifty years of experience between us as pastors, we have heard the cry from the heart of our people around issues of intimacy in private counseling settings. Yet we observe the reluctance to discuss such matters when we widen the

---

1. Thomas Troeger, "Holy and Good Is the Gift of Desire," 1988, 1991 © Oxford University Press, found in *Chalice Hymnal,* ed. Daniel B. Merrick and David P. Polk (St. Louis: Chalice Press, 1995), # 509.

conversation. For example, one of us offered a class on sexuality on a Sunday morning and only one person attended, a woman in her late seventies. When the usual crowd of adult Sunday School participants were asked why they didn't attend, one woman bravely admitted, "We wanted to come but we were afraid you would ask us to share what we think and we wouldn't know what to say!" Clearly we care about sexual intimacy and its connection to faith and we long to engage a wider audience in this urgent discussion. Where do we begin?

An excellent way for parents to engage delicate issues of sexuality within families is to leave out well-written books for the next generation to find, and then see what happens by way of question and answer. This simply works. Without wanting to patronize or matronize, we believe *Sex and the Spirit* could be such a book strategically "left out there" for adults to discover and subsequently discuss.

Our format for writing is simple. We take turns responding to real-life, candid questions from the heart in a simple, direct, heartfelt, and accessible question-and-answer format. At the conclusion of each chapter, the other of us writes a brief response to the work, much as you would.

According to these designs, we hope the book is at once impassioned and insightful, erotic and funny, faithful and personal, provoking ourselves and the reader to consider ourselves as sexual beings within what our Christian faith and theology teach about what it means to be human. We believe that an open, frank, and forthright conversation along these lines might even persuade some to consider returning to the Church, having dismissed it as out of touch with real life.

Of course, we two authors can only write from what we know. In this work, there are issues we simply do not address. For example, we don't write about same-sex or transgendered relations, though such explorations and conversations need to take place within the church. Much pain and misunderstanding continues in the church and we welcome this continuing discussion in other works. However, we choose not to address these issues because as heterosexual pastors, we do not want to speak for an experience that is not our own. We feel others are better equipped to support the questions and concerns of our same-sex brothers and sisters in Christ. We therefore look forward to an equivalent book written from other perspectives, but believe that we are not the best ones to write it.

Finally, we invite the reader to continue these conversations beyond this book on the *Sex and the Spirit* web site, blog, and at upcoming retreats. Warm up the teapot or pour yourself a cup of coffee. Find a quiet corner of your harried life to read. If one question doesn't quite fit your interest, keep reading. We hope you will then find the courage to discuss these questions in book groups or at the gym. And so it begins!

Verlee A. Copeland
Dale B. Rosenberger

Acknowledgement

While we have pondered writing this book in the abstract since the mid-90s, the firm plans for it set up during a Lilly Endowment–supported pastoral sabbatical to Isla de Margarita, thirty miles off the Venezuela coast, in 2009. As we gathered and met with other pastor-authors—all of whom were flown to this island courtesy of the Lilly Endowment—they charged us to fill this yawning void in the literature and consciousness of the mainline church. A seed was sown that now comes to fruition.

Full credit and thanks are due to the Lilly Endowment for creating room within the harried lives of local church pastors for projects such as this one. We are deeply indebted and this book would never have gotten past the dream stage and been completed without the generous support of the Lilly Endowment.

· I ·

THE BIBLICAL INVITATION TO WARM AND LIVELY SEXUAL PASSION

Dale Rosenberger

As religious writers treat sexuality, they refer a lot to Song of Solomon in the Old Testament. I looked it over. Wow—much more delight than naysaying! I can get with this religion. Tell me, how can I become a Song of Solomon-type Christian?

· · ·

I could gush over how magically different Song of Solomon is among the books of the Bible, but let me cite "purple passages" and then comment to allow the Song of Songs to speak for itself in addressing your query. It opens like this:

> Let him kiss me with the kisses of his mouth!
> For your love is better than wine,
> your anointing oils are fragrant,
> your name is perfume poured out;
> therefore the maidens love you.
> Draw me after you, let us make haste.
> The king has brought me into his chambers.

We will exult and rejoice in you;
we will extol your love more than wine;
rightly do they love you.
(Song of Solomon 1:2–4)

The woman who composed Song of Solomon approached her erotic poetry like Cecil B. DeMille did his film-making. "I like to start with an earthquake," he said, "and then build up to a climax." From the get-go we note she is unafraid. She is feisty. She is unashamed of fierce passion. Rather than apologize for it, she ramps it up toward culmination, then tamps it down to cool things off and collect it anew, before beginning to build slowly again in an upward arc. It is exquisite and undulating desire. We can compare Song of Solomon's structure to an Indian tantric master teaching the novice to build slowly toward the peak and then delay, to repeat that pattern several times before finally giving oneself over to satiation.

The purpose is not to idly toy with oneself or the beloved. The purpose is to cultivate deep yearning as we actually become trained in desire. Maybe that, and not its eroticism, is the biggest surprise of Song of Solomon to moderns like us: that our desire needs training. If it is true of sexuality, imagine: it could also be true of our consumerism, our sense of community, even of homeland security. Think of the many, wider possibilities for transformation embedded in the simple idea of retraining our desire. Because most of us naturally experience desire, we trust that we already understand it, know what it is about, and have mastery over it. We imagine ourselves experts in owning and sharing what and how we want in the courtly dances of love and elsewhere, as human desires come into play.

Song of Solomon, like erotic traditions in Tao and Hindu faiths, says otherwise. Less about governing our sexuality, more about freeing up our God-fashioned sexuality, it says, "Think again, life is full of surprises. There is a deep end in this swimming pool you haven't discovered yet!" It doesn't blink initiating us into the steamy, earthy attractions of man and woman. Yet it freshens and renews this energy without the tarnish of tawdriness, as though for the first time. So Song of Solomon potently combines first-time innocence and unabashed sensuality. Compare that with a more modern reference point, say, the likes of Marilyn Monroe's naive cooing in one scene, and then sultry purring in the next.

Imagine: desire is more than what we make of it left to our own devices. Yearning goes deeper than we expected as we first dipped in our toe. Nestled between the serious likes of Ecclesiastes and Isaiah, Song of Solomon claims that if we can sort out basic desire—like craving one another as woman and man—maybe we can climb other grand stairways of desire, the desire to learn and grow in wisdom, the desire to be just and concerned in discernment. If our wants can be shaped, maybe we can be wise and discerning, truthful and compassionate.

Deep faithfulness, like the sensuality in Song of Solomon, isn't about instant gratification. It is more about disciplining ourselves to wait with patience, to be found ready as the other arrives, whether that "other" is our beloved partner, or our beloved God. If we cannot recognize the shape and the dynamics of the most basic desire and primal yearning at our core, neither can we expect to become deeply aware and expressively grateful in life's other lofty arenas, like faith itself. Jesus said that he who is found faithful in little will also be found faithful in much.

In other words, if we can learn to love each other with all of our heart and soul, mind and strength, spirit and body, maybe we can also love God that way as well. So maybe including a book in the Bible that doesn't once mention God, but extols a woman in command of and enjoying her sensuality is not as deeply subversive as it might seem at first blush. By the way, my thinking here has been deeply shaped by Carey Ellen Walsh's splendid book, *Exquisite Desire: Religion, the Erotic, and the Song of Songs.* It is thoughtful,

SEX AND THE SPIRIT

poetic, insightful, provocative, and faithful to God, ever true to the spirit of Song of Solomon itself.

> Upon my bed at night
> I sought him whom my soul loves;
> I sought him, but found him not;
> I called him, but he gave no answer.
> "I will rise now and go about the city,
> in the streets and in the squares;
> I will seek him whom my soul loves."
> I sought him, but found him not.
> The sentinels found me,
> as they went about in the city.
> "Have you seen him whom my soul loves?"
> Scarcely had I passed them,
> when I found him whom my soul loves.
> I held him, and would not let him go
> until I brought him into my mother's house,
> and into the chamber of her that conceived me.
> I adjure you, O daughters of Jerusalem,
> by the gazelles or the wild does:
> do not stir up or awaken love
> until it is ready!
> (Song of Solomon 3:1–5)

That Song of Solomon made it into the Bible at all shocks us. But the more we ponder, the more we realize: it had to be in there. To grasp how Song of Solomon belongs, go to a concert of the soulful Al Green. Yes, Al Green. The winsome Mr. Green appears on stage with a joyous strut, shirt opened to his belt in a sequined black jacket. His band swings around him as his singing plaintively evokes a search for "Love and Happiness" amid troubles. A man of God is in the house. He is testifying. As he builds, he feverishly implores, "Can we go to church? Can we go to church?! Can we go to church?!!" Women from their twenties to their sixties stand, cheer, and uninhibitedly shake their bottoms. No contradiction. It makes perfect sense. Everybody is on board as this train is leaving the station.

After the intermission the Rev. Mr. Green appears in suit and tie as on Sunday morning preaching his sermon, leading worship at church. He dances with the smooth, fine, and easy grace of a matador in the arena. But there are also sparks as he tips the microphone sideways like Fred Astaire dipping Ginger Rogers on the dance floor to woo her. Women stand, shout approval and sway rhythmically. Nothing is inconsistent here. Nary a contradiction. It all makes perfect sense.

Song of Solomon similarly busts categories. It is aesthetically imaginative and thoughtful, developing original and lyrical metaphors of field and garden. But it is also deeply affecting, even arousing, scaling peaks and descending valleys of desire. It is public as the voice of the woman confides and confesses her desire, and as her stream of consciousness seems to unfold just outside of her garden window. But it is private because finally only the rhapsodic couple can fully understand the primal forces love unleashes, with which they must contend.

It is brazenly sexual, descriptively and explicitly reaching the brink of bodily orgasm more than once. But it is also chaste because the man remains at a distance, we are in the realm of visionary fantasy. And no matter how many times desire resumes after ebbing, climax never occurs. It is appropriate because this love poetry tells the rest of the whole truth of who we are as women and men. And Jesus said, when the truth is lifted up, it will draw all persons unto itself. But Song of Solomon is also bawdy because somebody somewhere told us we should never talk about such things, especially in church. So the Song also has a forbidden quality.

Actually, the author of Song of Solomon herself is a category-buster. Just picture all that she puts into play: she is fearlessly audacious and boldly erotic, yet not sleazy. No woman loving a man as much as she adores her beloved could be accused of sordidness, no matter to what reaches of bodily ecstasy she is transported. She is also a category-buster because—imagine this—millennia ago, this ancient woman modeled what women today effectively still want: the freedom to relentlessly search the truth of her yearning without being labeled and discarded as unwholesome, to live authentically as she fully extends herself by not giving up on her heart's desire, not settling for anything less than life's best and highest possibility, for which she deeply aches. Without asking anyone's permission, she confidently launches this exploration. Yet she is humbled, even reduced to trembling non-existence by the magnitude of the love the two share.

What does it mean to be a Song of Solomon Christian, you ask? Perhaps it is the willingness to allow the raptures of love to surprise flat expectation and defy facile categories. Perhaps it is the adeptness to see all around us in the poetry of God's good creation—irises and oaks, stamens and cedars, valleys and streams—the footloose power and exuberant imagery as God's gift of love pulses. Perhaps it is the unwillingness to apologize for or shrink back from how God has made us, male and female, to live that out as a joyous good gift from God, and to stand as an example of that for people to look toward across many generations.

Emboldened by this poetry, maybe we can more prophetically address both the irresponsibly promiscuous from without and self-appointed decency brigades from within the church to find a golden mean of holy sexuality that Song of Solomon imparts. Yes, if we only had faithful ears to hear it. After all, as Walter Brueggeman teaches, in the final analysis even the fiercest prophets were really only poets at heart. And true prophecy is impossible without the heart of a poet.

Back in high school, I spent a day at the Detroit Zoo with a girlfriend I was crazy about. It was a hot summer dog day of August. So we sat and rested on a grassy green knoll in the shade of a large tree. We held hands and smiled. The foreman of a zoo maintenance crew came by, leading his work detail. "Hey you," he shouted. "Cut that out. We don't go for that here. This is a family place." At first, I was certain he was addressing another. I couldn't believe he meant us. I mean, we were holding hands. As I unwittingly ignored his enforcements, he grew more strident, accusing us of corrupting the young children. I was livid. I protested so vigorously, we almost got booted, but my girlfriend calmed me.

Innocent love corrupts children? I thought. Wow, the world is in a lot worse trouble than I thought. What is it like to be that man's poor wife? I wondered. I quietly simmered all day. Finally, I recalled going with church youth and that same girlfriend to see Clint Eastwood's *Dirty Harry* at the drive-in just weeks before. Harry Callahan had the crowd counting, and even gleefully chanting, as "deserving victims" got shot: 36, 37, 38. No maintenance man, no local authority stood up to how obscene, how destructive of worth, how violating of families and youth, that unfolding carnage was. What can we say to a world for whom killing others is such acceptable amusement, but innocently loving another is obscene?

I understand that our culture idolizes romantic love to the sad point of worshiping lust. I understand that colors how some view the barest expression of love, romance, and affection. I understand that for us Christians, the romance between heaven and earth must come before any teen romancing some girl at the zoo. But can't we make some distinctions here? Song of Solomon helps us.

No less than prophecy is needed to project God's holy alternative in such a world, because no shallow free spirit can convey such a message. Song of Solomon isn't the thin iconoclasm of Cher, Madonna or Lady Gaga. It's more like Miriam's prophetic exultation song upon deliverance from bondage, escaping through a miraculously divided sea to dwell in a new place. (Exodus 15:20–21) A life-altering vulnerability is at play here. Both Miriam and Song of Solomon glorify God as they also radiate the confidence of never going back again. Carrie Ellen Walsh eloquently captures this soulful fearlessness:

> For the Song of Songs, the woman's soul is wholly invested in her lover. Such wholesale commitment, in which one's love defines one's existence, entails considerable psychological risk. There is a risk of loss of self in love at two junctures at least: once in love, in the loosening and melding of boundaries between two people, and once in lust, as desire rips the person beyond his or her own self. Orgasm is only the most visible form of this threat. It is something we both want and fear, the self's dissolution, if only for a moment. It is at once terrifying and exhilarating.[1]

Funny, isn't it, how we are never more splendid or more dangerous than when we are in love? Love is the movement from "I" to "we" that feels like going hard off the high board deep into a pool of Jello. To be that in love with someone is to forget oneself —never a bad thing for us self-absorbed human beings—and become consumed with another: always wanting to be together, losing sleep and resorting to poetry. Surely this is something like what Jesus had in mind quoting Genesis, "the two shall become one flesh." Surely this was what God had in mind at the dawn of creation when, after putting man within paradise, God still sensed something was incomplete, declaring that he simply must make a partner for him.

Our sexuality reminds us that loving each other is the most intimate and gracious thing we could ever do for one another. To expose ourselves to the gaze of another; to risk being seen by that person in all of our spiritual and physical nakedness; to trust in

---

1. Carey Ellen Walsh, *Exquisite Desire: Religion, the Erotic, and the Song of Songs* (Fortress Press: Minneapolis, 2000), 38.

our acceptability before that gaze where rejection is always a risk; to let our life become so caught up in the life of another that we don't know where we begin and the other ends—let's face it, if we pay attention, beneath the surface of our pleasure, all of this swells up into self-transcendence.

If the pleasurable paroxysms of erotic love are not exactly Jesus' self-emptying serving love, maybe they are also not so far off as we have been told. Maybe they are even related. While the Bible uses a few different words for our one English word "love"—this one being Eros, our cognate for the word erotic—in truth love is finally like the sixteen Eskimo words for snow we all learned about in Anthropology 101. In the final analysis, snow or love, it is eventually still one thing.

> I am my beloved's,
> and his desire is for me.
> Come, my beloved,
> let us go forth into the fields,
> and lodge in the villages;
> let us go out early to the vineyards,
> and see whether the vines have budded,
> whether the grape blossoms have opened
> and the pomegranates are in bloom.
> There I will give you my love.
> The mandrakes give forth fragrance,
> and over our doors are all choice fruits,
> new as well as old,
> which I have laid up for you, O my beloved.
> (Song of Solomon 7:10–13)

What does it mean to be a Song of Solomon Christian? All in all, it exclaims, isn't it grand our faith not only allows for, but even extols, this romantic and sensual part of being alive? And this earth-bound side of ourselves fully connects with the heaven-bound part that is our spirit, our soul. Actually, it would be painful and

SEX AND THE SPIRIT

confusing if this blessing were not forthcoming, since God has formed us with such sturdy desire for one another. Of course, the news of this blessing has not reached many quarters within church and society. Maybe being a Song of Solomon Christian means bringing good news of this spiritual-body blessing even in the face of the promiscuous, who give sensuality a bad name, and also the prudish decency brigades, who condemn our nature as unholy and unwholesome?

What does it mean to be a Song of Solomon Christian? I like the ring of that question. I like it because, if you have been in a church where community is honored and not squelched into uniformity, you know the sound of many voices. For the gathering of God's people is a chorus of differently gifted people, hitting varying notes and harmonies. Some fret that the gutters must work properly, others feed and hold close starving children, a few mystically connect to God through quiet prayer, still others deeply ponder and write about what Jesus' death means to us. The irreplaceable richness of this "multi-vocality" among God's people is why being alone unto ourselves as Christians is no substitute for being in community.

Thanks be to God, we also experience the richness of many voices in the Bible. In Genesis voices evoke the "who" and "why" mysteries of God's creation and purpose. In Exodus we hear God takes sides in choices amid oppression. In Job we learn that truth in suffering is better than happy lies that defend God. In Romans we learn obedience is grace, love is grace, judgment is grace, but grace is no easy substitute for skipping obedience. In Revelation we hear saint and martyr voices lift us as the world hates us for loving Jesus more than the world.

Whether we speak of the church today or of ancient canons of Scripture, all of this means that no one powerful point of view runs roughshod over the rest; that nothing of essential spiritual importance is left out; that there is something for everyone. Of course, in our hearing each other or in our reading, we tend to gravitate to the voices like ours. But the church and the faith are what they are because the full variety of our humanity gets reflected within these conversations.

The daring little text Song of Solomon makes room for people and parts of our humanity that many dismiss as incompatible with God's holiness. God has more room in his heart for the full-bodied passions of our hearts as men and women than we ever suspected. That this voice was not omitted from the ancient conversation of Scripture and from our conversations today means the world to us. Living so acceptably before God, we might also live as acceptable to one another. We might come to rest easy and strong in our assuredness. Such comfort and confidence within our own skin are what being a Song of Solomon Christian is. Maybe also it is to insist that we settle for nothing less than being so fully human. This is what the ancient fathers meant in the first place by including Song of Solomon within the biblical canon. With Christ's coming, both the divinity of heaven is made more human, and the humanity of earth is made more divine.

Carey Ellen Walsh writes, "This Song is worth the effort. It probes the limits of both language and the body; the assertion of identity, in a self-ownership that redeems desire from stalking—yearning having taken a hostage; and the terrible, delicious ache of waiting, the ecstasy and the danger."[2]

> Set me as a seal upon your heart,
> as a seal upon your arm;
> for love is strong as death,
> passion fierce as the grave.
> Its flashes are flashes of fire,
> a raging flame.
> Many waters cannot quench love,

2. Ibid., 9.

neither can floods drown it.
If one offered for love
all the wealth of one's house,
it would be utterly scorned.
(Song of Solomon 8:6–7)

. . .

CHAPTER 1 FEMALE COUNTERPOINT

VERLEE A. COPELAND

I hope that our readers have dusted off that Bible they received twenty-five years ago at Confirmation and finally opened the thing. It will no doubt be shocking to many that our God is a sexy God and our Bible is a sexy Bible. Every earthy, sensual and sexual experience known to humankind graces its pages. In the Holy Scriptures claimed by Christians, sexuality is exalted, misappropriated, abused, denied, bought and sold, and manipulated for personal or national gain. We find it easy to believe the worst of it: that sexiness and messiness are synonymous. Sexy women have long been seen as threatening and dangerous, leading to a lingering mistrust of women in every arena of contemporary culture.

That is why the Song of Solomon is so important to our understanding of God and sexuality. Here there is no judgment in the passionate expression of exquisite desire between a man and a woman profoundly in love. Like Romeo and Juliet, lovesick on a moonlit night, the unnamed couple in Song of Solomon barely contains their ardor. Unlike Shakespeare's tragedy, the Bible refuses the recurring cultural theme that passion this intense will get you killed.

Though you have not said so, a Song of Solomon Christian does not have to live a compartmentalized life, with all things religious on one hand, and all things sensual on the other. At best, this creates an uneasy company in one body. Rather, consider that a Creator God made us of the right stuff, both sex and the spirit.

In the pages that follow, there may be much that delights, surprises, dismays and provokes us. We carry within us the cultural myths of family history and religious folklore, married to bad psychology and the uneasy superstition that we're going to hell for the things we really think and feel about sex, not to mention how we actually behave. We invite one another to suspend our judgments, of ourselves, of one another, in the work that is to come. Imagine for a moment that your sexuality is a buried treasure that you falsely believe belongs to another but not to you. Here we consider that this precious and priceless gift is your birthright. Our powerful, passionate bodies make pies and make love, create community gardens and cuddle children. We fervently hope that this work to come will open windows locked and frozen, that the fresh breath of God's Holy Spirit may blow through all flesh, tender and hope-filled for what joy there may yet be.

· 2 ·

ECSTACY AND THE EROTIC
AS SACRED EXPERIENCE

Verlee A. Copeland

When I grew up, my mother was clear that sex was meant for marriage. I always knew what she wanted for me. As I matured in my sexuality, I sometimes wanted something different. Now I wonder, what does God want?

· · ·

What I'm going to say about sex may surprise you. The God we worship is a very sexy God who deeply desires us. God created us such that our ultimate desire is for God, without which we can never be satisfied. God wants us to live this side of heaven with joy. God made for us a new heaven, a new earth and a new Eden, that place where we can love passionately and wholly in the flesh with the fire created in us from the beginning.

When you think of sexuality, what is it that you imagine God wants for you? First, our sexuality gives us hints of heaven with God. There is a story told about St. Francis of Assisi, that he one day asked God if he could hear the music of heaven. God told Francis that he did not know what he was asking, for just as we humans see in a glass darkly this side of heaven, neither can we hear the music of heaven and survive the power of it.

Through our sexuality, God gives us hints of divinity, glimpses of glory, a single perfect note to stir our hearts to heaven. That melody of heaven, according to the theology of the body by the late Pope John Paul II, has to be translated into music we mortals can understand. That music is the power of human sexuality, made known to us through the erotic poetry of the Song of Songs in the Bible.

How remarkable that the early church leaders, thought to be so tired, chose to include such a sexy book in the Bible. Reading it for the first time, we may gasp, or at least blush. This love song between a man and a woman speaks of being drunk with love, giving oneself over to sexual ecstasy. While never fully consummated, the courtship of the early chapters becomes sexually explicit toward the center of the poem. We stand in the background listening to the knock of the beloved upon the door in the night. She rises to greet him, coyly remarking that she has already removed her garment and inquiring how she can put it on again?

We listen, as she opens the door of her chamber to him. "My beloved thrust his hand into the opening, and my inmost being yearned for him. I arose to open to my beloved, and my hands dripped with myrrh, my fingers with liquid myrrh, upon the handles of the bolt." Her lover is elusive, she opens to him, and he is gone. Here the dance between a man and a women hint at physical, sexual fulfillment to come, while pointing toward the deepest union between God and humankind.

We have only to recall that holy moment in our own life when heaven and earth moved, to begin to understand what it might be like to become as a lover to God, open, expressive, mutual, vulnerable. When we are lovers, our desire is to please our lover and the desire of our lover is to please us.

This understanding makes possible the adoration of a priest for God, the marriage of a nun in love with God, the celibate devotion of a monk. It also speaks to why our shallow infatuations prove to be false gods. While many came of age worshipping the Gospel of Hugh Hefner, there comes a point for most when the slick pages of a magazine pale beside the real live flesh of a human man or woman, and in turn, the divine power of our real-time God.

Sexuality is God's good gift that hints at heaven and draws us deeply into unity with God. Sexuality is also God's good gift to deepen and express our intimacy with one another as human creatures in the flesh. How then can our sexy, sensual selves be other than a good thing, a God thing? God created male and female and all creation and called it good. All of our flesh is good, created in God's own image: the deepest desires of our hearts, the aching of our breasts and genitals swelling in longing and holy delight.

Our God is indeed a sexy God, who loved us into being and made us just this way. We spend a great deal of energy trying to put our sexuality back into a box, or hide it, exploit it, abuse it, or use it to sell goods and services that leave us empty. Surely, God wants something different for us than this? How would our life be changed if we really believed that God wants us to enjoy how fabulous it feels to be passionately, sexually, wholly alive?

When we look more deeply into the history of monotheistic religions, those who worship one God, we discover that this teaching is consistent. For example, if you want to read something really sexy, skip the porn magazine and dust off that Bible your grandmother gave you when you were a kid. There, right in the middle of the Hebrew Scriptures (the Old Testament) is a deeply sexy book about erotic desire between two lovers. The Song of Songs, also called the Song of Solomon in the Bible, is considered a metaphor for the union of Christ and the church. For our Jewish forebears, it also served as an allegory for God's love for Israel. It is written in the genre of Egyptian love songs that express the marriage between human creatures and God. Yet the Song of Solomon also is what it is; sometimes a cigar is just a cigar. Song of Solomon is also about the erotic desire of two adolescents for one another before their engagement or marriage.

Imagine that you have gathered at the home of friends for an engagement party. The best gourmet foods are spread at a beautifully appointed table. Friends have been drinking and toasting with glasses of fine wine. A chorus of singers snakes their way through the guests and a lone female voice begins singing the erotic poetry of Song of Songs. "Let him kiss me with the kisses of his mouth!" She continues, "For your lovemaking is better than wine, in fragrance, your oils are exquisite, your reputation is poured out oil, that's why the women love you."

The writer explicitly describes in intimate details the sight, smell, taste of the beloved. They both drip with love such that we are tempted to turn away embarrassed, as if we are a bit voyeuristic, reading their love notes, listening in on the telephone, looking over their shoulders at e-mail intended for their eyes alone. How remarkable it is that such explicit sexuality is lifted up in the Song of Solomon, contrary to the more rigid conventions of its time. Here we glimpse desire that is mutual, passionate and untamed.

We are drawn to the edge of consummation again and again, teased in the singing. Then the song draws back, indicating that the completion of their union, while imminent, remains in the future. The Song of Solomon takes us to the edge of longing and leaves us there. This Song of Heaven expresses the deepest desires of the human body and the human heart, celebrating its intensity and affirming it's good.

We know what this erotic dance is like. We too have attended a wedding reception where everyone is ecstatic, perhaps under the influence of celebratory wine. The toasts begin blandly enough with expressions of gratitude, then turn a bit racy as they move toward speculation about the pleasures of the wedding bed.

The sexual tension heightens. Everyone at the wedding smells good. Conversation is lively. People laugh easily and have a great time. Sensually clad women, elegant gowns revealing their sleek feminine lines, lean closely towards glistening men who loosen their ties. They gyrate alluringly on the dance floor, often to horrible music, but no matter. As a pastor of over twenty years, I can tell you that no few marriages culminate as a consequence of awakened desire for intimacy, stirred by such events.

Our deep, human yearning for communion with another being is lighted by what the Greeks called Eros. This Eros, the root of erotic, is often confused with lust. Lust is the use of another person or the idea or image of a person for personal satisfaction. Eros is the opening of the body and the heart to unity, body, mind and spirit. When coupled with agape, the Greek form of love that considers the need of the other before self, the Holy Union grants a glimpse of glory.

When fulfilled, the erotic, orgasmic experience of making love with our beloved renders us spent at the edge of consciousness. For women, it is as if a Divine hand reaches into the innermost parts, turning body and spirit inside out. Only childbirth and death itself come close to this most human and profoundly sacred experience.

Eros is the gift of God for all God's people. No one is left behind. Just as not every, single prayer lights the hair on fire and lifts the veil to heaven, not every sexual encounter moves heaven and earth. Not every dinner is Thanksgiving, and not every broken loaf of bread becomes communion. Though any ordinary meal can become a Holy and fragrant offering that opens the way to God.

We do not have to experience wild, raucous sex with a generous lover to be the recipient of divine grace. We have only to recall that single moment of desire, experienced or fulfilled. In Zora Neale Hurston's groundbreaking novel, *Their Eyes Are Watching God,* she writes about the sexual awakening of a sixteen-year-old girl, lounging beneath a pear tree on a hot summer's day. There is no other human in sight, only the erotic awakening of her soul through nature made by God's own extravagant desire.

Hurston writes: "She saw a dust-bearing bee sink into the sanctum of a bloom; the thousand sister-calyxes arch to meet the love embrace and the ecstatic shiver of the tree from root to tiniest branch creaming in every blossom and frothing with delight. So this is marriage!"[1]

Created in the image of God, we were made for deep, intimate, abiding relationships, expressed in the flesh. Our longing and desires for union, one with another, hint at the longing of the human heart for unity with God. Our wildest couplings of body and soul this side of heaven, grant us but a taste of the glory that awaits us for eternity with God.

Thus, erotic love becomes one key that opens the door to intimacy and union with God. Theologian Christopher West writes "This doesn't mean that we all need an earthly spouse in order to enter into a mystical union with God. But it does mean that, for all of us, a pathway to a deep intimacy with God opens up as we come to understand 'sexual love as it was meant to be.'"[2]

And so we begin, the two of us as pastors and spiritual leaders within our communities, to initiate what we believe is a much-needed and candid conversation about our spirituality and sexuality as people of God. Consider that your sexuality is a good gift from a loving God, given for you to express love and intimacy with your life partner, and to give you pleasure.

What does God want? God expects you to enjoy your sexuality. Call it fire, flame, Eros, mojo or passionate delight. God is a sexy God. After all, sexuality is the gift of God for the people of God, drawing us ever more deeply into relationship with one another and into the very heart of the Holy Beloved.

---

1. Zora Neale Hurston, *Their Eyes Were Watching God* (Harper Perennial Classics: New York: 2006).
2. Christopher West, *Heaven's Song: Sexual Love As It Was Meant to Be* (West Chester, Pa.: Ascension Press, 2008).

CHAPTER 2 MALE COUNTERPOINT

DALE ROSENBERGER

It seems so elementary when posed like this, so natural and sensible and right, Verlee. For some, it fairly sings with good news. But frankly, many more resist the idea you put forward, the reconciliation of spirituality and sexuality as binary and contradictory opposites. Maybe it is because in our human "well-ordered universe," apart from how the Creator joined things together, we don't want a heavenly God to identify so heartily and intimately with our earthy selves. Maybe such a God is too threatening to us, invading our personal space, encroaching upon domain where we imagine that we are in control. Maybe we like to believe that our sensual, puckish, naughty selves are a rebellion against God, and that sex as come-uppance against all authority was our idea.

Maybe it sounds so novel because few have had the gall simply to say this, maybe for the fear of consequences. Or maybe in the same way we can't imagine our parents "doing it," we don't want to go there with God. For if the Living God can comfortably pulse in Spirit through such musky gyrations as ours, our familiar compass begins to swing wildly. People seem to feel deeply shaken.

Still, Verlee, your pairing of opposites that we have trouble joining together is good news, especially for those who uncomfortably live within divided selves. If we can warm to your suggestion—no pun intended—then sex can be sanctified and no less fun and satisfying. So many of us live as though we must choose between spirituality and sexuality. We set up false choices. Either we must become carnal and distance ourselves from God, or we must become godly and therefore cease to be fully human, male and female. These false choices have done us much harm. We need to be rid of them. Thank you for helping women and men with that. Keep singing this refrain, loudly and clearly.

· 3 ·

THE PLACE OF PLEASURE IN GOD'S GREATER SCHEME OF THINGS

Dale Rosenberger

For Christians, is pleasure bad? When can it be good? What makes sex holy?

· · ·

So how did a faith with daring erotic poetry like Song of Solomon nestled in its Scriptures get a reputation as against pleasure? Answer: we worked hard at it for a long time and still struggle to reverse the damage centuries later. This "Christianity-is-anti-pleasure" rap gets thrown at us for real reasons we can trace. So we must listen and can't wave off the protests as a simple misunderstanding.

Sadly, many do not give Christianity a chance because they would rather "laugh with the sinners than cry with the saints." Some of this hard-edged laughter is reserved for us for speaking of the gospel of Jesus Christ as good news on one side, and then acting joyless and dreary on the other, specifically as embodied human beings, gifted by God with our maleness and femaleness.

How did this happen? A brief history helps. After Paul the Apostle, the most formative theologian of the church was St. Augustine, the greatest of the early church fathers. His work decisively set the theological agenda of the church for centuries. He anticipated vital themes that Reformers like Martin Luther inherited 1,200 years later. His theology of sexuality, however, set the tone in anxious ways that still cause deep struggle for no few Christians today.

Augustine was not so unusual in that he had many torrid affairs as a youth. Then in his twenties, he took on one woman for the next thirteen years. In his Confessions, Augustine reports he loved this mistress and loved sleeping with her. This was not so shocking by the standards of his day, even for a future saint. During this era, though raised as a Christian, Augustine came to subscribe to Manichaeism. This religion, originating in Persia, taught that all things are either God's or Satan's, and all sexual activity serves evil powers. As a new adherent, Augustine now suddenly had sex as seldom as possible. Self-denial became his latest path to exaltation. So it was as a Manichean, not as a Christian, that Augustine uttered his now famous prayer: "Lord, make me chaste, but not yet."

When Augustine moved from Africa to Europe, he was baptized Christian. His mother Monica found him a twelve-year-old bride whose family was close to Bishop Ambrose of Milan. His mistress returned to Africa. Augustine resolved to wait two years for his well-born fiancée to come of age. But unable to control himself, he took a new mistress, "a slave to lust," in his own words. Alas, we sense in his gathering storm clouds a very human predisposition for a massive conversion experience.

It came one day in a garden, while reading Romans 13:12–14. The text struck Augustine like a lightning bolt: "Let us live honorably as in the day, not in reveling and drunkenness, not in debauchery and licentiousness, not in quarrelling and jealousy. Instead, put on the Lord Jesus Christ, and make no provision for the flesh, to gratify its desires." Of course, Paul sounded forth like this convinced of Jesus' imminent return, thus rendering irrelevant not only sex, but also marriage. But for the new Augustine the verses became his paradigm for the old Augustine.

Why did Augustine feel powerless to control himself? Because in effect he had no choice, no will to decide, he realized. So rather than become responsible for his choices before God, he declared Adam and Eve's rebellion had ruined things not just for him, but for all people in all times. Adam's semen transmitted their wrong across the generations. We live expelled from their garden paradise and are thus born contaminated. Because sex is inherently polluted, the sexual act is like a toxic EPA site waiting to be remediated. All it can be is less filthy.

Of course, after a youth filled with consorting with prostitutes, Augustine is transparently self-referential in declaring all humankind powerless to choose not to sin. The die was cast: because he felt helpless, so are we. We have no agency in sexual expression. Adam and Eve forfeited our freedom. All of the blame is shifted to our primeval parents in Eden. "Original sin" became both the cause and the effect of lust. Further, notice as Augustine decided humankind suffered from the sickness of pleasure, he appointed the Church as the doctor to prescribe the cure. Sad? Yes. Too convenient? Yes. Forms of this thinking have resonated throughout Catholicism and Protestantism since time immemorial.

Most have heard of Augustine. Some know his story. But hear also of Julian of Eclanum, his Italian contemporary, who took exception. Julian's view, that our sexual impulse is God-ordained, was mainstream. He publicly rebuked Augustine's teaching on original sin (sin is not biologically transmitted), free will (we are responsible for our actions), and the human body, with its pleasures. "God made bodies," Julian wrote, "distinguished the sexes, made genitalia, bestowed affection through which bodies would be joined, gave power to the semen, and operates in the secret nature of the semen—and God made nothing evil." What Augustine scorned as "the diabolical excitement of the genitals," Julian praised as "vital fire." As the smoke cleared from their exchange, the Roman church fatefully sided with Augustine, likely because he was faithful in other questions where much was at stake, questions where Julian was less wise.

What can we learn here? All are welcome to help plumb the mystery of our sexual nature. But we don't need dialogues dominated by those whose past licentiousness has morphed into reactionary rejection of sex. Nor do we need our sexuality appraised by those despairing of sex and rejecting it as ungodly. Think of it. Why should those who hate sex, those smitten with guilt, and those uninterested in sex call the shots here? It still happens. Someone defined a prude as that person seized by the dread fear that someone, somewhere might have fun. But the Jesus of the Gospels was no prude. He was firm but empathic toward his companionable warm-hearted sinners. He bristled at and avoided the proud, power-seeking, controlling cold-hearted sinners who finally murdered him.

All of this is worth saying not only because of key moments in church history. It is also worth saying if your upbringing was anything like mine. I recall the church people weighing in most vehemently on such matters were too often either haunted by a past or terrified of the searing intimacy that authentic sex involves. My modest proposal? That these camps no longer have the final word. We all need to hold ourselves accountable to one another as witnesses and to our God.

So that is a brief history of sexual pleasure and early Christianity. As the twig was bent, so grew the tree. When can sex be good, you ask? Historically, a waiver in this strict sexual regimen was allowed for procreation. That is, having sex to make babies, pleasure was at least excusable. (Augustine still believed sex necessarily sinful even within marriage and family.) This attitude carries over today. No few religious types still claim sex can be wholesome and healthy only in service to a nobler good than its lascivious self.

The Bible—in its candid and forthright earthiness—begs to differ with this. It surely does not endorse our lopsided cultural obsession with sex. It sometimes commends celibacy as a way to freedom and joy in serving God. (Matthew 19:10–12, 1 Corinthians 7) But Paul also exhorts us "to glorify God in your body." This means not only refraining from Augustine's brand of indiscretion. It also means something positive as well. Our bodies can become temples for the indwelling, and even our owning, by God's Spirit. (1 Corinthians 6:19) In any case, sex is never something that happens privately and alone between consenting adults. For Paul all that happens in every relationship has wider implications for our relationship with God and especially our place in serving to advance God's reign.

But Paul also adamantly opposed any whiff of what we might call hyper-spirituality, leading couples to renounce sexual relations. For married couples, they not only may have sex, they must. It is essential to keep marital promises. Most are unaware of Paul addressing "holier than thou" Christians in Corinth who refrained from sex, posturing as superior: "The husband should give to his wife her conjugal rights, and likewise the wife to her husband. For the wife does not have authority over her own body, but the husband does; likewise the husband does not have authority over his own body, but the wife does." (1 Corinthians 7:3–4)

The text is incredible. Its mutuality hits hard against men imagining women belong to them—sexually and otherwise—in ways men don't also belong to women. Its mutuality undercuts the reckless autonomy of becoming a sexual free agent. Paul charges us to fulfill our commitment as lovers implicit within our vows to couple as husbands and wives. Why? Retreating from sex, posturing as super-spiritual, that person and the partner will likely seek gratification elsewhere. Paul anticipates the John Updike novels of married couples playing a charade of sexual restraint with one another so as to indulge clandestine extramarital affairs.

The Apostle is clever and not at all stodgy. He doesn't deprecate sex. For him sex is good, necessary, and fulfills a holy promise. In fact, here Paul argues against those rejecting sexual intercourse as inappropriate. He instead affirms a place for sexual satisfaction without any qualifier requiring procreation to make sex wholesome. Some detractors have no idea this side of Christianity exists, but instead operate with priggish "church-lady" stereotypes from popular culture. While it is true the anti-pleasure strains within Christianity are traceable, it is also true that many people have false and silly caricatures about sexuality and the Spirit.

Take the Puritans, for example. Puritanism is such a synonym for prudery that we hear "puritan" more often than prude to describe the narrow and uptight. But did the Puritans mortify the flesh, eschew pleasure, and sneer at sex as unspiritual? Not even close. In my first class at Yale on the spirituality of the Romantic Movement, the teacher stunned the class by reading passionate purple passages from Puritan diaries and journals. They affirmed married sex as pure and necessary. They weren't squeamish about the body or human erotic contact.

Many Puritan writers cited the story of Isaac's fondling of Rebekah (Genesis 26:8) to argue the legitimacy of erotic love. Why did this capture their fancy? No idea. Let's just call it soft-core Puritan erotica, and let it go at that. In truth, the Puritans often held forth about sexual intercourse without using the word. Instead they spoke in code of the "act of matrimony," "cohabitation," "matrimonial duty," "mutual communication of bodies" and their favorite, "due benevolence." Far from settling with sex in marriage as merely valid, Puritan writers barely blushed to celebrate full erotic exuberance. As one anonymous Puritan rhapsodized, when the two become one in marriage, they "may joyfully give due benevolence one to the other; as two musical instruments rightly fitted do make a most pleasant and sweet harmony in a well-tuned consort."[1] We could envy this intimacy in any era.

---

1. Charles H. George and Katherine George, *The Protestant Mind of the English Reformation, 1570–1640* (Princeton: Princeton University Press, 1961), 285.

Or get this. The First Church of Boston excommunicated James Mattock in 1640 for denying "conjugal fellowship unto his wife for the space of two years." Imagine the self-styled enlightened, the painfully open-minded of some secular circle today having such a candid, open conversation to advocate on behalf of a woman. No way. But it surely would improve the closed circuit TV of our local City Council. And notice with "conjugal fellowship," the Puritans coined more terms for coitus than a rugby team, even if they were less florid, more dignified.

Finally, I can't help but mention the excruciating irony of waxing poetic about sensual spirituality on these pages. The contract to write this book was offered by The Pilgrim Press, the oldest publishing house in the western hemisphere, founded in 1620 by, you guessed it, the Puritans, of course. So who considers Christians killjoys? Mostly the uninformed. Broader conversations like this allow in some light and air, about then and now. C. S. Lewis once ventured, "We must picture these Puritans as the very opposite of those who bear that name today: as young, fierce, progressive intellectuals, very fashionable and up-to-date. They were not teetotalers; bishops, not beer, were their special aversion."[2]

So Christianity sheds its pleasure hangover. For a while now our faith has celebrated sex as God's good gift, even if popular perception does lag. But does it make any spiritual or sensual sense to say sex can be holy? Is that defaming blasphemy? Or is it cherished possibility? To get at this we must face into confusing and painful convulsions about sex in popular consciousness today.

For the longest time those trading in "traditional values" and championing decency had us deal with each other as though God made us without sexual organs, as though sex were a rumor, necessitating the visitation of storks. This couldn't last. Rebellion

---

2. C. S. Lewis, *Studies in Medieval and Renaissance Literature* (Cambridge, England: Cambridge University Press, 1966), 121.

against suppression and repression has been robust and pervasive for many decades now. But how much better is what fills this void?

Our technology-addled, 24 hour sex-saturated society is more obsessed with sex than any since ancient Rome. This agitated, profit-driven marketing of things sexual might strike some as bliss. The problem is our high-profile manic sexuality has not resulted in people feeling more loved, more cherished, or even more erotically charged. Deep feeling is in short supply these days. If the fig leaf in art once obscured genitalia to conceal, it now shifts to hide our faces with the same censorious effect in the electronic media. Once people felt guilty if they "did it." Now people feel guilty if they don't do it, don't do it often enough, don't do it in an endless variety of positions, or must do it the same way twice. Oh, please. Martin Luther observed how history moves like a drunk staggering from one side of the street to the other. Yes, staggering along is the operative image for our current sexual landscape.

So if Christianity would become more "sex positive," it needs to model alternatives to this scene, born from a counterculture apart from our faceless, programmed consumer sexuality. It was no theologian, but aesthete-eroticist Henry Miller who once observed that sexual passion remains ready at any moment to catch us off guard and prove it is the *mysterium tremendum.* No Sunday School boy, even Miller could see how sex might link us to the eternal. The latest favorite couples therapist of the *New York Times*, Esther Perel, comments, "Blatantness doesn't inspire you these days. But to talk about mystery is immensely inspiring."[3] An airbrushed, mechanized approach to the transmission of pleasure results in no one feeling the earth shift beneath them while in the throes of pleasure in another's arms. That we are so obsessed with technique is one reason sex loses the power of its mystery.

---

3. Esther Perel, as quoted in *The New York Times*, Sunday Styles section, "The Sexual Healer," 26 January 2014, 7.

Technique, with its objective and factual step-by step logic, breaks everything down into its smallest constituent elements, hoping to understand the whole through the sum of its parts. Let's face it, seeking prescriptive answers with an emphasis on sexual mechanics and technique isn't working. Instead we only become cold, fragmented, devoid of passion, desensitized to what once had power to enthrall and excite, to elevate and heal, a semi-miraculous foretaste of God's inconceivable wonders. Instead of starting with the God in whom all things come together, fixation upon technique splits things apart. It divorces body from soul, sensuality from spirit, information from meaningfulness.

Can sex be holy? What makes it so? The first answers are found in what makes it unholy. Fragmentation does not invite us to abide patiently in holy mystery, waiting for beauty and meaning and belonging to be revealed in their seasons of patient and enduring love, allowing the union of our souls and spirits to precede the union of our bodies, which is essentially the Christian take on sex.

Technique cultivates outwardness, not inwardness. What that means is fragmentation seeks quick fixes on the outside rather than wading through our untidy interior lives. You feel crabby because your deceased father's birthday hits you with his loss? You feel afraid because your boss makes threatening noises? You feel sad because your children struggle? As technique goes, none of these make for scintillating eroticism. So many just refuse sex with their beloved or find themselves refused. Instead we put all of those complex feelings and behaviors aside and simply find some pornography, fantasize about the unknown neighbor, or maybe locate another partner for relationship intimacy, if not an outright affair. This effectively splits off our sexuality rather than integrating joys and struggles within the prime relationship, and letting them give depth to our erotic lives.

But what if God would have us make love from inside out rather than outside in? What if our emotional peaks and valleys have everything to do not only with loving the other by talking things through, but also with what Marvin Gaye provocatively and invitingly called "Sexual Healing"? What if the big, untidy pile of love, life, and sex is one package, not compartments like lockers in a gym? What if sex is about more than performance and sensation? What if the body is more than machine? What if heart and head might unite in a cause greater than either? What if God has made holy our lovemaking as opposed to just having sex to avoid the emptiness of despair? Do we dare to live lives holding all of this together instead of splitting up the package, fleeing for simpler and shallower sex elsewhere, to cheer us up in our grim day?

If so, we run the royal and sacred risk of knowing (in the full biblical sense) our partner and lover in a way deeper than the isolation that modern secularism advances. If so, we take a chance on sex resonating and bursting from within rather than settling with merely distracting and numbing ourselves from without. Truly, soulful sex of this order is not easier to seek and find. It is a quest for more than fleeting effervescence. But sex as holy as this is finally the only sex worth having. Everything else is cheap imitation. Accept no substitutes. And to hold all this together we need binding agents like Christ, his Church, and vows of marriage. Why are these necessary? Because when it comes to the greatness of sacrificing to love another so passionately as this for a lifetime, we are all halting cowards.

Are you still glad you asked if sex can be holy? Will you accept something as risky and dangerous as this? Are you willing to have your foundations shaken? Be warned, once you try it, you can't go back. For it will take you from splashing in the shallows out into deep currents and far trade winds of life-defining journey, where love becomes deeply transformative rather than merely entertaining, distracting, or amusing. It will also enhance your pleasure because you need not count on the enhancements of variety from without. You have a deep spiritual well for pleasure from within, which is the basis for a lifetime of shared pleasure.

That is the power of holy mystery. That is the godly dynamic man and woman share in loving each other as Jesus Christ has loved us. That is God's gift of sex the church now no longer overlooks. Look out, world, we are now getting this right, changing the course of our history and world history, and getting our true message out there.

. . .

CHAPTER 3 FEMALE COUNTERPOINT

VERLEE A. COPELAND

We certainly have a great deal to think about here. To put it plainly, sex can indeed be holy. People of faith believe in a God who created all that was, all that is and all that ever will be. We trust in the God of creation who breathed into dust and brought forth all of life and called it good. If we believe we are inherently sexual as human creatures, and if God made us and called creation good, then sex can be a holy thing, a God thing. Like any gift, we enjoy it with gratitude when we practice loving another through this beautiful flesh that God created. The 139th Psalm affirms that we are "wonderfully made . . . . and intricately wrought." Our bodies become the means through which we act lovingly in service towards another for the glory of God. This is sex as it was meant to be.

When we honor God's gift of sexuality in such a way as this, God blesses our sexuality and its faithful expression. Unfortunately, the church historic has perpetuated guilt and shame around bodily functions, including our sexuality. The church cannot be entirely to blame for this. We humans have the tendency to abuse and misuse God's good gifts: for personal gain, for selfish desire or ambition, or to the detriment or harm of another. Our sexuality then becomes the occasion for sin, which means, literally, "missing the mark." When we use and abuse our sexuality only for what it does for us, rather than how it serves another, then we miss the mark. It's not that by missing the mark we will be cast into the outer darkness. Rather, when we misuse God's gift, we miss out on the present itself. Like a two-year-old at Christmas, we spend the better part of a holiday playing with the wrapping and ignoring the gift entirely.

God gives us this exquisite means of expressing deep love and intimacy through our lovemaking, or what might be more aptly named "love expressing." We don't actually make love happen by having sex, even with someone we love. But we do strengthen the bonds of love and affection between us when we cherish and honor one another with our whole being. God makes sex and all things holy.

4

SEXUAL FANTASY, HOLY PLEASURE, AND HEAVENLY IMAGINATION

Verlee A. Copeland

I've been in love many times. But no matter how satisfied I think I am, there always seems to be something missing. Even when I'm in a committed relationship, I tend to fantasize about someone else. What do I do about these sexual fantasies?

* * *

Love is in the air. Imagine that it's Valentine's Day and Walgreens is aglitter with stuffed animals, heart-shaped boxes of chocolates and singing cards. We're drawn to this holiday like insects to a light bulb.

Several years ago I took on the dreaded chore of cleaning out the back of the storeroom closet where I kept the boxes labeled "childhood stuff." I discovered the expected Barbie dolls and the adventure books I loved as a child. But what intrigued me most were the scrapbooks.

Pages were filled with the usual proud report cards and dorky school pictures. And then there were Valentines, lots of them. We bought a Valentine and those awful-tasting hard candies for every kid in the class. "Be mine . . . Kiss me . . . True friend."

I remember sitting with my best friend Darlene, poring over each word for a secret meaning about which boys liked us. Only later when I raised sons did I learn that the boys couldn't care less. As children our fantasies were quite innocent. I fantasized that the fuzzy bumblebee card that said, "Bee mine" meant that Donald loved me. In truth, the only thing I ever got from Donald was a kiss at recess, and therefore a bad case of measles in the second grade.

Our childhood fantasies have matured to be sure. Most of us have fallen in and out of love more than once. We may no longer fantasize that Donald will grow up to marry us, but we long for those grown up boys to ravish us just the same. We fantasize about expressions of passion that make us blush. As adults we look to our sexual fantasies to provide us what those grade school Valentines could not, evidence that we are profoundly desired and deeply loved.

The grown up version of sexual fantasy, of course, takes us places our childhood longings do not. While we still desire to be loved and cherished, we also want to express that desire with our beloved. When erotic images and imagined scenarios flow across our sexually stimulated brains, our sexual pleasure and erotic lovemaking intensifies. Just as children experience great joy when they fly above the highest mountains or swim the deep blue sea in dreams, so too our fantasies transport us beyond our tired flesh to ecstasy.

Most of us don't discuss our fantasies. We may think they are too perverse, or that there's something wrong with us for imagining things we would never do in real life. For example, many women fantasize about lying on a hot beach under the tropical sky of some exotic land. A scantily clad male delivers umbrella drinks and offers a massage, without expectation of anything in return. Sometimes these fantasies conclude with wild, raucous sex. For other women, it is enough to imagine the undemanding attention of a handsome man who finds her desirable. There is nothing more erotic than to be appreciated and desired.

The secret pleasure of fantasy can intensify lovemaking and enhance the relationship between partners. That's a good thing. Nevertheless, many of us feel guilty about our sexual fantasies. We wonder if they take something away from the love we have for a mate. We fear they may get in the way of developing a real time relationship. After all, how can any man live up to the idealized image of the sensitive, passionate lover we conjure up in our minds?

It may surprise you that many women fantasize about making love with another woman. This does not necessarily indicate sexual preference. The imagination, like our nighttime dreams, can project unfulfilled aspects of ourselves into consciousness, where we can see ourselves more clearly. That gorgeous, athletic, beautifully breasted and very sexy woman in our imagination may represent our own hidden sexuality yearning to be fully expressed.

Whatever you are imagining, you are not alone. Nearly everyone has sexual fantasies, even of the slightly dangerous sort. The person who claims not to have sexual fantasies may not be telling the truth or may lack the courage to admit it. Others may not experience dreams or sexual fantasies because they are taking medication or consuming alcohol that inhibits the world of imagination. The question remains. Is there anything wrong with sexual fantasy? And if so, what can we do about it?

First of all, there is a big difference between having a rich sexual fantasy life and acting on those fantasies. Fantasizing about being seduced by the body builder you met on the airplane while making love to your husband may heighten your mutual pleasure. Sharing that fantasy with him, or asking about his fantasies may intensify his desires. How great is that? Sex play that delights both partners and provides mutual satisfaction is a terrific way to channel fantasy life for mutual good.

When we do not have a lover, or even when we do, fantasy can contribute to self-pleasuring, a healthy release for sexual tension that lowers stress and contributes to sleep. Many wives and husbands fail to grasp that self-pleasuring can have a rightful place even in a strong and stable married life. No, masturbation won't make you blind. No, your hand won't fall off. No, you won't go to hell. Yet the prohibition against self-pleasuring and sexual fantasy runs deep through the collective psyche of our culture.

When certain passages in the Hebrew Scriptures prohibit the spilling of seed on the ground, it is a poetic way of discouraging male masturbation. Is it any wonder that many people assume faith and sex don't mix? Well-meaning but misinformed ministers still preach against self-pleasuring as a path to sin. They confuse biblical scholarship with folklore. The Leviticus prohibition against male masturbation in the Hebrew Scriptures had nothing to do with moral behavior and everything to do with primitive understandings of human biology. When reading scripture, we look at the context in which it was written, the time in history and the intended message for the audience hearing it, among other concerns. When we do so with this passage, we remember that people in ancient times knew very little about human biology. In a time long before modern medicine, microscopes, x-rays, MRI's and blood tests, ancient peoples had a primitive understanding of reproduction.

At the time the Old Testament covenants were written, the interior workings of human anatomy remained a mystery. People believed that there were miniature people inside the male seed, and that these miniature people were sacred. This sacred seed was planted in a woman through intercourse, where the seed could grow in her fertile ground. Male masturbation and homosexuality were prohibited for similar reasons. It was forbidden to spill the seed on the ground or otherwise to waste it by placing it where it could not grow.

We live with remnants of shame and guilt over expressions of sexuality whose roots we do not know or understand. That's why it's so important to talk about sex. Sexual fantasy and self-pleasuring can provide physical, spiritual and psychological benefits that enhance every other aspect of our life. They can take some pressure off our partner and off of us.

Self-pleasuring and fantasy in the context of lovemaking can enrich our relationships and deepen our pleasure and mutual pleasure and desire. You may wonder if there is ever a time when sexual fantasy is simply not O.K. The answer to that question is "yes" although only you and your partner can determine where to draw the line. When in doubt or uneasy about any sex play, including fantasy, consider the extent to which it strengthens your capacity to express pleasure and increase intimacy.

For example, not all fantasy builds up relationship. Sexuality has the power to bind a couple together, and also the power to wound and rend apart. When sexual fantasy moves from imaginative play to real life temptation for the muscled and fit car mechanic, it may signal that it's time to back away slowly from that fantasy. In like manner, we may choose to avoid entertaining certain fantasies that might create hurt or pain for our partner in real time. It can be unfair and hurtful to compare a real, flesh and blood man or woman with an idealized, airbrushed symbol of unattainable perfection. We may want to talk frankly with our partner about that which opens up deeper intimacy and sexual expression, and that which leads to shame, guilt or anxiety. The bottom line is that fantasy can enrich a healthy sexual relationship between two adults who trust and honor one another in the flesh, but it cannot replace it.

When we spend so much of our time in the world of fantasy that it encumbers our real life relationships or when it threatens our fidelity, then it may be time to turn around and walk away. Fantasies tend to feel a little bit dangerous. That is why we are drawn to them in the midst of our humdrum routine. They can intensify desire and pleasure. But fantasies may become destructive when they are not only more exciting than the pot-bellied, middle-aged man we live with, but they are also more idealized. When we hold out for the perfect fantasy we may miss the pleasure and joy of our here and now partner, warts and all. Sex becomes holy when it exists in the very mix of the mundane and transcends the weaknesses of both parties.

Our imagined wanderlust may not have anything to do with the risk of sexual infidelity or a gnawing dissatisfaction in our relationships. For Christians, ever drawn to "something more," there is a sense in which there can be no satisfaction apart from God. All other loves only hint at the real deal. Human love and friendship is a glorious thing, the passion of lovers, the depth of friendship, and the sustaining comfort of family. All these are fabulous and they give us hints at glory. But ultimately, when we look to the love of another human creature to satisfy all our needs, we will be disappointed. Only God can satisfy the deepest desires of our hearts.

Some years ago when I was still teaching school, a colleague of mine was struggling deeply in her marriage. Her husband had been a scoundrel and cheated on her numerous times. The two of them reconciled but a breach remained in their relationship, like a scar that heals imperfectly after an injury and always pulls just a bit, reminding you of the wound when you least expect it.

Occasionally the two of us would get together before school to pray. Sometimes we prayed for our students, but often our prayers shifted to the loves of our lives. Though she was committed to her marriage, her unsettling dissatisfaction was never far beneath the surface. One day as we were wrestling yet one more demon to the ground, I said to her what I still believe. "Dear One, Jesus is the only man for you." I did not mean of course, that she should fantasize about Jesus or that her relationship with Jesus was sexual. She understood right away that while sex is a great thing, and we're hard-wired to long for intimacy, she was expecting love to fill a deep chasm of need beyond the capacity of any man.

What this means is that we sometimes tend to expect more from our relationships than any human relationship can deliver.

Even the greatest of human loves pale in comparison with the promises of the Holy One to love us unconditionally, even to the end of time. That is why we conclude the liturgy for marriage in our tradition with these words: "Forgive as freely as God has forgiven you and be truly loving. Never expect the other to be more perfect that you are yourself."[1]

A long time ago, God sent a Valentine into the world. It didn't sing, or crack jokes. It wasn't fuzzy with a cute message like "Be Mine" and it wasn't made with dark chocolate. God's Valentine lit up the sky with the life of Jesus, the ultimate lover of our soul. You are passionately loved and cherished for who you are by God, the only one who can truly love you unconditionally. All romance and sexual fantasy this side of heaven are measured by their grounding in this divine romance between heaven and earth.

You are a sexy, sensual creature, created in God's own image. Whether or not you have hoarded a shoe-box filled with funny Valentines to make you feel loved, whether or not you lay awake in the watches of the night thinking about some imagined lover just out of your reach, the love you seek is near at hand. If you are blessed at this point in your life with a real, live naked human being lying next to you in bed, reach for him or her with abandon.

Sex is a good thing, a God thing. Your imagination too is a gift from God. Enjoy your wild and rich fantasy life without guilt and with abandon. Allow the blossoming of your beautiful sexuality to please yourself, your lover and your God. For you may recall that even the most titillating fantasies that intensify the pleasures of love play only hint at the satisfaction that ultimately comes from God. We ground all of our loving in this final truth: You are Christ's beloved, and there is nothing on earth or in heaven that can ever take this love away from you.

---

1. *Book of Worship, United Church of Christ* (Cleveland: Local Church Ministries, Worship and Education Ministry Team, 2009).

. . .

CHAPTER 4 MALE COUNTERPOINT

DALE ROSENBERGER

It is amazing to ponder the extent to which fantasies dominate our day and the degree to which we don't acknowledge or discuss them. You rightly point out why, Verlee. They are indeed dangerous. But properly assimilated into a healthy and strong marriage, this could be exactly the dose of daring we complain is lacking. Indeed, it is a good instinct, if we experience something sexy, to bring it into our marriage or relationship rather than live it outside of couplehood. Within the marriage, it has power to deepen intimacy and lend zest; fantasies always kept outside the relationship cannot strengthen a couple and could become a wedge, like any significant part of our lives we refuse to share with our beloved.

Often the choice is more complex than the simple binary, to share or not to share. If, for example, we have a sexy dream about someone known to both husband and wife, we might want to mask the identity of the dream lover, and go with a neutral description. We want to take the right kind of risks, to discern which will bind us to grow together in new ways, and which might wound. We can trust our partner to help us with these distinctions, if we truly listen and have ears to hear. Generally, sharing fantasies is difficult for couples, especially at first. But the potential upside is the very creativity and imagination that most couples decry as in short supply. Remember, if we do not find variety and zest within the marriage, the natural consequence among humans will be to seek it from without. Did you hear all of that? Say it slowly and out loud. This is important.

As it is true in love, so also in sex: the one who loves (and risks!) the least often ends up setting the rules and holding the power. The partner courageous enough to venture a fantasy becomes vulnerable to ridicule and even condemnation by "the decent-minded." Fantasies are silly and idiosyncratic; ridicule happens easily. Rejection is always painful. What can be done?

Perhaps couples might develop a presumption of grace in favor of the one who risks venturing something so personal as a fantasy. It is very Christian to protect the vulnerable. This is in effect to make both partners responsible, each asking, "How much am I willing to bare my soul and trust my mate?" Intuitively, we know that in most marriages we need to push our limits with a dash of boldness. Can the promise of creative but dangerous fantasies be turned for good by trusting couples? Frankly, it all depends how much intimacy we would dare. We will never know until we try.

5

HOW WOMEN AND MEN
MIGHT CONNECT BEYOND OUR
REAL DIFFERENCES

Dale Rosenberger

When my wife and I find the courage to look each other in the eye and really talk about sex, we talk past each other. She dismisses what turns me on as crude or shallow, so I feel reduced. I can't for the life of me grasp what her comments have to do with sex. So she feels like I don't "get it." What would you suggest?

. . .

First, let's notice how tough it is to talk candidly, boldly, and vulnerably about sex with the one you love. When you love someone, it unfolds in such close proximity, hurt comes easily, often unintentionally. Vulnerability is profound. So much is at stake. On the heels of that, let's affirm how essential such exchanges are as couples seek to keep things lively and avoid getting stuck in ruts.

We ask ourselves, if I am honest with my mate about my desire, will it later be used against me? If what I say is too intense, will he or she think less of me as friend and life partner? We fear how damaging implications might overshadow a relationship. And let's not forget the immediate, showstopper fear putting the brakes on honesty: will my candor ruin my chances for making love (also called "getting any") tonight? For a myriad of reasons, the conversation gets put off and then never occurs. Still, the bold drama of sexual intimacy at least minimally begs for a script. Or at least maybe a few stage directions, for goodness' sake.

It is surprising how often we feel more at ease talking with former lovers, special friends, counselors, and strangers exploring intimate sexual desires, themes, and questions. Witness the growing popularity of Internet sex chat rooms and how free some become as anonymity and confidentiality remove the fear of judgment. Some women talk with girlfriends about sexual details, perhaps because they do not feel permission to share openly with their partner. Why do they not feel permission? Many passionate women feel little room to be deeply or explicitly sexual for fear that men or society might find them unacceptable. Let's face it: women have less leeway as sexual creatures than similarly passionate men do.

This is all sad. For in this our sexuality falls far short of sacred, intimate, and deeply alive. Intimacy with our one and only is meant to be a sanctuary. But here we settle for something less than a safe, shared retreat where we feel emboldened by freedom, strength and security to explore new forms of closeness.

Suffice it to say trust is holy, vulnerability gets us outside of comfort zones to transform us, and rejection, even in small things, is always painful. Suffice it to say few of us excel at being nonjudgmental, even with those we profess to love, maybe especially with them. Maybe we all need training in withholding judgment for our sexuality to become sacred. Maybe we should read in bed to each other what I Corinthians 13 claims love is not: envious, boastful, rude, arrogant, petulant, irritable or resentful. Reckless judgment in the face of each other's nakedness can forestall untold shared intimacies and cast shadows for years.

Briefly, practical reasons around our socialization make it difficult to look each other in the eye and be honest about desire. Many men imagine we should already be sexual experts, as though anything less is unmanly. As women expect their man to take the initiative, they further expect him to know what he is doing, and not be a fumbler. Men can be overly sensitive around suggestions of doing things other than how we usually do them. "Are you saying I wasn't doing it right?" Moreover, women can resist specifying what they like. "What if our sex becomes wooden, rote or formulaic instead of spontaneous, heartfelt sharing?" Let's face it, for couples the whole encounter can be stacked against honesty about sex.

Secretly, a woman might feel that if her man is the right man, or if he really loves her, he should know what to do without ever needing to be told. He should anticipate all of her needs and desires. Or she might believe that a truly sexually knowledgeable man will automatically be able to please and satisfy her. All of these common assumptions and dangerous myths are hurting and holding back many couples. Finding a better way is why your question remains worth hearing.

But your question implies even deeper differences, limiting how men and women communicate about intimacy, differences based in our core as men and women. Let's start from the beginning. When boys and girls inevitably notice anatomical differences, and girls wonder about him "having more" down there, the wise mom responds, "Honey, here is how things are: boys are complicated on the outside. And girls are complicated on the inside." Now there is enough in that little saying to give boys and girls, men and women, pause for reflection. Actually, this simple statement is wise beyond our anatomy, and suggestive of matters delving deeper into souls, spirits, and psyches, both male and female.

Even children can see it: boys and girls are different. And if boys and girls are different, men and women, with our endocrine systems roiling from adolescence on, are even more different. How can we account for such real and powerful differences without letting them be used to treat women as something falling short of being male and to treat men as something inferior to being female?

We talk so much about communication in relationships, it becomes cliché. We struggle so with communication because an inherent impasse exists between men and women. This divide can only be overcome with careful listening, selfless love, persistent effort, and gallant understanding. But for those couples determined to enter new places spiritually and hot places sexually, it is worth it.

First, let us notice that both tendencies—men disdaining women as falling short of our maleness and women dismissing men because we are not female—occur frequently, even naturally. We human beings are egocentric creatures. In part, that is what Christianity means by sin. That same brokenness is on full display in our sexuality. Here, "egocentric" means assuming what pleases me is what pleases my partner. It ain't necessarily so! And it is arrogant. Men and women do this in different ways. Our self-absorption undercuts the prospect of making deep and enjoyable connections. In other words, it might be funny when *My Fair Lady's* Henry Higgins belts out "Why Can't A Woman Be More Like a Man," but who wants to live with someone like that? No one I have ever met.

Where to begin with this impasse? For women, the prospects of the relationship, with its stability and security, make sex possible and enjoyable. The two are inextricably linked. The relationship is where she feels protected enough to become fully available, vulnerable, and alive as a sensual creature. For women, talking and feeling close make sex possible. In this regard, with the intricacies of the relationship as the gateway to her sexuality, women are more sexually complex than men. Whatever men do to show their awareness of this—sweet notes in her briefcase, really hearing her out instead of only listening so we can talk next, knowing and asking about things truly vital to her—all qualify as foreplay. This is why calling her the next day matters—even after decades of marriage. It screams, "I get it. I understand you. I bow to the relationship. I meet you there. I am in it for the duration." Men have trouble grasping how erotically women will respond to the thousand creative ways we convey this awareness.

Yes, men, that's right, such seemingly non-sexual behaviors have power to entice, enthrall, arouse, and excite your woman. Believe it! Of course, for women who are asexual, none of these suggestions can thaw desire frozen deep within an iceberg. But even if getting outside ourselves to see it from her view is no cure-all, do not miss this golden insight: for women, fully honoring the relationship is the gateway to deeper intimacy and greater sexual pleasure.

Consequently, we might say women are more direct about relationships and more indirect in their sexuality. Gentlemen, let me translate. This means as women share the detailed complexities of your relationship, they provide us with helpful insight into and clues toward their sexuality. Frankly, many of us guys miss that much of the time. Do we have eyes to see and ears to hear precious information about sex with her encoded in a foreign language called "relationship"?

For men the prospects around sexuality, with the affirmation and validation it provides us, make the relationship possible and enjoyable. The possibility of sex makes vulnerable sharing and feeling close real in the relationship. The two are inextricably linked in the opposite direction. Within the sparks of attraction and how that plays out, men feel unique, desirable, valued, cared for and manly enough to live in relationship. In this regard, men are more simple and straightforward in their sexuality. Sex is not encoded in relationship. Sex is straightforward sex.

For men, you can't tell where the sexual side ends and the relationship begins. Sexuality and its attractions are the gateway into the relationship, as his beloved makes love to him in ways affirming, exciting, caring, and daring. So yes, breezily and wordlessly serving him dinner braless in a silk blouse unbuttoned to the waist should not be dismissed out of hand as "slutty." Same thing as surprising him with a naughty quickie in a moment and setting when he least expects it. It surprises women how meeting a guy where he lives shows understanding and empathizes with who he really is. It can lead to deeper connections, that is, if the man is made of the right stuff. Of course, for emotionally immature men who fear authenticity and real, lasting relationships, no insight or sacrifice or effort can make men out of such mice.

As a result of this divide, we might say men are more direct ("complicated on the outside") and woman are more indirect ("complicated on the inside") in our sexuality. We might say don't be surprised if your man is more direct sexually and more indirect relationally. So, women, as you hear your man talk about your sex life—rejoicing or bemoaning—prepare to learn real and important things about your relationship. Are you willing to meet him on his terms by being generously erotic with him sometimes without long, constant, and drawn out assessments on the relationship's status? Without accusing him: "That's all you really want from me?" Do you have eyes to see and ears to hear valuable relationship data, which to you is encoded in the foreign language of "sexuality"?

A few words about actually discussing sex analytically with your lady, guys: talk before or after having sex, but not during. She may not be as verbal as you are in the act. Besides, such a conversation in the heat of the moment is not as romantic as a sexy conversation to plan and prepare for lovemaking. She will love that as it builds from the relationship toward the sexual encounter. What to ask about? Listen closely to her sighs and moans during lovemaking. They are fraught with clues. To put both of you at ease, talk and share after a memorable lovemaking session: a moment of less fear, more flush with triumph.

Remember, men, you are direct in your sexuality, she is indirect, more complex, more subtle. Apply this across the board. Be more casual and playful (spontaneous and from the heart) than formal or interrogative (no charts or graphs, please!). Instead of clinical (vagina, mammary glands, glutes), or vulgar (pussy, tits, ass), try the poetic side of romancing her (fragrant flower, breasts, derriere). You can all make simple poetry, gentlemen: "Your skin is softer than silk . . . I love it more than I can say to share our lives and our bodies . . . Your breasts are incredible; your ruby lips are perfect." If you need a primer in sensual poetry as a practical help in talking about things sexual, re-read Song of Solomon. If you feel silly doing this, know that she will swoon. Just make sure you mean it and say it feelingly. Or to begin, whisper such phrases. You think she doesn't need to hear how attractive you find the temple of her sexuality? You are wrong. Trust me.

Clearly, the more willingly we transcend ourselves to experience sexuality and relationships from the other side of the gender divide, the better the communication, the deeper the bond, and the hotter the sex. Clearly, this is a lifelong project and real work, being naturally self-involved and egocentric by nature. Instead men would rather stamp their foot and go out with the guys to the sports bar and ask why women can't be more like us and just "go for it"? Instead women would rather complain to their girlfriends that guys are pigs and just don't get it. Let's admit it: being self-centered, we all prefer shortcuts. But nothing great happens without sacrifice, even in sex. Does greatness interest you?

Transcending our limited perspective to understand the other so our lovemaking might become exalted loving service and not merely self-satisfaction? That is asking an awful lot. It is excessive, some will protest. Too much bother. Too much work. Who has the patience for it? Perhaps excessive, yes. But excessive in the sense of William Blake's reckoning where the road of excess leads to the palace of wisdom.

Getting over and beyond ourselves to get inside the heart and mind, the spirit and soul of the other, trusting that deep connections of intimacy will follow? Yes, this requires much time, effort and sacrifice. It is never finished within any lifetime, so profound are the mysteries God puts in place around our differences. But it is the spiritual definition of sexy. And it is why Madeleine L'Engle wisely observed about Christian sexuality that God intends us to explore each other's hearts and minds, souls and spirits before exploring each other's bodies. As you privilege first the perspective and needs of your partner before your own (even if it is not enough to bond deeply with your mate), discover exciting new sexual sharing, and fulfill God purposes in bringing you together, consider how your willingness to stretch yourself toward her or him will transform you personally.

Men, it is shocking how often we are lonely and close to no one as we make our way in achievement and performance-based daily routines. Our emotional landscape is often barren. Moving in wide circles, we still often live isolated lives. For many of us, our wife or partner is key to expanding greater intimacy and deeper connectedness with others. Face it, we need more than pleasure. We also need meaning, belonging and love. Sex rooted in a real and lasting relationship liberates us to learn to feel in new and deeply human ways.

Again men might ask, why bother with all of this? The move to understand and be understood is a royal road to wholeness as creatures not equipped to network as naturally as women are. Face it, we need nurture no matter how tough and independent we fancy ourselves. Often we don't grasp this till we are older. The approach to our manhood where we honor first her womanhood takes us beyond a shallow, minimalist sexuality of hormonal hydraulics and mechanical release into a realm of deep and life-changing mystery. Surprisingly, in all of this relating to her in ways that reach out to her and meet her in the middle, we might also discover physical pleasure heightened to boot. That shouldn't surprise us.

Women, by keying into his sexuality and inviting him to focus lavishly on yours, even before all of the relationship dynamics are figured out—or even as a way to access those dynamics—you gain a moment in the sun front and center where your needs are recognized, affirmed, and honored. Sex honestly exposes our needy creatureliness, just as food and meals do. Women can live so much in real and imagined relationships that they dwell too much way up in the sky. Sexuality is grounding, immediate, and satisfying. It lives here and now, and forces us to do the same. Sex can open you up to possibilities of the moment to discover fulfillment you deserve now in favor of a distant romantic ideal that never comes.

But this requires you to confront directly what you prefer erotically and what you crave as a sexual being. If you haven't felt permission to be "this kind of woman" or to make room for this dimension in your life, I officially give you that permission now. You can quote me. If you like, I'll even send you a card: "I am a sexually alive and fully empowered woman. Deal with it." Put in your purse, your briefcase, or on the bathroom mirror. Read it as your nerve falters, thinking you should set your mind on "higher things." Having the courage to center yourself in earthy satisfactions over against your many sacrifices might better balance your life.

We feel sexuality become something holy when getting outside ourselves to live in and love through our partner is no mere duty or method, but a cherished place we appreciate, enjoy and celebrate. After making us male and female, God blessed and celebrated our differences as good. (Genesis 1:27, 5:2) Reuniting male and female, instead of keeping them far apart, accesses this primeval, garden-like goodness.

The Psalmist reminds us the male-female divide runs through all of life, and that we are fearfully and wonderfully made. (Psalm 139:14) That sounds to me a lot more like joy and festivity than rolling our eyes and heavy lifting. Men and women, as we get beyond tolerating, to appreciating and celebrating the other, beyond judgment and rejection, new heavenly panoramas and perspectives open to us, as we learn to see as God already sees. Wonderful are the dynamic differences of our man/woman polarity; awe-filled is how this makes us feel as we delve into our origins and discover our destiny as sexual creatures.

. . .

CHAPTER 5 FEMALE COUNTERPOINT

VERLEE A. COPELAND

Men and women may have a tendency to approach sexuality differently, as you have said. You insightfully observe that men approach sexuality as the gateway to relationship while women view the relationship as the gateway to sexuality. That said, we remember once again that sexuality is both fragile and fluid. Other factors such as culture, age and experience shape our sexual responsiveness. For example, one parishioner described to me that her greatest sexual frustration was never being able to initiate sex with her husband. From the outside, we could easily misread her circumstance. It would appear as you have described that her male partner viewed sex as the gateway to the relationship because he was the one consistently initiating their lovemaking. She appeared to prefer the role of responder, as if lovemaking were secondary to relationship needs for her as a woman. This observation would have been wrong.

This woman lamented that her husband was unable to obtain an erection if she approached him directly, that somehow he felt anxious and pressured whenever she initiated sex. When she wanted to make love with her husband, she had to be very oblique so that he would catch the clue and initiate the act. The female indirectness you describe was culturally learned and not innate in her womanhood at all. Her experience is not uncommon. One secret that women share is a counter-dance to what you have described as male courtship ritual: the language of love, the art of appreciation, etc.

More important than how we communicate our desire and willingness to be sexually intimate is what we want from one another. In *The Four Loves,* C. S. Lewis describes Eros as the state of being in love. He writes that sexual desire without Eros wants "it," the thing itself that we call sex.[1] When we are in love, we don't just want to have sex, we want the Beloved herself, himself.

There is an anonymous saying splashed across t-shirts and on bumper stickers that reads: "I know that you know that I know what you want." It sounds quite suggestive, as if all the person wants is sex, plain and simple. Yet for both men and women of faith, committed to marriage with a beloved partner and friend, what we most desire is different than that and quite straightforward. However we say it, what we long to communicate is this: "What I really want is you."

---

1. C. S. Lewis, *The Four Loves* (New York: Harcourt, Brace & Company, 1988).

· 6 ·

WHEN A PRETTY GOOD MARRIAGE ISN'T ENOUGH

Verlee A. Copeland

I am jealous of my best friend who makes love with her husband three times a week. She says just the thought of her partner makes her feel frisky. They make it look so easy. We have a pretty good relationship. What can we do to strengthen our marriage and improve our sex life?

· · ·

Sex is a revealing microcosm for everything else happening in a relationship. Few questions about sexuality have more power to suggest a full inventory of a relationship than this one. Deeply satisfying sex begins outside the bedroom, long before the lights grow dim and come hither looks are exchanged. Let's begin with your characterization of a "pretty good" relationship. One way to move from good sex to great sex is to move from a pretty good relationship to a deeply intimate and mutually satisfying relationship.

Passionate sexuality flows from desire for the taste, smell, and touch of the beloved. Along these lines, you may want to re-read the few chapters of Song of Solomon in your Bible. The thread running through it is precisely this yearning of the beloved for one another, expressed in deeply sensory and sensual poetry. The lovers are temporarily separated and their longing for one another knows no bounds. It is evident they are at a wonderful place as a twosome, their shared love having become a living sanctuary. The imperative to create this intimate space is holy.

We open sexually to one another when we feel completely safe, cherished and embraced as a human being without judgment. In other words, our "Generosity" in expressing love in a thousand daily ways multiplies the mutual satisfaction of our lovemaking as human creatures.

You are insightful when you observe that recovering a sagging sex life begins with improving your relationship. To strengthen marriage, many couples begin with a series of frank, open and loving conversations about what seems to be working best in the relationship. A spirit of gratitude and what we call hospitality as people of faith lays the groundwork for trust and intimacy. Whether couples choose to work with a capable psychotherapist, or set apart time over a cup of coffee or a glass of wine, checking in with one another regularly about the relationship is step one. The sensuality you share or not, may indicate how things are going between you.

It's funny how focused we can be in setting goals for our work life, education, even parenting, and how casual we can become in our approach to the most significant relationship of our life. We would not expect to be successful in our work without setting goals, working to achieve them, and then reflecting through some evaluative process on our success. Yet many couples enter a relationship that they hope and trust will endure for several generations, without the same care and mindfulness that they give a job that may last but a few years.

"Couples time" needs to be scheduled like everything else that matters. Given the other pressing commitments of life, we often relegate the time we share as a couple to leftover moments at the end of the day. At that point, we are often too tired to care. We pat one another on the back affectionately; offer a peck on the cheek and a smile, and drift off to slumberland. This passes for a pretty good relationship for many couples. But why settle for so little when so much more is available to you?

We are hardwired as passionate, sexual human creatures, a trait we share in common with the animal kingdom, where friendship behaviors have been observed through creatures as diverse as the family dog to foxes in the wild. Friendship requires time hanging around with one another. Companionship is the most undervalued blessing in your relationship and a hidden cornerstone for elevating your friskiness. Who knew? After all, Hollywood makes more movies about eroticism than companionship, about non-committed sex than friendship. Yet research on marital satisfaction indicates that effective communication patterns outside the bedroom form the bedrock of satisfaction in all other areas, including the tenderness, vulnerability and joy of great sex.

Think about how relationships begin. We start by noticing one another and begin hanging out with one another. That early friendship may turn into hours on end of talking about everything from favorite foods to what we believe about our common life purpose. Once we move from friendship with much in common to a deepening relationship as a couple, we can't seem to get enough of one another. From those long, languid conversations and mutual engagement in activities we both enjoy, an awakening of mutual desire to express that growing love emerges. We want to embrace our beloved so closely that we literally desire to pull them into our very being.

When there is a disconnect between husband and wife regarding sexual desire, we may want to examine the relationship itself and find ways to re-engage when one or the other has taken marriage for granted. Scheduling what might be called couch time, to talk with and listen to one another in a relaxed way, helps to recover intimacy.

Next, find ways to enjoy activities with one another. Over time it's easy to mistake being compatible as roommates with a deeply satisfying marriage. While it's important to effectively work out who cleans the garage and who shops for groceries, it's not enough to make sex hot in the bedroom. We're rightly grateful for the mutual reciprocity of picking up the kids and doing the laundry, but it takes more than this to fire the libido. A mediocre marriage leads to boredom in the bedroom.

The second step, then, to mutually satisfying sex is the date night, a regularly scheduled time to enjoy one another. This may sound too simple; after all there was a time when we couldn't wait to be together. Nobody had to tell us to go out and enjoy ourselves. Yet many couples who have become entrenched in a routine benefit from the simple encouragement to set aside mundane tasks, quit the house, and have a little fun.

Take turns choosing the activity so that you can participate without resentment. When you engage in an activity your partner enjoys, it communicates that you enjoy them and appreciate them, even if the activity is something you might not choose on your own. She may need to ask him to attend her favorite sporting event, for example, while he may ask her to go bowling. It doesn't really matter if we love bowling or not. We go because we love our partner.

I once knew a woman who went to baseball games every weekend when she was dating. He was shocked to discover after they were engaged that she didn't like baseball. She still goes to baseball games sometimes, just because he loves the game so much and wants to share it with her.

It doesn't really matter what we do, whether we attend an expensive concert, or take a picnic to the park. What matters is that we hang out together for the sheer purpose of enjoying one another. Isn't it funny how going out once a week after two decades of marriage seems like a lot? Yet that is exactly what sexually active couples tend to do. If we want to be intimate with one another as couples, we have to actually prioritize time with one another apart from work, chores and children. We can claim that we care for one another, but if we are unwilling to make time to be together, it just isn't true.

The weekly date needs to include times of being present to one another as well as engaging in activities. While it may be fun to catch a ball game, it is even more important to go out afterwards for a burger and beer. Intimacy increases when we look one another in the eye and talk about stuff, even if it's just the triple play in the third inning. This means it's time to turn off the cell phone, computer and television at a certain point. Create a sanctuary for your relationship, for conversation, play, and sexual exploration. Then watch the sparks fly.

Once your relationship satisfaction has increased through regular conversation and scheduled couples time, you can turn your attention towards the bedroom. Just as communication outside the bedroom increases intimacy, conversation about what happens inside the bedroom matters. Think about any other important part of life, from how we resolve an issue with our third-grader who is failing math to how we fill out our taxes. We have to communicate effectively in order to function in a mutually satisfying way. You see where we're headed with this.

By now you may be thinking that this is an awful lot of work just to get laid at the end of the day. While initially this may seem to be true, remember that you are laying essential groundwork and developing new habits of the heart to make love last.

All that said, there are three barriers to passionate sexuality in any relationship. The big three libido crushers include anger, fear and grief. Unexpressed anger, unacknowledged fear, and unresolved grief or chronic sadness can profoundly affect sexual interest and satisfaction.

Anger is a natural human response to disappointment or frustration that our wants and needs are not being met. Every intimate, meaningful relationship experiences moments of anger. We sometimes misunderstand one another. Our attempts at loving one another fall short or we miss the mark of one another's expectations. Tempers flare in such as time as this. We wonder how we can work through it. Nevertheless, we know that if we want great sex, we have to check our anger at the bedroom door.

Most marital frustration has little to do with sex per se. Worries about money, disagreements about parenting, personal anxieties over work or health issues can cause us to snap. There are times however, when we do become angry over sexual issues. There is no other aspect of life where we feel so vulnerable. Our tendency as humans is to become irritated, disillusioned, and even angry when what we want and need sexually is not met. When we are sexually aroused or desire to make love and fail to receive the hoped-for response, we become cranky. Much as we may think we have a right to be distressed, crankiness and unspoken demand do not constitute effective foreplay. An attitude of "you owe me," thinly veiled, unspoken, can be easily perceived by our partner. The non-verbal pursed lip, distant look and body language reveal our feelings whether we express them verbally or not.

The wisdom of our faith tradition informs our response to anger. Hebrew and Christian scripture urges us to resolve our anger before the sun goes down. Sacred texts acknowledge human creatures sometimes become angry. Nevertheless, we are encouraged to resolve our anger to avoid sin, to avoid damaging our relationships.

It doesn't take a degree in theology to see that it's a bad idea to go to bed mad! In other words, if you want to have a deeply satisfying relationship, work out your anger before you get to the bedroom. If you resist touching your partner or being touched, you may wish to ask yourself what you're so mad about, and you may be surprised with what you discover.

We see the relationship between conflict resolution and intimacy in the Christian approach to communion. To engage in the intimacy of shared life in Christ through his body and blood, we are urged to first go make peace with our brother or sister before we come to the table. Then when we are reconciled, we are invited to return and feast together. Whether feasting at the table of the Lord, or feasting in the intimacy of mutually shared desire, we first need to reconcile with one another if we hope to open ourselves wholly and holy to the other.

Fear, like her brother anger, can debilitate sexual intimacy. We are afraid of many things. We are afraid that our belly fat or lumpy thighs are a turn off. We are anxious that we don't know how to please our partners. We experience shame from unresolved childhood body image issues or outright abuse. All this and more can impact sexual satisfaction for both men and women. Again, the scriptures of our tradition can be our guides. "Perfect love casts out all fear."

Through the eyes of love, the lumps and bumps of physical imperfection all but disappear. Sexy is the one who looks us in the eye adoringly with unspoken desire, "I want you." I've never heard of a partner adding, "But first go get some liposuction and take care of that backside."

Sex is one of the few human experiences that can be satisfying even without experience and when poorly enacted. That is not to say that mutual satisfaction cannot improve through experience and the nuance of knowledge of one's self and partner. Nevertheless, fear, like anger, has no place in the bedroom. While we may be able to engage in sexual intercourse when we feel angry or afraid, we simply cannot open fully to physical intimacy with mutual vulnerability.

The third encumbrance to exuberant sex may be unresolved sadness or grief. This is not to say that sex cannot be deeply satisfying during seasons of grief or loss. In fact, physical intimacy can provide the nurture and care that contribute to successful recovery. Wise is the partner who envelops the beloved in her arms, his arms, with reassuring whispers that all will be well. Silent holding and caress in such seasons speak volumes about our willingness to be there for one another, until such time as joy returns on the far side of sorrow.

Apart from these three potential libido busters, there may be other individual or relationship issues that encumber healthy and enthusiastic sex. When sexual dissatisfaction persists over time or when other issues of the marriage remain unresolved, further work may be needed to resolve those issues and withdraw demand.

While most of us marry with the expectation that passionate desire may flow freely and receive fulfillment and satisfaction within our marriages, satisfying sexual expression always comes as gift. Great gifts carry an element of surprise and delight well beyond the expected or perfunctory, mutually given and received.

There are of course, no guarantees. People are wired differently when it comes to sex, and there is a full range of normal hormonal drive than can vary for both men and for women. But sex in the context of a deeply intimate, mutual and committed relationship is about much more than orgasmic satisfaction. Being lovers means engaging sexually through the mutual expression of affection, respect, honor, love, trust and gratitude. Passionate sex expresses love between two human beings who want to share not only the bedroom but also all of life.

. . .

CHAPTER 6 MALE COUNTERPOINT

DALE ROSENBERGER

It is such a helpful reminder, Verlee, that sex is not only intensely enjoyable, but also an unmistakable indicator of how things are going for a couple. Putting couples on guard for the three libido busters of fear, anger, and grief is to give them a tool box they can carry into the bedroom. Let every couple keep these basics within reach! Yes, we need practical and grounded strategies to fix things in our vulnerability, not just dreams of more fireworks.

When I began preparing couples for marriage over 30 years ago, I would repeat with you that communication was the major virtue to be guarded to keep things healthy. I don't now neglect communication. But I don't say that anymore. I believe, as our faith teaches, that forgiveness and acceptance matter even more. When there is a major impasse in desire, for example, you can communicate till the cows come home, and the couple will still be as unhappy as before, perhaps even more frustrated after all of the rehashing from umpteen different angles. With such an impasse, without a spirit of mercy, grace, and forgiveness, given that our natural egocentrism reigns, communication could maybe even make things worse.

I recall the scene in the movie *Annie Hall* with the split screen where Alvy and Annie both talk to their therapists at the same time. Alvy's therapist asks, "How often do you sleep together?" Then Annie's therapist asks, "Do you have sex often?" Alvy answers first, lamenting, "Hardly ever. Maybe three times a week." Then Annie answers, annoyed, "Constantly, I'd say three times a week." How much more will communication help here? How easily could communication become the veiled attempt to make the other more like oneself?

You mentioned that at the beginning of a relationship, conversation and communication are shared at great length. It is also true early on that little hurt and collateral damage have yet occurred. Expectations are not yet thwarted or disappointed. Over time, without even realizing it, people change and break vows made at the altar. The differences never get reconciled. Honest, sincere, helpful communication gets blocked by our broken dreams, if they are not first dealt with.

Perhaps I really agree with you, but instead add not just communication in general, but forgiveness, as communication in particular is the essential beginning point and the last place of repair for all couples. Perhaps I am only more specific and theological as we both attempt to commend the same healing, hopeful message.

· 7 ·

MARRIAGE AND THE IMPULSE
TO REDEEM ITS FADED GLORY

Dale Rosenberger

Fewer young people marry these days. They are uninterested in marriage. The vows just don't appear on their radar. Some older couples wonder what marriage means, now many decades into it. For young and for old, is marriage still viable?

. . .

Such candor as you dare to venture in your query unsettles our familiar landscape of expectations. As love, romance, and family shift as dramatically as they have within a few generations, the ground trembles beneath our feet. So your concerns are real and daunting. Marriage is indeed in noticeable decline. In 1960, two-thirds of all twenty-somethings were married. About fifty years later, only one-quarter of those in their twenties are bound in wedlock. People marry much later now, or not at all. In 1960, just over 70 percent of adults were married. About fifty years later, just over 50 percent of adults are married. Still, despite this deep and rapid flux shaking and shaping the life of couples, it remains true that a whopping nine out of ten Americans will marry by age forty-five.[1]

Many assert cohabitation as an alternative to marriage; it has doubled since 1990. Yet couples who live together before marrying divorce even more often than couples who do not cohabitate. Maybe living together is not the fresh, hopeful alternative it seemed back in the day. Maybe the bright alternative is right before us but overlooked because, obsessed with meeting our needs and making our choices, the countercultural nature of deep commitment is buried under layers of unnerving uncertainty. Freedom is not found in making things up as we go along. Freedom is found within a structure that gives us a foundation to improvise and play, venturing outside of ourselves. Deep and abiding commitment is not only the road less taken, but also the bright light showing us the way through a couples' wilderness.

I put forward binding ourselves in lifelong vows not just as a source of personal hope and social stability. I re-introduce and re-launch marriage here as a sacred sanctuary for the best and happiest sex. Marriage is a gift from God. It was God's idea and invention, not ours. If we revisit God's intentions around marriage and trace the lines of this encompassing divine architecture as opposed to half-hearted notions clogging our assumptions, we can glimpse the garden where God would have us dwell. In a word, could the loftiest theology of marriage also be a place of passion, where we are not sexually stultified but more fully satisfied?

First, we must ask: what do we expect out of marriage? What is its purpose? Is it some private retractable dome within which couples scamper for mutual pleasure and self-fulfillment? Is marriage alone and unto itself expected to serve as our vehicle to claim

---

1. D'Vera Cohn et al., "Barely Half of U.S. Adults Are Married—A Record Low," Pew Research, Social and Demographic Trends, Dec. 14, 2011, http://www.pewsocialtrends.org/2011/12/14/barely-half-of-u-s-adults-are-married-a-record-low/.

our right to personal happiness and bliss? And if it does not turn out well, does that mean we married the wrong person? If we say yes, let's realize we can romantically freight marriage with burdens of expectation it was never intended to carry, more encumbrance than this staggered institution can realistically be expected to bear. Modern love, with romance front and center—rather than at the side—often takes on a shape like this. Of course, there is nothing wrong with personal fulfillment. On the face of it, one would be hard-pressed to make a case against that, and you won't hear it here. It is a wonderful gift. But Christian marriage unfolds differently and perceives fulfillment differently.

The reason Christians marry is simple: two of us can glorify God more by uniting our spirits as one than by living as separate individuals. For people of faith, becoming one in marriage means God's purposes stand a better shot to be fulfilled over living singly and apart. And leading with the fulfillment of God's purposes, our own personal fulfillment follows in surprising and wondrous ways. Faith in God asks our willingness to trust and risk that as couples. It is truly as basic as that.

Can you see how this broadens the horizons for love, marriage, and romance, putting Christ at the focal center and romance at the periphery? Can you see how this lends what we might call proportionality in all the right places? Can you see how Christ as our partner reduces pressure on couples to succeed as we move ahead, mediating a mercy and grace from without much bigger than we are, giving us an essential margin to prosper and rejoice within our lifetime?

Christian marriage is less centered upon human fulfillment and more upon God-fulfillment. We are part of a larger movement and not a "self-project." We play our small part in advancing purposes in the greater scheme of things we call God's kingdom. As married couples freely offer their distinctive gifts through the Christian community to feed the hungry, to heal the broken, to reconcile the conflicted, to bring hope to the despairing, to teach the unaware, the possibilities for love open before us in profound and life-giving ways. So the time-honored architecture of Christian marriage is grander and soaring, more like a vaulted cathedral gathering in a congregation. I am talking about couples offering up our spiritual and physical union as our life's worship of God. We don't see it drawn up like this much anymore, but that is the essential design. The modern romantic ideal for marriage is an isolated cozy seaside shack where the couple retreats. Christians put romance to one side, as a smaller story within a grander narrative.

And here is the kicker. By focusing more directly on God and the greater good and less directly on our own happiness and fulfillment, it ironically frees us up for, yes, greater personal happiness and fulfillment. Receiving life's best and highest gifts as a byproduct of our relatedness to God rather than our own personal initiative is paradoxical and counterintuitive to the common sense psychology of finding our own way, by ourselves. Taking the direct path, these gifts elude us, like sand escaping through our fingers on the last warm day of summer. We know the seasons change. They *must*. The Christian life agenda is bigger and grander than any human self-project. In a word, we cannot mediate unto ourselves the life of grace that we require and yearn for. This grace is God-mediated, or in our case as Christian people, Christ-mediated. Only he can finally fully reveal what love, forgiveness, forbearance, compassion, generosity, and patience ultimately mean. Only Christ has the power to renew their meaning and transform us.

As we receive happiness and fulfillment as the fruits of living in right relationship with God and partner rather than directly chasing them on our own, we can also hope to become less selfish, less insistent upon our way, less strident about our rights at the expense of others. This is no small feat in the tug of war of wills that many marriages devolve into. And this was Jesus' pregnant and enigmatic meaning in saying: "But strive first for the kingdom of God and his righteousness, and all these things will be given to you as well." (Matthew 6:33)

Beginning my ministry a few decades ago, building my pastoral library, a book sat upon my shelf to help couples navigate the rocky shoals of spirituality and sexuality, righteousness and romance. I frequently loaned it out. This book is devout to the point of pious. It covers all aspects of lovemaking, but with wholesomeness and reverence. It doesn't dodge any aspect of our arousal or anatomy, but is careful, thoughtful, and chaste in its approach. Written by a lifelong committed Roman Catholic married couple, however, the suggestive title of this book fairly screams off its red cover, *The Freedom of Sexual Love.*

Anyway, one day a faithful and committed church member named Betty sat in my study discussing some routine matter of church business. But over my shoulder on my shelf were a few copies of this red book. I had them handy to dispatch to searching couples asking questions about shared intimacy. A few days later I received a letter from this stalwart church member. It expressed mild outrage that her pastor had sold our faith down the river and bought into a permissive society bent upon cheapening what was precious and held dearly between married couples. At first I had no idea what she was talking about. Had I said something to give her the wrong idea? So where did her ire originate? By the letter's end she elliptically referred to the title, and then it became clear to me.

I called and invited her to stop by my study after Sunday worship. I placed the book in her hands and asked her to read it, and note exactly where it woefully misled the reader. I would gladly respond and take responsibility for putting it out there. To Betty's credit, she carefully studied the book. She then delivered it back into my hands. Realizing she had jumped to conclusions, she apologized. She said the title had given her the wrong idea about the contents, which were orthodox and traditional in the conviction that a force as powerful as sex properly belongs protectively set within lifelong vows of marriage. She lauded the couple for writing on such a controversial subject in such a faithful way. Kudos to Betty for getting beyond reactionary knee-jerk responses, opening her heart and mind.

Beyond the obvious point that we can't always tell a book by its cover, the story is suggestive of even greater things. First, as Verlee and I hazard this conversation on sexuality and spirituality, it will doubtless scandalize some elements, like Betty peering from a distance and misjudging. Yes, it is true we are permission-giving in the sense of wanting to empower and restore the many who have given up on sex as a blessing within God's greater purposes. Yes, we are permission-giving for those who have never experienced their sexuality as a God-given gift to be fully shared and celebrated because of fear, guilt, distortion, or ignorance. But that does not—in our estimation—implicate us in what gets called the general permissiveness contributing to the slippery slope of moral breakdown and the collapse of civilization. In fact, we see ourselves as raising standards by bringing God back into the equation and declaring that holiness is not hopelessly at odds with our carnality. As John's gospel opens: "The word became flesh and dwelt among us . . . full of grace and truth." (1:14) We hear this promise without flinching.

Second, Betty's story tickles me because placing sex within the sturdy foundation and soaring architecture of Christ-centered marriage—an idea often dismissed as a conservative encumbrance to keep people down and diminish pleasure—actually leads to the hottest sex. Perceiving that, and, I hope, even experiencing it, maybe that is why Joseph and Lois Bird gave their traditional and demure book on Christian sexuality a rather racy and wild title, *The Freedom of Sexual Love.*

A single woman disclosed to me that her therapist, a faithful and observant Jew, confronted her reluctance to date a practicing Christian, thinking him stuffy and plodding, pleasure-reluctant and fun-impaired. The psychologist challenged her narrow bias, "Don't you know the truly religious people are the ones having the best sex? Don't judge him by the worst of his faith." Her outlook came as a surprise. But over time she came to see the wisdom of this view, even agreeing with her, and credited her therapist for insight she had missed.

Another church couple was abashed to admit that while away on vacation, after a lovely dinner one evening, they walked by a posh sex salon selling every imaginable X-rated item, from videos to lingerie to dildos. Their spontaneous visit was a first for them. They stayed but a few minutes and wandered back out. As they left, the husband smiled to recall her flashing a smile over her shoulder, and saying, "I would rather be in love." The implication was clear. Loving each other spiritually from the inside out, as God invites, rather than from the outside in, as neon sex-for-sale screams, is the most potent and vivid immersion in sexual pleasure we can know. That's why Paul wrote to rowdy and ribald Corinth "We look not to the things that are seen, but to the things unseen. For the things seen are transient. But the things unseen are eternal." (2 Corinthians 4:18) Sadly, this spiritual variety of free and unfettered sexual love remains a secret. Can we get the good news out?

Third, we are at our best as humans as we make promises bigger than we are, promises greater than we could invent, and then spend our lifetime growing into them. Of course, this is not the easiest way to live and love. Frankly, not everyone is called to marry. And not marrying is better if we must insist upon an "I-gotta-be-me" way of life. But in my view, we humans are neurologically hard-wired for binding ourselves in covenant promises. The God who created us and gave us Jesus Christ as a companion to couples understands our needs better than we do. That is why God our Creator is also God our Redeemer.

It is also why the loving-through-trusting-God-first-in-order-to-better-love-one-another model for marriage has existed forever and remains compelling today. Wrapping our lives as couples in this vast overarching commitment of Jesus' self-emptying love creates a safe and secure haven, giving couples freedom to explore and experiment, improvise and extemporize, dabble and play, tease and tantalize, and push the boundaries of what we might find hot and sexy. Perhaps this is why that conservative Catholic couple titled their book as they did.

Let's face it, love and sex intrinsically create tremendous vulnerability. Instinctively, we can sense that as we disrobe and expose ourselves to each other in the buff. Getting naked can be exhilarating, yes, but it is also deeply frightening. Am I desirable? Am I acceptable? That fear side reminds us of why love and sex inherently beg for a structured, committed context lending safety, security and continuity.

Loving each other for now, only to play the field as relationships become difficult or boring, creates uncertainty that reflexively makes us pull back on investing our inner selves to make love wholeheartedly and unselfconsciously. Binding ourselves in God-given promises to love as selflessly as Christ loves frees us to relax and erotically explore in an adventure that never grows old and stale. Of course, this doesn't happen automatically. It demands of couples creative sexual imagination from within, requiring courage and effort. This discipline from within replaces the shallow and easy substitution of new partners from without. Do we dare consider erotic imagination to be a spiritual discipline? Why not? It is all of that in a good marriage, replacing variety from without with variety from within.

The simple words introducing the wedding ceremony express something easily overlooked: "Let all who enter it know that marriage is a sacred and joyous covenant, a way of life ordained by God from the beginning of God's creation."[2] This means marriage was God's idea for us, God's gift to us, not something we cooked up for each other. This means we were made for marriage and marriage was made for us. This means that marriage is not a two-sided pact between a couple, but a three-sided covenant between the couple and Christ, who mediates our love from a higher ceiling than we can when left to our own devices.

---

2. *Book of Worship, United Church of Christ* (Cleveland: Local Church Ministries, Worship and Education Ministry Team, 2009).

Living in a marriage with Christ as our covenant partner, holding husband and wife accountable to God's higher love, establishing foundations and creating equality on bended knee before God is a world of difference from staging a Ken and Barbie wedding in a church and calling it "Christian marriage." In a day when all varieties of marriage falter, when external supports for living marriage as a sacred and joyous covenant are removed, we can no longer take this for granted as people of faith. Of course, we should factor this in not only for marriage, but for every aspect of being Christian in a post-Christian, done-with-God world.

Maybe what Christian marriage promises isn't clear until we consider the alternative, which is one encounter before wandering to the next one, a kind of serial polygamy. But hear this if that sounds promising. When sex is reduced to a form of amusement or entertainment, it enforces superficiality upon our life. Random recreational sex keeps us from plumbing life's depths, where the most powerful and essential sacred mysteries are found. Rather than working our way through together and emerging on the other side at a place of trust in the face of testing and obstacles, we opt out only to start over once again. This is not a formula for spiritual or sensual greatness, giving up and moving on rather than persisting together and pushing through adversity for a deeper bliss.

We root our living in discipleship instead of coasting through the motions of "yeah, whatever . . ." because the external props in society that used to support Christian marriage are now removed. With outward supports no longer there, we look inwardly within the heart of what marriage means and within our community, where we attempt to find our way forward together through joys and struggles. In a day when marriage has become self-invented rather than "a sacred and joyous covenant, a way of life ordained by God from the beginning of God's creation," we recall the purpose of marriage as God defines it, not as we do.

Does this mean Christian marriage is less romantic and less sexy? No, it means romance is less anxious because it occupies its proper place instead of carrying all the freight of the relationship, only to cast itself upon rocky shoals. It means romance can be light and fun. It also gives the chance to make marriage more deeply erotic because sex has been placed in its rightful context. This is how God in Christ gives the freedom of sexual love. Truly, I could not possibly commend to you anything sexier than that.

. . .

CHAPTER 7 FEMALE COUNTERPOINT

VERLEE A. COPELAND

When we covenant with another human being to live as marital partners, we place ourselves in something bigger than ourselves, as you have said, Dale. Our relationship is for us but also for the world, a sign of what God can do through the unitive love of two persons for one another. The relationship becomes a sign of hope for others, as well as an encouragement and a comfort for the two who choose to marry.

Here we speak about faith-based marriage as distinct from the countless other reasons people choose to wed. As people of faith, we marry to pledge the whole of ourselves to another as the primary companion and partner of our life. It is no small thing to give oneself to another for a life we cannot imagine. We cannot know, for example, when we pledge to love one another through sickness and in health, what it will actually feel like to do so: when we clean the bedpan and change the bandages of our partner of fifty years as cancer eats away at their life. We cannot see the consequences of our promise to stand by one another in plenty and in want until one loses a job and the expectation of plenty becomes the cruel reality of want.

The world tends to believe that the purpose of marriage is to make us happy. Our faith teaches us that the purpose of marriage is to serve God together and bear witness to what God can and will do for all God's people through our mutual service. We want to be loved and cherished by the one we love, and we rejoice in the privilege of loving and cherishing them. In marriage, God gifts us with the opportunity to love another as God has loved us, to practice loving deeply and faithfully so that we can love others who frankly are harder to love: those most different from us who nevertheless God counts as our neighbors.

We believe as Christians that contrary to slick media, the best sex is married sex. As we have said, married sex is about more than wanting a regular partner with whom to have sex. Marriage is about wanting the person, and wanting the best well-being for that person. Marriage is about self-sacrificially wanting what our partner needs, before having what we think we want. In marriage we practice forgiveness, never expecting the other to be more perfect than we are ourselves.

Deeply satisfying sex happens when we open ourselves to God's intention for us to live in a safe, mutually caring relationship of love and delight. Though you may think otherwise from reading our work, sex isn't all that complicated. When we love God with all our heart, soul, mind and strength, and love our neighbor (in this instance our spouse) as we love our own self, as Jesus said, then we will be satisfied with our life.

Blessed by God, we create a sanctuary for love to grow. We nurture a context within our home whereby we can reach for one another sexually and both give and receive pleasure. Our sexuality within marriage becomes a gift from God, and for God. We might even say that through our sexuality, our deeply embodied self, we worship God, praising God through love's luminous expression in body and spirit.

When we are married in such a way as this, we reach for one another upon sleeping and upon rising and in the watches of the night. We turn toward one another entwining body and spirit, safely held in the arms of our beloved, whatever the world may render in our waking hours. Whatever befalls us, we return to the marital bed at the end of the day, knowing that we may be met there by one who most deeply desires us and loves us as we are. Here in this sacred marriage, we receive a hint of God's love eternal that waits for us on the other side.

· 8 ·

THE TRUTH THAT SETS YOU FREE

Verlee A. Copeland

My partner wants me to be honest about my sexual past, but I worry that this will damage our relationship. How can I tell the truth in a way that increases intimacy without risking our relationship?

· · ·

This question is a sticky wicket, destined to snare the sexually experienced in a web of half-truths from which he or she may never recover. Alternatively, the honest among us, eager to please the one we love and clear the memory of a past we cannot change, may create a deep relationship rift by telling too much. We may find ourselves in the unfortunate position of wounding our relationship by sharing details that no longer have power over us, but assume disproportionate importance in the imagination of our lover. Often we err by assuming that our partner is asking one thing when in fact the question asked may be something else altogether.

We begin by asking whether or not God always wants us to tell the truth. We may assume that God desires truthfulness given Christian teaching through scripture that invites us to plain speech. "Simply let your 'yes' be 'yes' and your 'no' be 'no'. Anything beyond this comes from the evil one." (Matthew 5:37, NIV) We also recall the words of one of the Ten Commandments: "You shall not bear false witness." A false witness testifies in court that something happened a certain way when it did not, or tells a partial truth that implies a different outcome than what actually took place. That is why the historical oath in American courts asked witnesses to "Solemnly swear to tell the truth, the whole truth, and nothing but the truth." We may no longer say, "So help me God" in court, but we promise it as Christians in our relationships. We count on one another in Christian community to share the truth about our lives.

The Bible encourages us in this way, "Instead, speaking the truth in love, we will in all things grow up into him who is the Head, that is, Christ." (Ephesians 4:15 NIV) In both Christian community and committed relationships, truth-telling in love is essential for healthy intimacy to grow.

I know of two churches that suffered through crises due to sexual misconduct on the part of clergy. These communities handled the crises in very different ways. One community, upon legal counsel, did not speak of the situation at all. The truth remained hidden, underground. By the time the case settled out of court two years later, the community already demonstrated signs of distance and estrangement that can occur when secrets are tightly held, the truth never spoken. The other community painfully acknowledged what had happened and took responsibility for their part in it and their response in the aftermath. The clergy was appropriately disciplined and removed from office. In small group settings, people were encouraged to express their anger and grief.

Through deep trust in God and one another, through effective intervention and fervent prayer, the latter community healed and was able to move forward once again as a vibrant and faithful church. We create a safe and sacred container for our lives when we trust God to hold the whole truth of who we are and whose we are, and to remain with us regardless of anything we may have said, thought or done.

In Christian community we can hear things about ourselves that we don't want to hear, and receive the forgiveness we may not believe we deserve. God is merciful like that. Through the Abrahamic covenant of the Hebrew texts shared by the major monotheist faiths of the world, we believe there is a God who made heaven and earth and all that was, is and ever will be. We affirm that this God created all things and remains intimately involved in creation. From the beginning of our story as human creatures, we were created related. The intention of creation is that we live in harmonious relationship with one another and with the God who promised to be our God and claimed us to be God's beloved people. When we live in committed relationship with one another and with God, we can confront another whose words or actions are causing us harm and trust that they will hear our underlying desire to be reconciled with them, because God has revealed to us that this is not only possible but desirable for us as human creatures.

When we are willing to face the truth about ourselves and come clean with it, we can trust that God will do what God does: "Create in me a clean heart O God, and renew a steadfast spirit within me." (Psalm 51:10 NIV) God makes possible what we cannot, the reconciliation of human creatures to one another and to God. Simply stated, our faithful response to a God who loved us into being and loves us still is to behave in ways consistent with our creation in God's image.

That said, we remember that of the roughly 300 questions asked of Jesus, only a small number of them were answered. Jesus understood our insecurities and fears. He listened deeply to the questions underneath our questions and addressed those instead. Asked about use of money, he called for a coin and inquired whose picture was on it. When the reply was Caesar, he told his inquisitors to give to God what was God's and to Caesar what was Caesar's. He refused to be trapped in such a way that one answer made him disloyal to Caesar and another disloyal to God. He gave them a real question to replace their trick question. When Job questioned God about how he, a righteous person, could so profoundly suffer, God didn't answer those questions directly either. Rather, God gave Job better questions.

When asked about our sexual past, we need to listen for the deeper questions too. We may think that we readily understand what is being asked, but we may want to pray about this and listen for God's wisdom in order to answer rightly. On the other hand, it can be tempting to manipulate the question in order to avoid answering it altogether. For example, when our partner asks if we've ever slept with anyone we weren't married to, we may squirm saying something like, "I've always been as faithful as I could be." If in fact we had a two-year affair with the mailman, saying that we were as faithful as we could be may be true, but that isn't what our partner is asking. Here we may sidestep, asking back, "How about you?" "What makes you ask?" Or, we may say, "No, I've never slept with anyone." What we may mean is, "I had sex with Joe Smith fifty times but we didn't actually ever sleep together." However we respond, God calls us to do so lovingly, motivated by a deep desire to assure our partner that they are loved and wanted.

Sometimes when asking about our sexual past, our partner wants us to affirm that they are good enough as lovers. Many people hope to hear that they are the only or the best lover we have ever had. This is not a category in which anyone wants to win the silver or bronze medal. They may want to know if we desire them above all. They may worry that we linger over the memory of someone we wanted more or remain haunted by memories of some great lover whom our current partner can never match.

When our partner wants to know that they are the best in bed, what may be most needed is the loving reassurance that we are sexually satisfied, that we are hot for our partner, and that we have never known anything like what we experience today. Regardless of our sexual history, we can tell our partner that all other loves or experiences fade and dim in memory such that you couldn't honestly bring them to mind any longer. If that is not true, it may be better to praise specific things we enjoy about the one we are with, the unique gifts that person has brought to us rather than say something that is less than true just because we think it will make our partner feel better.

All that said, there is the possibility that our sexual history is taking up more space in our current bed than we would like. We need to be honest with ourselves. An honest self-appraisal may be in order to discover whether or not our fantasy of another enhances our current experience with our partner, or leaves them and us wanting. There are times when a current lover simply cannot compete with the idealized image of that perfect man or woman, frozen in time and space at a body perfect and ripe age. That wrinkling, paunchy guy on the other side of the mattress may not be able to compete in your imagination with the fling you once had or wanted on a moonlit beach in your youth. Get over it. The guy in bed next to you wins hands down, because, well, he belongs to you. That's sexy.

While most people fantasize about another from time to time, real or imagined, what can you do if your partner is worried for good reason? If our fantasies of a former lover, real or imagined, keep us from being fully present to our husband or wife, we may need the help of a competent therapist, priest, minister or rabbi to be healed of such memories and let them go. If we find that we are in fact not happy in our current relationship, and/or that our sex life falls far short of what we had hoped or imagined, we may benefit from couples' therapy to remove any blocks in the relationship that get in the way of playful delight with one another both in and out of the bedroom.

If we struggle in the bedroom, we may want to begin to increase our intimacy somewhere else. I often tell couples that prayer is more intimate than sex. They seldom believe me, until they try it. The mutual vulnerability of placing ourselves together before our God who is so much bigger than ourselves can open us profoundly both above and below the navel. We are created of a piece: body, mind and spirit. There is a direct correlation between our sexual satisfaction and the shared intimacy of passion outside the bedroom. With hands held in a quiet chapel or on a local park bench, heads bowed in prayer, a connection is forged that expands our physical embrace of one another. Pleasure shared through an emotionally moving concert or a breathtaking sunset can open us more deeply to one another physically as well.

Prayer in particular makes of us something we cannot of our own accord make of ourselves. For example, a woman once told me how excited she was to be marrying her husband as a virgin. I knew for a fact that she had been sexually promiscuous by the age of fourteen and had enjoyed a series of boyfriends in high school. She was sexually active with a number of them. She looked at me knowingly. She knew that I knew her history, and could tell from my expression that I was at first perplexed. "You see," she said, "God has forgiven me. God's power released me from the past in all ways. I am a spiritual virgin. The past is over and gone."

God's forgiveness for this young woman completely restored her: body, mind and spirit. It freed her to give herself wholly and without reservation to her husband, and neither she nor her husband ever felt the need to talk about her past. Her early sexual experiences were over and gone as God promises.

This is good news for us and for our partners. No man wants to hear his wife describe in detail the top ten sex positions she enjoyed with a previous lover, unless it is personally non-specific in the context of foreplay, learning and growing, and he is eager to try them too. What woman really wants to know that her husband made love to a woman morning and night every day for the year they were together? She would likely feel deflated and inadequate before their honeymoon was over, especially if she were less sexually experienced.

One woman came to see me for pastoral counseling saying that she and her husband had been struggling with their sex life for more than a year. One day in his misguided attempt to come clean with the truth, he blurted out that while she was a petite, short-haired brunette, what really turned him on was large-boned, big-breasted blondes . . . like his former girlfriend. Marital counseling became divorce counseling in short order. Can we rehearse how things might have gone if the standard of "speaking the truth in love" had been better understood and heeded here?

Another couple, eventually married for decades, had a most rocky start. During one of several lengthy separations early in their married life due to the husband's numerous affairs, the wife found comfort for one night in the arms of a dear male friend. At the time she did not believe that her husband would return, but return he did. While they did eventually reconcile as a married couple, a deep rift grew and deepened after she confessed her brief liaison. While she did find through faith a way to forgive his sexual exploits outside their marriage, he was never able to release his rage at her infidelity, treating her with unwarranted mistrust for years.

You may wonder at this point if speaking the truth in any form is worth the risk. Should we lie to avoid telling the truth or leave out critical information that has profoundly shaped our story? That brings us back to the sticky wicket where we began this conversation. When do we tell the truth and how much truth do we reveal? Whatever our partner asks us, we may want to think before answering. We can do this with a response such as: "That's such an important question that I want to give it some thought."

Set a time to come back to it as a way to honor and value the question and the one asking it. Then resist the temptation to pretend the question will go away. It won't. Think about how to most faithfully respond and consider the following. Pray alone or with your partner about what might be gained or lost by disclosure regarding your sexual history. Unexamined disclosure is unlikely to contribute to intimacy or alleviate anxiety on the part of either of you.

Explore with your partner the potential motivation behind the questions. Is he looking for proof of your current love? Does he wonder if he can satisfy you sexually? Is he deflecting conversation about his own sexual history? What's at stake in this conversation? Does your partner have an unnatural and unhealthy sexual interest in what you did before you met?

Acknowledge honestly your own underlying motives *not* to disclose. Is it to protect your partner from hurt or harm, or is it to protect yourself from shame, embarrassment and the risk of potential loss? How can you faithfully address what you discover about yourself? Discuss together what it means to be people of character, people who can count on and rely upon one another to live a life of fidelity and authenticity.

There are of course legitimate reasons to provide a straightforward answer to a straightforward sexual question. When asked if you used condoms or other protection against pregnancy or other sexually transmittable diseases, you need to answer the question directly so that your partner can make an informed choice. If you protracted a sexually transmittable disease, your partner has the right to use protection and you have an ethical obligation to give them the information they need to care for their own physical health.

Another reason to answer the question directly is when you sense that the two of you have a deep trust and loving context for the question. Then you may know that your best response is to enfold your beloved in your arms and tell them that you love them, you adore them, and whatever your past there never has nor ever will be another like them. As one of my parishioners said most succinctly: "I've been to more than one prom, but I saved the last dance for you."

. . .

CHAPTER 8 MALE COUNTERPOINT

DALE ROSENBERGER

You give sound practical counsel, Verlee, in an area where most couples have little idea that land mines ominously linger beneath the surface calm. In the moment we inquire about our partner's sexual past or volunteer information about our own, we naturally sense that we navigate dangerous waters. But it is hard to gauge how explosive even an innocent, tossed-off remark might be, and how lasting the damage. Words have such deceptive power and they can only partially be taken back once they are out there.

As we talk about "speaking the truth in love," it might be helpful to break "the truth" in two and keep both parts equally in mind as couples enter this minefield. After all, for us Christians, truth is an expansive and encompassing tent housing people beloved to God, not an accumulation of factoids, as the modern world has it. First, truth has a factual, objective side where we must reckon with what actually happened apart from the spin we want to give it. This is what you mean, Verlee, by "the truth, the whole truth, and nothing but the truth," as a court of law seeks to have events narrated in a neutral and accurate way.

Second, truth has a personal, subjective side of keeping good faith with another human being and always seeking their best interests, most especially someone we love and want to spend the rest of our lives with. Every relationship brings obligations, and by fulfilling them, we remain true to that person. All of this and more is implied when we talk about "being true to the one I love." Can you hear how personally all of that rings?

The factual, objective side is what most normally mean by "the truth." Still, if that is all we are aware of, we likely end up

occasionally wielding the truth like a club, intentionally or unintentionally, and find the person we cherish reduced to tears. And
then we will defensively mutter something unhelpful like, "Well,
you asked . . . ." If we are aware that the personal, subjective side
of truth, which is the integrity of our relationship and the generosity of our love, is no less important than "the facts," then we will
prayerfully devote ourselves to matters like when to say what, how
to say it, what to skip entirely, and, as Verlee insists, what question
is actually being asked of us. This asks a lot more of us than simply
reporting the facts. This requires devotion, imagination, sensitivity,
and willingness to get outside of our skin and dwell for a few key
moments in the skin of one beloved to us. Are we up for it? We
had better be if we speak of love. Much is at stake where we are
so vulnerable, body and soul. Maybe this is why Shakespeare said,
"Speak softly, if you speak of love." Hear the bard. Tread gently.

9

THE GOOD, THE BAD, AND
THE INDIFFERENT AROUND
SELF-PLEASURING

Dale Rosenberger

I recently walked in on my wife pleasuring herself. Was I surprised! She looked embarrassed and we haven't discussed it. What is the place for self-pleasuring?

. . .

We badly need a fun fact here to begin. For if we join this discussion without a sense of humor, all is lost. Question: what do graham crackers, corn flakes and cold showers have in common? Answer: the cold showers tip us off that both graham crackers and corn flakes were invented as "mild foods" to decrease sexual desire, specifically to prevent masturbation among young people. Dr. Sylvester Graham, a New Jersey Presbyterian pastor came up with the graham cracker in 1829 to mute carnal desire. Dr. John Harvey Kellogg (yes, that one, from Battle Creek) was a Seventh Day Adventist physician who created corn flakes in 1884 in the ongoing warfare against passion, particularly "self-abuse."

Such thinking hearkens to Dr. Samuel-Auguste Tissot, a Swiss doctor. In 1758 he indicted masturbation as a perilous threat to the human species. He theorized that losing an ounce of semen equals losing forty ounces of blood. In the Middle Ages, the body was seen as the devil's dominion. Enlightenment civilization next saw the body as a bank on the brink of collapse. Any withdrawal of what Tissot called *liqueur seminale* risked organic and spiritual bankruptcy. Self-pollution, as he dubbed self-pleasing, caused irreversible decline in the nervous system. Before we roll our eyes at his assessments, it must be said that Dr. Tissot was no quack, but a respected man of science. Yet because of his reactionary fear around masturbation, the church no longer stands alone with its nutty histrionics on sex.

Notice also that as we consider self-pleasure, we enter the theater of absurd. Popular culture has lampooned our overwrought fears. For example, Federico Fellini's film *Amarcord* shows Italy in the 1930s through the eyes of youth. A priest specializes in ferreting out boys ruining their lives through feeding and fomenting adolescent fantasies: making too many withdrawals "from their bank." Over and over in the confessional booth, speculating on their furtive secrets from the dark circles under their eyes, he accuses, "You are a toucher, aren't you!" They squirm and fidget. But they remain undeterred, finding refuge in a tiny car whose headlights bob under the cover of night, relieving themselves en masse. The confessional booth scene gets funnier as it recurs throughout the movie. "You're a toucher! I know it." The priest has appointed himself watchdog as the future of Italy threatens to squander its vitality through masturbation. But the priests are so worried about boys' self-touching, they miss Mussolini's thugs seizing power as violent despots, visiting ruin and loss on an entire generation. What did Jesus say about straining at gnats but missing logs? It is seemingly Fellini's point also.

Of course, today is very different. Counselors and other therapeutic experts go out of their way to commend masturbation as normal and healthy, not only to be expected, but as natural as buttering your toast in the morning. Just be careful about the setting (not appropriate public behavior) and the frequency (do your homework first). Such blithe, *carte blanche* approbation feels again like overcorrection to the centuries-old demonizing of sex and masturbation. Perhaps a more nuanced consideration is in order. Perhaps our spirituality can inform these reflections.

First, let us beware of puffing ourselves up ridiculing past errors and anointing ourselves scions of reasonable progress. Arrogance is hazardous. For example, while Drs. Graham, Kellogg, Tissot and others got wrong the theory of spermatorrhea—men having only so much seed and needing to retain it at all costs to remain vital—they did know something lost on many contemporary observers. Sex is no mere amusement, distraction or entertainment. It is never disinterested happenstance biology. Sex powerfully shapes us for good or ill, even alone by ourselves. Sex—including self-pleasure—is about hearts and minds, souls and spirits. As Frederick Buechner succinctly summarizes, sex is always to be treated like nitroglycerin. For it has power to heal hearts or to blow up bridges.

Now, for your question, having cleared some space beneath the frippery of these historical and social trappings. Masturbation is a natural, wholesome, and perhaps preferred course in our early sexual self-discovery. If we are lucky, it is how and where we begin to unfold as sexual creatures, male and female. In that regard, we should be grateful our initial forays into becoming sexual creatures can happen in a neutral solitary ground to learn how we are made, how our bodies function, and the delicate interplay of creative fantasy as symbolic beings with our primal physicality as earthbound creatures.

These complexities of human arousal are the same for no two of us, their interplay is delicate and arcane, and the connections involved require the craft of much subtlety. For example, it is a fact that most women cannot achieve orgasm without clitoral stimulation. If efforts toward that cherished goal start only as a woman reaches today's marriageable age of twenty-seven, having waited for decades under the age-old banner of restraint, she may never achieve orgasm, having come too late to the party, please pardon the pun.

God knows we all already feel ridiculous and misbegotten enough crossing this threshold into our developmental sexual maturity. At this turn, we typically feel like something must be wrong with us, that we are like nobody else, and that we are the only ones burdened with such urges. Not to be coarse, discovering our sexuality in self-pleasure, we can grope and fumble without an audience to mock us. Given how vulnerable we all feel discovering ourselves as sexual creatures—and let's face it, our first orgasm brings home this reality as a shock to all of us—we should be grateful. Being alone by ourselves to figure out the vagaries of how God equips us and taking our sweet time according to our individual timetable to become sexual are both good things. I have met people who by their own description seem incapable of self-pleasuring. In these and other regards, they may be operating at a disadvantage in today's world.

Also, first discovering ourselves as sexual creatures alone in self-pleasure, perhaps we can be less vulnerable to being exploited by someone older and more powerful looming over us in our naiveté before we "know the score." In a day when we are newly aware of the appalling extent of sexual abuse, this poses distinct advantages for good, personally and socially. This is not to mention avoiding the damage done by sexually transmitted diseases, which morph from nuisance to life-threatening in our lifetime.

As hinted a moment ago, self-pleasuring becomes even more important as the average age to wed and the opportunity for the Christian ideal—sex nestled in a marital covenant of belovedness—now occurs on average a full fourteen years later, more than double the age, of three centuries ago. We do know this much. We are not developing sexually later than in generations past. The sexual urge within us will not stand idly by, dormant, as sociology and demographics shift. As the blues artist John Lee Hooker put it with primitive eloquence in "Boogie Chillen' No. 2," "It in 'em and it gotta come out. Let that boy boogie-woogie." No, Hooker didn't mean Tissot's precious seed, but the mojo of being made a sexual creature, equipped with a dynamic God-given force, animating life and populating society. Teens are sexual creatures. Why does it seem to surprise the decency brigades that we will not soon convince them otherwise? This dialogue is about how to mediate God's intimate gift of sex in ways at once holy, healthy, and right.

Is it possible that what once was denounced as "solitary vice" might become "solitary virtue" as new threats in our developing life stages present themselves? If that sounds like a brave new world or a slippery slope into vulgarity, consider again the Puritans. Despite modernity's caricature of them as uptight prudes, were the Puritans ahead of us? Consider how the Puritans practiced "bundling." Bundling allowed young people in love to bed together with a large board down the middle to separate them. This allowed the couple to talk, to touch, to view, to feel, even to release. But at the same time there was a line to be respected, and neither party was to cross over it. I do not advance this as some magical remedy today, these centuries later. But if we take seriously the sexuality of young people, respect their situation, and give them options, sex need not become all or nothing at all. This is what Puritans of 300 years ago can teach painfully enlightened moderns.

If we can talk about a place for self-pleasuring within God's greater purposes for young and single people, then let us also talk about married couples, which is where your question originated. What is perhaps most amazing is the many who marry only to assume and expect that self-pleasuring is over. Or it should be. Of course, in an ideal world, pure freedom is a whole, full giving of ourselves sexually to our husband or wife out of mutually shared love, all of the time. God knows we don't live in an ideal world.

What about periods of lengthy separation for couples such as military service or business trips? What about couples being away from one another to attend to urgent family duties like infirm relatives? What about being apart because increasingly scarce good jobs require long commutes, with perhaps one taking an apartment in another city? What about the grinding routine facing young couples with pressures on several fronts as they prove themselves in the workplace at the same stage their young and needy children are most dependent at home? That usually means either the breadwinner or the childcare-giver collapsing into bed at 9 P.M. leaving his or her partner to wonder what happened to the sensual magic that launched their lives together way back when. Is it forever gone and lost?

In all of the above, self-pleasuring could possibly become a compassionate alternative to always having to ignore and stuff insistent erotic feeling and living without in a landscape devoid of gratification. In all of the above, masturbation can also be a hedge against affairs outside of marriage and give spouses what we need to survive until a less mean season of life arrives. As we assess its place in the lives of married couples, none of these dimensions should go underestimated or unappreciated.

Further, what about the individuals who, for whatever reason, never marry but are gifted by God with erotic energy? Or what about the couples who marry never suspecting the difference in their sex drives is a great and wide gulf? What if this difference in desire changes significantly for couples over the decades? If you are one of the rare couples waiting till marriage to consummate your sexual relationship, as Christianity traditionally taught, the chances skyrocket of a painful mismatch in desire happening. Are such as these to be without recourse? Are we to sing to them our own righteous, self-satisfied choruses of "all or nothing at all?" None of that sounds to me like the working of the Holy Spirit or the way of the God who was in Jesus Christ, reconciling the world to himself.

This next remark sounds odd, but give it a chance. It is entirely possible that God could have made us such that any auto-erotic release would be impossible. But that's not how we are made. Instead God endows us with soaring imagination and powers to magically lift and transport us beyond immediate circumstances. Read Song of Solomon again and appreciate the free and lofty erotic ceiling God gives us. Song of Solomon 5:5–6 is an erotic dreamscape, essentially a woman's wet dream, if truth be told. As the Bible's sole masturbation scene unfolds, it is unexpected. It is even shocking. This is the Bible my grandma gave me? Most of the yearning in Song of Solomon occurs as the couple is apart; all of the vivid arousal it describes is absent of her beloved other. Auto-eroticism is implied from the beginning and to the end of this erotic masterpiece. Maybe suggesting God's greater purposes might be served within the auto-erotic impulse—for many stations, including marriage—is not far-flung, misplaced, and wrong-headed.

Notice as we discuss masturbation for couples from a Christian point of view, it is as a proximate, not a final form of sexuality. It is a bridge, a way-station to elsewhere, a safe haven in a rights-based sexual wilderness screaming self-assertion. This is important. This matters in a day when sexual materials abound to inflame and own us, and when hyper-individuality sadly carries the day at the expense of the riskier yet more rewarding work of living in authentic relationship. This matters as it displaces and replaces sex between husband and wife. As lonely self-pleasuring becomes the goal and the intimate connected vulnerability of husband and wife is discarded, we lose something precious. We have been compromised. Masturbation becomes pathetic sex rather than solitary, alternative sex. We become stuck at a diminished level of sexual expression that makes us less able to enter the risky intimacy and tender intricacy of deep eroticism in true love.

The more self-pleasuring becomes the consumerism of instant gratification, the more we run the risk of becoming consumed with it, as in becoming addicted. The world does not know, but the church can teach that sex lodges deeper in our spirits and souls than, "Where do I itch? How soon can I scratch it?" In his fine book *Kosher Sutra,* Shmuley Boteach makes a case for sexuality that transcends the satiation of biological urge. If we want sex as more than hydraulic release, sleeping pill, or tension reduction, he invites us to consider the merits of delayed gratification. What if the husband saves his desire for his wife rather than always caving in to "blow off steam?" Frankly, men who cultivate restraint make better lovers because their yearning increases. Whenever yearning increases, Boteach reminds, deep longing for the other increases. Yearning and longing are what Song of Solomon are all about. "I am faint with love," (5:8) writes the author. "Many waters cannot quench love, neither can floods drown it," (8:7) she says.

Like this, before we know it, we find ourselves with our spouse in a place we can call true eroticism. We find ourselves escaping the humdrum many married couples complain about. This can't happen as we always satiate ourselves apart from our partner when our partner might only be hours or a day away from us. Resist the shallow impulse in order to feed the deeper one of a more complete union with your beloved. It is how boys spiritually mature into men: delay of immediate gratification for the sake of greater fulfillment. Notice how this spiritual conversation of masturbation—Jewish and Christian—diverges from the blander advice ("as long as it's not hurting anyone") of counseling orthodoxy in this regard. This is what I meant by a more nuanced and spiritual consideration of self-pleasure.

We cannot discuss masturbation and ignore its relationship to pornography or erotica. How do pornography and erotica differ? Gloria Leonard joked it is the lighting. Surely the difference is in the eye of the beholder. But no one can deny that Song of Solomon is graphic erotica cast into poetry. Read it in its original Hebrew and the craving sizzles even more in its imagery. Anyway, as for the relationship between masturbation and erotica/pornography, let us invoke the law of male versus female sexuality lifted up elsewhere in this book. Remember, we men are more direct, transparent, and straight ahead, sexually. What you see is what you get. Women are more indirect, mysterious, and complex. What you don't see is better yet.

First, let's talk about the male side. When explicit sexual materials are not only an alternative in times of deprivation, but a replacement for genuinely relating to a living, breathing human, they become addictive. Women complain about men fixing upon and obsessing over young and perfect bodies. They feel intimidated, diminished and replaced. That isn't necessarily the biggest problem as masturbation becomes a lonely, addictive pastime for men. Frankly, most men are more grateful for their wives' bodies than women believe; yes, even despite their flaws. Frankly, the truth is that most women are harder on their own figures and the figures of other women than men are. Women would know that if they spent any time in men's locker rooms. If Madison Avenue has done a job on us and our bodies, it has been subtly done on women more essentially than on men.

While idealizing the impossible figures of pornography can hurt couples, what is even more troubling is the manipulative complete control of an isolated "one" displacing the more complex and difficult interplay of "two," the meeting in the middle that is essential to mature relationship and sexuality. Frankly, many men look to excuse, withdraw and exempt themselves from the complex back and forth of intimacy that occurs in real relationships. Escaping into reclusive or obsessive masturbation becomes this bunkered hiding place for no few men. A glimpse into this withdrawn world is in the 2013 film *Don Jon* as he ticks off his priorities: his pad, his car, his body (exercise), his family, his church, his girls, and his porn. It is a source of real consternation as "his porn" outshines "his girls." He indulges in porn even right after lovemaking with his companion.

But Christianity is about holding sex and relationship together, and not allowing sex to be split off and apart from a committed, living and breathing, beloved union of two persons. We maintain here as elsewhere that a faithful theology of sex is about two spirits, two souls, two minds, two hearts becoming one as the two bodies become one. Even more than body parts, this requires commitment, loyalty, tenderness, dedication, constancy, playfulness, unselfishness, humor, imagination, generosity, and especially faith.

We might also discuss women and pornography. No, I don't mean women viewing graphic body linkages found on the Internet, although the popularity of that grows among women these days. The female pornography I mean is the romance novel, a.k.a. "the bodice ripper." Let's face it, female pornography is mostly socially acceptable whereas male pornography is not. She buys it at an airport newsstand in front of everyone without blinking. It is well-understood that women buy these paperback erotic novels not so much for their romantic chivalry, but to get lost in long, extensive tales of seduction. Instead of the stark plumbing shots of male pornography, female pornography is carefully coded as his "throbbing manhood" meets her "dewy flower" giving rise to "her shivering, shaking resolution." It is another instance of how female sexuality tends to be more indirect.

Instead of male pornography's unattainable ideal of a young, lithe, voluptuous Barbie, romantic novels conjure a man who is wealthy, muscled, attentive, and able to anticipate her many needs without even hearing them articulated. Of course, the guy in these romantic novels never endures a tyrannical boss to hold down a job he hates or fixes clogged garbage disposals. And here is the point: no man can compete with and live up to this ideal any more than women can compete with an impossibly curvaceous Barbie of male pornography.

What is the difference? Both are remote, unattainable, and unsustainable in real life. Both are fully pornographic, in that sense; they are a self-involved, immature recoil to replace the demanding work of negotiating with another in the middle, relationally and sexually. Women retreat and hide in their fantasies; men retreat and hide in our different fantasies. Maybe we best bring our fantasies in the open to share them with our beloved. Maybe honesty is the best playing field for these matters to be worked out. Maybe what we allow to separate and divide us can unite and passionately fuse us together. What a notion!

What is the place of masturbation in marriage, you ask? Much as couples first measure intimacy by their willingness to leave the lights on while making love, perhaps another benchmark is the willingness to instruct your beloved in what pleases you by demonstrating how you self-stimulate. Think of it: if you will not teach, how do you expect your beloved to know? And is there any better teaching than demonstration? Of course, this might be too candid for some. It might be startling. But it is real, vulnerable and full of clues to your beloved's unknown hidden self, for those not too faint of heart. Remember what is not hidden and kept from each other, but brought out and shared, is robbed of its power to divide, and even charged with new power to unite you.

Reaching a level of honesty where you do together without shame what you had always furtively done alone can confer trust, banish distance, and endear with tenderness. Same as looking into each other's eyes as you make love rather than closing them. Same as kissing long, passionate, wet kisses rather then curt pecks. Same as luxuriating over a long time cherishing and exploring each other rather than making a beeline to orgasm only to roll over and snore. Self-pleasuring within marriage could fit in this category.

Maybe it is time you look her in the eye with new honesty before, during, and after the next time you make love. She might be holding her breath and waiting for you to take the lead in this. Vulnerability requires much courage. Are you ready to move to the next level together?

. . .

CHAPTER 9 FEMALE COUNTERPOINT

VERLEE A. COPELAND

Graham crackers may have been invented to temper passion, but the inventor clearly misunderstood the capacity of humans for naughty pleasure. What could be more fun than snuggling up at the backyard fire pit on a crisp fall night to roast marshmallows, and, you guessed it, a graham cracker. Ask any woman to choose between sex and melting marshmallows? Add the perfectly toasted jewel to a slab of Saratoga dark chocolate from Blommer's and you'll hear a long pause! No wonder they're called s'mores!

Perhaps the issue of self-pleasuring, like no other, points to distinct differences between men and women. You've spoken here about the benefits of self-pleasuring for men in general, as a safe and healthy release when shared mutual intimacy is not possible. It's helpful to de-mystify and de-moralize sexual relations with oneself. While we both affirm the primacy of scripture to guide our lives, we understand scripture in new light based on our emerging insight into God's creation over time. You may recall that we have discussed previously how our understanding of biology has changed since our ancestors first prohibited the spilling of male seed on the ground. We now fully understand the role of both male sperm and female egg to produce a child. We thus re-interpret scripture over time as we become more clear about how God's creation works. The prohibition for men to self-pleasure continues primarily in those religious traditions that affirm sex only for procreation.

Theological ethicist Margaret Farley describes sexual relations with oneself as morally neutral.[1] There are risks of course, as with any sexual practice. We humans have the capacity to take any good

1. Margaret Farley, *Just Love: A Framework for Christian Sexual Ethics* (New York: Continuum, 2006).

and corrupt or misuse it. You've explored the potential risks of addictive reliance on the practice: withdrawing from the greater complications of relationship to the lonely release in some private quarter. While masturbation does have its place, it cannot substitute for the Song of Solomon embrace of lovers we celebrate as God's good gift.

For women, self-pleasuring in twentieth century North America became an avenue for awakening desire and exploring sexual understanding. In the last half of the century, women began to discuss in greater detail their sexual experience rather than simply describing what went on "down there" as if sexual response were somehow detached from the body. Like the experience of their male counterparts, women discovered much about their own sexual response through self-pleasuring. And like men, many women practice self-pleasuring when sexual practice with a partner is not possible.

We also know that the intensity of desire builds differently for women than for men, sometimes taking a longer time to peak, and then remaining at peak long after her male partner. His tendency may be to roll over and fall asleep, as hormone levels drop swiftly immediately after orgasm. Her response remains heightened. Self-pleasuring for her can contribute to his capacity to remain present to her longer response time, thus playing an important role within lovemaking. A man also learns what pleases his lover by participating with her in self pleasuring, as our complicated anatomy differs not only from men, but also from one another.

Understanding and accepting our own bodies contributes to self-acceptance for women that can create a greater ease with one's partner. The more we know about ourselves and accept the unique and complicated anatomy of our human form, how it works and what brings us pleasure, the more we have to share with our partner. Men who love us want to please us sexually. They want us to want them and to want to please them sexually. Insofar as self-pleasuring increases our comfort in our own skin, the practice contributes to satisfying mutual sexuality in our marriage. Once again, that's a good thing, that's a God thing.

· IO ·

COME ON BABY, LIGHT MY FIRE

Verlee A. Copeland

My husband and I have fallen into a comfortable love with about as much sexiness as a pair of old gym shoes. I'd like to light a fire, but frankly it's been a long time and I don't know how to begin. How can I seduce my husband?

· · ·

What a playful and hopeful question you pose! Clearly you want to experience a kind of seduction outside the bedroom that leads to hot sex with your partner. Sexy starts in the room furthest from the bedroom. It begins slowly, a dance of seduction so subtle it may not at first appear to have anything to do with sex at all. This seductive dance begins with a mindful awareness of the presence of the beloved. In the Song of Solomon, two potential lovers open to one another in a sensual awakening that can be described as a feast for the eyes.

> My beloved is all radiant and ruddy, distinguished among ten thousand. His head is the finest gold; his locks are wavy, black as a raven. His eyes are like doves beside springs of water, bathed in milk, fitly set. His cheeks are

like beds of spices, yielding fragrance. His lips are lilies, distilling liquid myrrh. His arms are rounded gold, set with jewels. His body is ivory work, encrusted with sapphires. His legs are alabaster columns, set upon bases of gold. His appearance is like Lebanon, choice as the cedars. His speech is most sweet, and he is altogether desirable. This is my beloved, and this is my friend. (Song of Solomon 5:10–16a)

We imagine that the bride ravishes her beloved with her eyes before the barest touch of a finger brushes his skin. Powerful words describe his physical being as like that of towering cedars. The hearer of these words from Song of Solomon can imagine the strength of muscled thigh, sinewy belly, and unyielding arms. Hebrew scripture does not mince words. The physique of a beloved man is a vision to behold. Imagining his legs as alabaster columns and his arms as rounded gold are enough to make the raptured woman swoon. Such erotic language awakens the senses such that every nerve ending is afire with desire.

Compare this to the following scene from the average American household. ESPN blares the latest sports event from the foot of the bed on the big screen television set. She crawls into bed wearing a pair of paint stained yoga pants from that last project in the basement, her oversized gray t-shirt touching her knees. Now that the kids are finally tucked in for the night, she texts her friend across town.

He sits beside her on his half of the king-sized bed, finishing up the last of the late night work emails while the television provides white noise that drowns out the wordless silence that would otherwise settle between them. Samson, the golden retriever, jumps up on the bed and plops down at the foot, forcing one of the two to scrunch up slightly beneath the covers to make room. The husband in this scenario belches and then tries to scratch a body part he can't quite reach. She pulls out a small mirror and set of tweezers, and then begins to pull out a few stray hairs, examining her face in the mirror for signs of the betrayal of years.

With unspoken agreement they turn off the bedside lamps from either side, after setting their e-clocks to wake them separately at their appointed hours. They mutter good night as she rolls away from him, war-torn and weary from the challenges of the day. He just now thinks how nice it would feel to get laid before falling asleep. Does this sound familiar?

There is nothing very sexy about this picture, is there? Is it any wonder that she stiffens at his touch? "Just let me fall asleep," she says inside her head. Or perhaps she's the one who reaches her hand across his belly, snuggling up from behind. He then freezes at her touch. "Maybe if I pretend that I've already crashed out, she'll leave me alone," he says to himself. Regardless of who initiates, the other lies perfectly still at the uninvited touch of the other, feigning the heavy breathing of sleep.

If asked by a friend about their marriage, either would say they have a pretty good one, maybe even better than most. Yet they seem baffled by the growing distance between them and wonder if they'll ever experience that heart-rending desire they once knew just at the sight of the other entering a room. Given the nature of our social, familial and work patterns, Americans fall near the bottom on commitment to leisure and vacation time. Is it any wonder that sexual satisfaction for the average American falls near the bottom of the list among developed nations of the world as well? If you want to have a sexy life, move to Greece, or Italy. You may wonder what those peoples have over you; after all, your great-grandmother came from a little village just south of Rome.

There are few studies that indicate DNA has much to do with sexuality. However, much can be said about developing a culture of desire that makes lovemaking not only more satisfying, but more likely to occur. Given our workaholic, competitive culture, lack of extended familial support for child rearing and addiction to electronic toys as a kind of parallel play, it's a wonder Americans ever manage to procreate. The only time our national birth rate seems to rise, according to cultural myth, is when there is a national disaster: blizzard, electrical blackout, hurricane, earthquake or some other phenomenon that extinguishes the electricity long enough for us to reach for one another in the dark. We want to believe this because we long for a time without distractions when we have permission to reach for one another.

Great sex then starts with noticing the other and letting the other notice that you notice. Find something positive to say about the other. Anything. Couples often complain that their spouse no longer sees them. Women joke that they can spend $150 in the hair salon and their husband doesn't say a word. He goes out of his way to put on clean gym shorts and shave on the weekend, and then wonders if it's worth the trouble when she doesn't come closer to him than a ten-foot pole.

Then comes appreciation. Men wonder if women have any idea how much expressed appreciation boosts libido. When one half of a couple expresses appreciation for something the other does, well, the libido factor shoots straight up. If you want your partner to get hot for you, just admire his skill at making the perfect Béarnaise sauce after watching the cooking network, or praise her thoughtfulness at changing the batteries in the smoke detector so that they don't beep every fifteen seconds when you're trying to hear the end of a game.

One man who struggled in a near sexless marriage lamented that all he wants is for her to say that the nightly dinners he prepares taste good. "I fix her car, and cut the grass, and haul the kids to practice. You'd think that once in awhile she'd say 'thank you.' Every night I take a shower and kiss her good-night, then nothing." This man's exasperation is coupled with her insistence that he never listens to her. Their marriage is in peril, their sex life dead. By all accounts, this marriage could be saved if he would simply ask her to tell him about her day and really listen to her, and if she would use real words to express gratitude over little things on a regular basis. This seems like a small price to pay to avoid divorce court. Though their relationship is headed that way, they both say they love the other and wish their relationship were better. If wishing were sufficient to give us what we want and think we deserve in life we wouldn't need to have this conversation. News flash: Everything worthwhile in life takes a certain amount of effort, even sacrifice.

It isn't that difficult to develop the art of appreciation. Appreciation can be expressed with a once-over look of amazement. It's nearly a lost art. Appreciation and then gratitude are followed by some expression of relationship that indicates the other is known or loved for who they are. For example, my husband tends to be a bit obsessive about safety details, driving well below the speed limit and reminding me to do the same, to my frequent annoyance, and tending to lock all the doors even when we are at home. On a recent vacation abroad, everyone in our corner of the village was robbed, while they were home, because they had left their back doors open. My husband had locked the door when we went to another part of the house, and we were spared. When I told him how safe that made me feel, knowing he was looking out for me and protecting our family, he started beaming from ear to ear. I knew then and there that the chances that I'd get lucky later in the evening went up exponentially.

Seduction then begins with mindful attention and expressed gratitude, followed by verbal foreplay. To increase both the frequency and passion of sex, talk about it. Verbal foreplay is hot. When we open our verbal communication and deepen intimacy as a couple, physical expression of that intimacy is more likely to follow.

Sex talk can happen anywhere, anytime. It's free. But it does take a bit of planning. Though some may be able to pull it off, seductive conversation works better when you're alone with your feet in his lap than when you're rushing to pick up the kids from a birthday party. It's less than satisfying to wedge conversation about sex between mowing the lawn and the grocery shopping. My mother once said, "Don't start something you can't finish." Perhaps that wisdom applies here.

It's seductive to run your hand lightly across his forearm as you ask your partner what he finds most satisfying about sex. Always begin with affirmation. Be specific. Ask how he likes to be touched. Inquire about what feels great, what gets him cranked up. You may already think you know this, but he'll get excited thinking about it and saying it out loud.

Ask how he prefers to initiate sex, and how you can better express your desire for him. This may open the door to sexual intimacy that feels inviting and loving rather than demanding. If appropriate, ask him to show you what he likes.

In this sacred conversation, continue to touch your partner as you discuss this. Stroke his thigh, making eye contact as you continue. It's even sexier to initiate sex in a public place: at a restaurant or in the car on the way home from the movies. One look can communicate, "I want you" and seal a promise that lingers. Touch him again, anywhere. This will fire his hope, among other things, increasing the chances that you may end the day entangled, limbs akimbo, between the sheets.

Every couple expresses their own secret language of desire: caressing the hair at the nape of her neck, casually stroking his back through his shirt. If you do not have such a silent code, you are never too old to develop one. Recall what made you moist and luminous when you first crossed that bridge from friend to lover. Cross that bridge again.

Surprise one another. Take off your shirt in his office, door closed perhaps. Run your bare foot up his pant leg under the dinner table. Get risky to get frisky. The kids will never know what makes you smile.

This isn't all that complicated. You're married. He pledged his body to you. She pledged that lovely bottom to your keeping. No one cares whether it sags or folds. If she wanted the mailman she would have picked him. If he wanted a movie star, he could have married the prom queen. Instead he chose you. Trust me, nobody cares about your physical imperfections. We just want to love and be loved for who we are.

One man approached in this way then responded to his wife: "Now that you have my attention, what are you going to do with me?" Much has been written in countless magazines and the popular press about how to physically achieve an orgasm. There are plenty of materials available in the bookstore or on the Internet to help you with that. By themselves, what they offer seems empty, vacuous. Step-by-step books take the mystery out of what was hinted at in the underwear section of the Sears and Roebuck catalogue when I was a child. All the focus on visual stimulation and mechanical detail can take the pure joy out of looking a man you love in the eye and then giving him the once-over while brushing your hand against his backside as you pass by. Trust me, at a certain point; you'll both know what to do.

Practice the unexpected. Reach out and touch his arm as you pass in the hall on the way to the bathroom. Lean over and kiss her neck while she's pouring her morning coffee. Touch each other, anywhere, often, without demand but always with appreciation. I can't tell you how often a couple will sit sulking in my office, arms crossed, eager to share the grievances the other has enacted against them. How quickly the impasse dissolves when one takes the risk of asking: "What can I do to cherish my partner?" This approach tends to produce greater results than recounting all the ways his wife, her husband has disappointed.

Seduction involves a kind of moving forward and drawing away, a hint of possibility that something good might take place later beneath the sheets, but not yet. Flirt with her. A tender word, appreciative touch, or loving gaze counts as foreplay, no surprise here. But foreplay can also be as ordinary as walking in from work and unloading the dishwasher or wordlessly cleaning the baby's crumbs off the kitchen counter. Every time one person in the relationship puts a simple, decent meal on the table, or folds another load of laundry and puts it away, it is as if saying: "I'm here for you. We can do this life together. I've got your back." Then when the lights go out the distance between "Not tonight dear, I've got a headache," and "Why not now?" collapses considerably.

For many couples, sex just seems like too much work. It takes time. It's slow. It can't be tweeted or texted or friended. Seeing one another, really noticing and responding to one another requires a kind of poetic imagination. Our beloved, though perhaps not head turning handsome, nevertheless radiates the beauty only love can reflect.

In every culture, the sexy brain awakens the sexy heart that in turn awakens the sexy loins. Imagine this from a contemporary woman in the Caribbean. "His thighs were like Cuban cigars, firm and fragrant, his belly a set of steel drums, resounding in the innermost dwelling place where the flowering heart resides." It matters little if the language will win a writing contest or not. It only matters that you fully embrace your beloved, first with your eyes, then with your heart. When you do this, your body will follow. Embrace your beloved visually, and you may be rewarded with a passionate love that will make you miss your favorite television show, and you won't care. At first it may seem awkward, messy and complicated, a fumbling in the dark, but it's your sweet, complicated mess to enjoy.

God created humankind in God's own image, male and female God created them, and God called it good. Sex is a good thing, a God thing, from alabaster thighs to rounded gold everything.

. . .

CHAPTER 10 MALE COUNTERPOINT

DALE ROSENBERGER

The world has had a slow food movement over the past twenty years, and we are better off for it, healthier and happier. Maybe we are ready for a slow sensuality movement in a world where sex is too often driven by a manic intensity bent upon instantaneous gratification, at least on this side of the Atlantic.

Seduction loves slow and sultry, to taste and tantalize and unabashedly tempt. Sexuality grows best within unhurried gardens, teeming with fragrance and color, drenched in shadows and sunlight, with room to swell and expand. For these reasons, Verlee, you identify seduction with taking the time, making the effort, and the placement of little loving sacrifices like hidden notes in her purse or surprise naughty texts to his cell phone. Seduction is taking the time to build up something intimate or tender in a demanding world forever shredding such breathless closeness. At its best, the time we couples spend seducing one another, playing up to each other's sexiest features and strutting our own, can become a counterweight that offsets the acute awareness we have of each other's flaws and faults, living in close proximity over so many decades together.

But let's back up. Maybe we must self-consciously reclaim the word "seduction" before we can advance this movement. Seduction, of course, is often associated with the rake who wants nothing more than a woman's body, willingly manipulating and exploiting circumstances until he gets it, before he moves on to the next victim. But we have been at pains to emphasize that context is everything when it comes to sex. Seduction in an endless string of conquests differs from seduction within a caring covenant to love one another for a lifetime. In the former, it is a kind of sexual swindle. In the latter, for a committed couple enduring the slings and arrows of life together, it is the determination to keep the magic within the mundane tasks of staying alive. Here it becomes a timeless appeal to the youthful signature of what originally drew you together.

Seduction is an art form as surely as working in oils. It is full of poetry and presentation, nuance and suggestiveness, distance and intimacy, alluring and teasing. I like how you spoke of praise and appreciation, Verlee, to elevate the relationship. In the case of seduction, however, it seems more about risqué playfulness, full of teasing and tempting, revealing then drawing back, advancing and then retreating, an erotic relentlessness that wears the other down until resistance is in tatters. Seduction is less about genial affirmation and more about exploring the enticingly forbidden and the sizzling side of things, where we too seldom arrive together as couples.

Of course, this is the way of all of life, not just human beings. Birds do it. Bees do it. Even educated fleas do it, if you have ever watched the elaborately choreographed mating rituals of scarlet macaws or streamlined gazelles. It seems no matter which way we turn, Verlee, we end up back in that primeval Song of Solomon garden, which is not just about pleasure, but no less about wisdom.

· II ·

THE MYTHS OF MANHOOD
AND THE QUEST FOR FAITHFULNESS

Dale Rosenberger

Why do married men so regularly fall into sexual infidelity? By now we know it is a bad idea. So what can we do within our marriages to make this less likely?

· · ·

This one is a tough call. But if Henry Kissinger was right that "Power is the ultimate aphrodisiac," the more status and ambition are in play, the more likely men (and increasingly, women) will stray. The concealed powers at work here are formidable. The constraining forces shrink. The titillating, forbidden factor around adultery sizzles; sanctioned incentives for fidelity all but vanish. Other irresistible powers are on the rise.

Let's face it, our society lives in thrall to celebrity so much that media stars take on the proportions of gods. Did we think the idolatry Moses found at the foot of Mt. Sinai in the Golden Calf is ancient and gone? Think again. It lives today as *Entertainment Tonight* stalks an uncomprehending Angelina Jolie or *People* magazine voyeuristically reveals what Christian Bale ingests for breakfast. Moderns follow these details of popular culture like the ancients memorized David and Bathsheba, or Zeus and Callisto.

Remember, systems are more powerful than individuals. So what system of meaning do we live out of? Which is our primary reference point? One innocently passed off as the latest scoop of gossip? We cannot live in thrall to these powers without impact.

Consciously or not, we hold up such as these to measure who we are, what it means to be human, what we want and need. Our aspirations become caught up with theirs. As they act with the vain impunity of gods and plummet earthbound in disgrace, we villianize them for not being gods after all. So the next, fresh set of cosmetic gods—usually younger than the previous group—is produced for our vicarious enjoyment.

Trace this matrix a bit more with me until we turn back toward our own lives. Gods feel unlike the rest. The rules mere mortals live by don't apply to them. Gods have unique pressures and loftier roles. Therefore, they are entitled to certain privileges and benefits above those of the masses. As for boundaries, gods become a law unto their own desires in the moment. Tiger Woods was honest enough to say *all of this* in his carefully orchestrated televised public apology after his fall. What was stunning was his utter unawareness of such forces as they *owned* him. In this, the infidelities of towering celebrity gods do not differ from those of the regular person next door.

Living lives re-narrated by pop culture, even paunchy Joe the plumber repeats Tiger's refrain after straying. How can celebrities be so self-deceived? How can we so foolishly follow? A telling scene in the movie *Hoosiers* helps explain. Gene Hackman plays a gifted, vitriolic coach stepping down to a small town job for a last shot at redemption. Barbara Hershey plays a teacher wanting education and a future for boys caught up in the quasi-religion of Indiana basketball. She wonders aloud: what's the big deal about being a sports hero? "You know," he answers, "most people would kill . . . to be treated like a god, just for a few moments." This is the social medium in which we live and strive.

The oldest struggle—since the tree in Eden—is whether we bow before the true God or become gods unto ourselves. Fidelity to God correlates to all other forms of fidelity. How do we respond as temptation invariably presents itself?

It depends how full we are of ourselves. Does godlike entitlement fill our soul? Listen for it: "*I* have suffered from such neglect from her that I deserve this. *I* have sexual energy she can never understand. *I* have sacrificed for her and the children in ways no one sees, giving up so much. So *I* owe myself this. And who'll look out for me, if *I* don't?" Such protests may be heartfelt, at least partially valid and overdue for attention. Still, adultery destroys relationships as it asserts unmet needs. The ruin comes at our most vulnerable place: trust. Even a little trust violated takes a long time, as in a lifetime, to rebuild. Or maybe never.

In another film, *The Family Man*, Nicholas Cage ponders a dalliance with a sultry, willing neighbor. He mentions the chance for conquest to a close friend, played by Jeremy Piven. Piven is incredulous because he perceives Cage's wife as incomparable. Can't Cage see most men would give up everything to get what he already has? Piven quietly seethes, and then cautions, "The fidelity bank and trust is a tough creditor. You make a deposit somewhere else, they close your account—*forever*."

If you scratch your head at how men rationalize fooling around, like they are "treating themselves" or doing humankind a favor by scattering their seed, as though it were pixie dust, then such a man-to-man scene gets at something essential. And it raises an important question. Why do men not call each other to accountability like this more often? Why is there an unstated man code that you protect a male friend's infidelity? Why isn't faithfulness to one's wife considered manly, at least by Christian men?

Think of it. Adultery often amounts to a kind of cowardice. That is, men often have affairs because they lack the courage to face into a marriage with its long list of daunting issues needing attention, demanding deep new resolve. Men committing adultery are often cutting and running from facing marital problems head-on by initiating physical intimacy with someone new, where infatuation is free and easy, without any heavy lifting. The breezy new escape from the hard work of staying married beckons no farther than a few desks away. We run, hide, and take refuge in arms where we are lauded as gallant new hero (for a few weeks anyway) instead of owning our part in fixing the fissures and fractures that appear in all marriage vows. What if men were to call other men on adultery as cowardice instead of wearing new conquests as notches on our belts?

The slope here is so slippery. Rationalizations come fast and easy once we view ourselves as basically good people who are victims, unlike the "bad adulterers" out there, responsible for the demise of the family and the decline of America. Of the great majority of adulterers admitting what they do is wrong, it is amazing how many *don't* see themselves as seedy, like the lecherous boss running off with the ditzy secretary. It is striking how easily we make ourselves the exception to our firm boundaries for others. Then again, let's face it. We all write our own story in such a way that we are the hero. And we rewrite our story in our own minds until we are that hero. So when we do something destructive, we go easier on ourselves. "They did it for disgusting reasons, but mine are sound and make perfect sense."

One Christian writer observed we moderns feel cheated by marriage in that we only get to sample one mate as lover across the sweep of a lifetime. But in truth, he affirms, we might be grateful God gives us one partner as wholly and utterly ours. Having a life partner so completely ours is God's generous gift. In marriage there is such complete sexual freedom as cannot be found elsewhere.

Knowing each other's bodies, learning each other's unique pleasure, sharing our secrets, enjoying each other's trust, anything goes and freedom reigns, short of frightening or damaging the other. The abiding truth of this sexual freedom gets lost as we idealize forms of pleasure demanding a variety of different "stops." For entitlement is the opposite of gratitude. So how can we learn to live together for decades without taking each other for granted? This challenge ranks foremost for couples in sustaining good satisfying sex. With longer lifespans, marriages stretch over more decades, further testing our fidelity.

I am struck by men who fancy themselves special advocates for women because they hold the door, listen sensitively with a furrowed brow, and wear pink bows for breast cancer research. But then they get wrong the most essential thing, the one behavior at the root of "men are pigs" resentment. That behavior is failing to honor the sanctity of shared sexual intimacy with our one and only by wandering off and frittering away such precious intimacy with another woman.

Men living out of the American myth of "self-made man" (a godlike myth) or as "lone rangers" (another godlike myth) are most vulnerable. Let's face it, all of us are tested sooner or later. If we share anything that matters in our lives with other men, and our lives are rooted in a culture of manhood predicated on integrity rather than multiple conquests, we are miles ahead. We can only hope the church might be such a counterculture to the good-ole'-boy egging on of popular culture.

To become this counterculture, the church can't stop at declaring, "You shall not commit adultery." (Exodus 20:14) Even more, we moderns, so full of ourselves, might re-narrate our lives with words like these from Philippians 2:3–8:

> Do nothing from selfish ambition or conceit,
> but in humility regard others as better than yourselves.
> Let each of you look not to your own interests, but to the
> interests of others.
> Let the same mind be in you that was in Christ Jesus, who,
> though he was in the form of God, did not regard
> equality with God as something to be exploited,

but emptied himself . . . he humbled himself and
became obedient to the point of death—even death on a cross.

Our distinguishing mark as moderns is the arrogance that no one—not even God—has a right to tell us what to do. We are accountable to ourselves. Centuries have shown the only power that promises strength enough to counter such hubris—male or female—is God's self-emptying love of Christ on the cross. This is the spiritual counterculture the church forever has the chance to become.

Closer to home, speaking more practically, other reflections on fidelity merit our attention. We mentioned how deadly it is to marriage to take one another for granted. This obviously applies for keeping up our attractiveness and not assuming that because you have your husband locked in by vows, it no longer matters.

My teacher, Paul Holmer, a masculine and fiery man, also adored his wife, even unto the latter stages of cancer, caring for her in ways far surpassing the eloquence of his lectures. He charged men to win over our beloved's hand anew each day as though we had never done so before. More than a helpful attitude, he urged it as a spiritual practice, serving it up as hedge against our inevitable apathy.

Correspondingly, perhaps wives could inventively find new ways to attract husbands, effectively banishing sweat suits when he is at home. If this seems too fixed in dated gender roles, why not reverse them as a test of our equality? Women, seek and desire your man anew daily, finding new ways to project that. Men, kindly delete those paunches and nose hairs for your wife. The interplay of conquered and conqueror between men and women is delightfully complex. Women, know that men are much more complex than the sexual heat-seeking missiles popular culture depicts us to be.

If women could trust how visual men are sexually, that gives multiple clues to how to increase variety in marriage, rendering outside variety less tempting. You feel silly wearing exotic lingerie?

Believe me, if you feel silly, he feels blessed, interested, and aroused. So value your sexuality, ladies. Imaginatively invest in your own sensuality. The more you do, the more we will. Bring attitude; you have what he wants. You need to believe that first. Bring the strut that entices. None of us looks like we did in high school. So what? You are alive now. So is he. The real issue is the voltage of the sparks flying between you. How often did Ann Landers urge lonely wives to turn up the heat in the bedroom? Frequently.

Try this. Go to a lively watering hole, ask hubby to sit at a distance for a while, and then respond flirtatiously to the men who sense your availability and offer to buy you a drink. Husband becomes the *gallant* rescuing you from the meat hooks of those cads. But once he realizes your desirability in that open market, I promise you, neither of you will take each other for granted. Playfully remind him.

These ruses are too obvious, you say. Is there a subtler way? Sure, alternatives abound for any with imagination. Just before arriving at your niece's wedding, weakly protest you forgot to wear undergarments. Beneath a lidded gaze, shift with suggestive agitation, asking whatever are you to do? Use the power of gently rubbing your thighs together to arrest his attention. Ignore your mother's advice by wearing no panties. Be prepared for what unfolds and embrace it; a little imagination goes a long way. Sexual creativity can flourish in marriages where the one willing to step out and take such chances does not get ridiculed. If this seems contrived, indecent, or immoral from a faith perspective, remember that the flirting and fantasy in Song of Solomon is much more graphic and racy than this. That is, juicier scenarios are found in the Bible, of all places.

Still, if you insist exotic flirting is not your style, try simple appreciation. A big reason men fool around is because, like women, we feel unappreciated. Both breadwinner husband and breadwinner wife can feel invisible in households where the stay-at-home spouse calls the shots for their social life and forever has the final word on child rearing. The benefits the breadwinner brings by way of income support are indirect, in the background, mostly assumed, that is, until he or she becomes unemployed. Then he or she commonly feels some version of impotent or useless. Not taking the "outsider" for granted, being grateful and treating him or her royally, will increase his or her desire. Much of the breadwinner's self-worth is tied up in productivity and performance. Letting him or her know that you are impressed stokes our hormones in the right directions. Such erotic marital advice is the ounce of prevention that is worth a pound of cure.

The aforementioned professor, Paul Holmer, was once on a commuter flight from New York to New Haven. Seated next to him was a fellow flying back from D.C., having just visited his mistress. Feeling pretty chipper, he gushed how far society has come not to get so bent out of shape as we go about "meeting our needs." Holmer listened patiently. His response? "It's called adultery, and is a sin against God and mankind." Rumor has it the rest of their flight was silent.

Holmer's reply sounds severe, old-school, hopelessly out of step with modernity. Why such a tone? No, there is no excuse for adultery. But it can be forgiven. It can even help redeem a relationship by surfacing issues where too much has been taken for granted for too long. Marriages can be healed. But consider what adultery does to our faith in God. It might seem like nothing has changed as he wanders. In fact everything has changed and hubby is missing it.

In the Garden of Eden, the serpent asked the couple why they had not enjoyed the forbidden fruit. They informed the tempter if they ate it, they would die. The serpent dripped with disdain, "You will not die." Rather, claimed the Evil One, you will become more like God. And God forbade you from this delectable item because God is jealous. So Eve and Adam reevaluated the forbidden fruit, appearing so luscious.

They ate of that fruit. And they didn't die. Or did they? Physically, they were the same. Spiritually, however, their trusting love of one another wasn't the same. And their relationship with

God—compared to before—had indeed died. I know of Christians, basically unperturbed in their extramarital dalliance, unaware that their relationship with God is dying. Sadly, they would be the last to know.

As Catholicism speaks of "mortal sin," it sounds like Paul Holmer. Maybe mortal sin isn't that grievous unforgivable sin sending us to hell. Maybe mortal sin is rather how the wrong we do has the power to kill our relationship with God. Maybe that is reason enough not to be cavalier and carefully tend the home fires.

. . .

CHAPTER 11 FEMALE COUNTERPOINT

VERLEE A. COPELAND

I appreciate the risk you take in calling men to task on infidelity, Dale. This is bold on your part, as men traditionally wander with the wink of an eye. Cultural expectations persist that women remain faithful "till death do us part," although this double standard has loosened in recent decades. From the earliest writing of the Ten Commandments, adultery has been forbidden. But adultery is forbidden for reasons other than what many moderns imagine.

We wrongly assume that "thou shall not commit adultery" is an injunction against moral failure. This construct did not exist in the ancient world as we understand it. Adultery had little to do with sexual immorality and everything to do with theft. Women were the property and responsibility of men. If another man violated your woman through sexual intercourse, he damaged your goods. Thus the last commandment in the Hebrew text reads, "You shall not covet your neighbor's house; you shall not covet your neighbor's wife, or male or female slave, or ox, or donkey, or anything that belongs to your neighbor."

When contemporary adults think of adultery, they think of betrayal and sexual infidelity, or cheating on your wife or husband. If adultery isn't primarily about the sexual ethics of faithfulness to covenant promises made through marriage, how then can moderns understand adultery? I might suggest that we revisit and reclaim the original intent of this commandment.

Giving to another what has been promised to one's spouse is indeed a kind of theft, isn't it? It is not as though adultery is an unforgivable sin, but rather that it disrespects the marriage covenant that provides a safe harbor for intimacy between persons and before God. Such intimacy becomes a sign and symbol of our intimacy with God.

When we cheat on our spouses, we betray the trust of those who love us. As in all matters this side of heaven, such an offense hurts our spouse, whether they know of the theft or not. Infidelity hurts us too, as we become less open to other relationships when we live a divided life. Protecting a secret life creates an invisible wall around us that separates us from other significant relationships with family, friends and through our work. Those who love us may sense that we are less than available emotionally, without understanding why that is so.

Finally, infidelity hurts our relationship with God. I think God is deeply concerned about what we do with our genitals and how we express our desire, because God cares intimately about what we do with our lives. The discipline of sexual fidelity ultimately reminds us of who we are and to whom we belong.

· 12 ·

IS THE GRASS EVER GREENER?

Verlee A. Copeland

After twenty years in a pretty good marriage I find myself increasingly attracted to the husband of a close friend. We spend a great deal of time together as couples and the two of us especially enjoy one another's company. How can I enjoy our friendship without putting our marriages at risk?

· · ·

Two couples mingle in the kitchen over a glass of wine, swapping stories about the latest escapades of the kids. It's a Saturday night like any other, laughing with your best friend, the guys just in from flipping burgers out on the grill. Then it happens.

Fingers brush at the passing of the ketchup, eyes linger a moment too long, the scent of a man not your own at once unfamiliar and tantalizing. You look away blushing. Your nipples suddenly perk up and you experience warmth in the nether regions that takes you by surprise. For just a moment, you wonder what it would be like to be in bed with the husband of your friend next door.

The first time it happens, you think you are imagining things. Anxious, you hope no one noticed. You try to shake it off and let it go. A few weeks later at the kids' soccer game, he reaches over and touches your back in a familiar way. You feel the touch long after his hand drops as if it never happened. By the end of the game as you talk with other parents; you notice that you are leaning toward one another, shoulders nearly, but not quite touching.

The body language of courtship has begun. Unchecked, you know that this behavior will escalate. It's titillating, a bit thrilling, and dangerous even. "No harm, no foul," you tell yourself. After all, you haven't really done anything wrong, yet. Soon you find yourself fantasizing about the guy next door when you make love to your husband. You discover that it increases your arousal and heightens your sexual response. You are not alone. The guy next door is probably doing the same thing, but perhaps for different reasons, as we will discuss.

What is really happening here? Are you falling in love with your neighbor? Maybe. Are you at risk of breaking up your marriage and that of your best friend? Potentially yes, but don't panic. Most men and women regularly engage in sexual fantasy, often while making love to their partner. This can heighten arousal with your spouse, is within the "normal range" of behavior among happily married couples, and can potentially enhance your relationship if the sexual energy is expended at home. In fact, studies show that 99% of such fantasies remain just that, never enacted in real life.

Once we pass the animal brain stage of early adolescence, healthy adults tend to have pretty good impulse control. We know that the primary sexual organ does not reside a foot south of the belly button, but upstairs in the brain. Long before human creatures engage in sexual behavior, the brain initiates responses to the sight, smell, touch, taste, and sound of a potential partner. Physiologically, we know that pheromones, the individual scent of a person, can attract two people like bees to nectar. It remains a mystery why we are attracted to one person and not another.

We do know some things about human sexual response and learn more all the time. For example, research indicates that women respond more to scent than men, and men tend to respond more to sexual cues that are visual. The longing that begins in the brain translates to the physiological responses we have previously described.

Women have a greater tendency than men to respond sexually to relationship cues as well. The most seductive thing a man can do is to look a woman in the eyes and listen intently to her tender discussion of just about anything from what happened at work that day to her dream of starting a creative new venture.

Women who have affairs are more likely to say, "My husband never listens to me," than "My husband seldom brings me to orgasm." Attentive partners are sexy partners. For men, the motivation may be different. Sleeping with an unavailable woman ranks among the most common of male fantasies. The woman next door is mysterious, unattainable, a challenge worth pursuing, at least in his mind.

So what's the big deal? If this is a common fantasy and we know that most fantasies are never enacted, does this mean that you should simply relax, indulge the life of the mind, and enjoy it? The answer to that question is likely "No." You wouldn't be asking the question if you didn't think this particular fantasy created a risk to your marriage.

While imagining what it would be like to make love with the man or woman next-door ranks as a common fantasy, it is an especially dangerous one. What makes this so is that the fantasy is tied to a real person, a real relationship, in a real social setting. Proximity, relationship and opportunity increase the chances of follow through. Sixty percent of affairs take place with someone you know and see regularly, rather than through a casual encounter such as at a sporting event or the local bar. Unless you are willing to risk your marriage, your friendship, your neighbor's marriage, and the secure home environment of all your children, you may want to stop now.

It may be time for a reality check. Just because you get all hot and bothered when the guy next door comes over to borrow a power tool, doesn't mean it's time to run away with him. We human creatures are hard-wired to desire one another. If that were not so, the population of the United States would not be expected to double in the next thirty years. The promulgation of the species depends on our psychological and physiological response to a desirable other. Yet physical desire does not translate into the necessity to act.

Take, for example, the dying embers of sexuality between the characters of Tommy Lee Jones and Meryl Streep in the 2012 film *Hope Springs*. In a sometimes reluctant, tentative effort to save their marriage, the two head off on retreat in coastal Maine to work with a marriage therapist. The husband of the couple appears to have left all sexual thought in a drawer at home next to his fourth grade report card until the therapist asks him about his sexual fantasies. After stuttering about, he eventually owns up to his fantasy about a threesome with his wife and a neighbor across the street. His wife, on hearing this news is shocked, "The one with the Corgis?" As the couple returns home from their successful therapeutic journey out east, they emerge from their car to the friendly wave of said neighbor out walking the dogs. All wave and smile as the wife mutters to him, "It's not going to happen", while continuing her cheerful greeting.

Not everyone seems to understand this difference between fantasy and the temptation to make it real. We sometimes make fun of the sequestered life of earlier generations, when women seldom appeared in public and men and women were separated in Sunday worship to left and to right. These archaic practices point to the not altogether unwarranted fear that given the chance, we won't be able to keep our hands off of one another. Whenever human beings spend a great deal of time with one another with affiliation and affection around a common purpose, some level of sexual tension is likely to occur. At issue is not whether we will desire one another, but what we will do about it. Unless you are willing to blow up your life, consider the following alternatives.

You're going to hate the first choice. You can cut off the friendship and limit the amount of time you spend with the one you desire. Painful as it may be, you may need to walk away from the relationship if there is more than sexual attraction. Ask yourself if you are forming a deep, exclusionary spiritual intimacy, if you increasingly spend more time with your "friend" than with your spouse, or if you no longer place your husband first. If the answer to any of these questions is "yes," then you may want to walk away. In this instance, the answer to your wonderment about what to do with this increasing attraction may be simply, "run."

Translated in faith terms, this can be a call to repentance, that is, to stop what you are doing and return to right relationship with God and the one with whom you have a deep and abiding covenant. However effective, this situation will likely repeat itself in the future unless you address the underlying hunger in your soul that made you vulnerable to this nearly irresistible attraction in the first place.

Another strategy is to confide your attraction, not to the one you desire, but with your husband. "What," you protest. "Are you crazy?" No, not at all. In the right environment, a shared fantasy can stimulate your partner as well. Tell him you find the guy next door sexy, but that man doesn't have the one thing your husband has, you. Then draw him into bed with a flirtatious invitation to "take me to bed or lose me forever," to paraphrase a famous movie line from *Top Gun*.

If the confession comes across as invitation to play out the fantasy with you, it can draw you closer together. If, on the other hand, you share a tearful confession that you are falling in love with your neighbor that will likely produce fear and anger in your spouse.

Check your motivations. If you want to hurt your partner, this latter strategy will work, but at considerable cost to you and your relationship. Confessing your thoughts and temptations to your partner may draw you closer together if you have an intimate, trusting, well-grounded relationship. Nevertheless, do not mistake openness with your spouse with your need to relieve your guilt over these thoughts at your partner's expense. If what you are seeking is forgiveness or absolution, seek the counsel of your spiritual leader and discover how you might be forgiven. If you want to recover your life and return to your marriage, discuss this situation with a competent therapist who will help you sort out your intentions. When you are clear about these matters, you will be in a much better position to discern the path to recovered intimacy within your marriage, and to once again affirm your wedding vows to "forsake all others."

Many years ago I worked with a couple as their pastor who over time independently confessed their flirtations with infidelity. The husband made clear with his wife that if ever she was tempted, he would want to know about it, and early on, so that together they could find a path through it. He promised her that if she maintained such integrity, he would always stand by her. Her honesty demonstrated to him that her intention was to honor their marital vows. Her confession to him was a mark of fidelity as she sought to maintain the primacy of their relationship. When in fact she did develop a friendship with a man to whom she was attracted, she was able to keep her behavior in check by discussing her feelings with her husband before the relationship with her "attraction" developed to the extent that it jeopardized their marriage. In this situation, her honest, if painful discussion of the attraction made it possible for the flirtation to diminish as this couple worked on the fundamental relationship issues that had made her vulnerable to such temptation in the first place.

Years previous to this, he had engaged in an affair with a colleague whom he had grown to love and admire over an extended period of time. Both he and his lover were married to other people and hoped to remain so. They chose to keep their relationship a secret, in part because to do otherwise would bring it to an end, something they were not prepared to do. At the same time, they did not wish to hurt their marriages. They convinced themselves that their relationship enhanced their marriages by taking pressure off their spouses in all manner of ways, sexually and otherwise. Neither had to face the diminishing libido of their spouses. Neither had to negotiate the usual arguments both petty and grand that are the consequences of living intimately with another human being for an extended period of time. Their relationship was like a perpetual honeymoon, whereby both were at their best behaved and most beautiful when they were together. Who wouldn't want that?

This scenario, unlike the one previously described, ended in heartbreak. The husband decided to spend more time at home with his wife. Living a double life and keeping secrets began over time to diminish the abandoned joy he at first experienced with his lover. He came to see what would be obvious to anyone looking at this situation, that he could not fully care for his wife as a lover, partner and friend so long as his primary energy focused on the woman with whom he was having an affair.

When he finally gave up the extra-marital relationship, it was at considerable cost. His wife suspected, but proclaimed that she did not want to know. However, she asked him to return to her, and to affirm his fidelity to her going forward. He agreed to do so as it became increasingly clear that his behavior was jeopardizing his marriage, something he had not previously believed to be true. His lover was deeply wounded, as she genuinely loved him. The grief they both experienced at letting go of their relationship was private, painful and protracted. By necessity, the loss of the relationship remained hidden, as had the affair. However, the woman, utterly bereft at the loss of her lover, could not find her way back to her marriage and the marriage ended, at great loss for her now former husband who loved her and their children. One could argue that their marriage would have ended in any case, and perhaps much earlier, if so many of the relationship needs had not been fulfilled in the affair. But in truth, none of the players in this scenario will ever know what might have been.

This case study represents countless others, including perhaps your own. Primary prevention saves paramount grief. Once you know a person intimately, physically, you cannot put what you know back in the box. You cannot forget, and you may be haunted by it for the rest of your life. How do you return to your ordinary spouse when the man next door turns out to be a better lover, more richly endowed, kinder, or a better listener? Unless you are the master or mistress of depersonalization and compartmentalization, you will become someone different for having gone there. However this chapter of your life ends, and it will, your life will be changed in ways that you cannot control or predict.

Prevention is hard work. Great relationships do not fall out of a wagon. If a "neighbor" tempts you, focus on what's happening at home rather than on your feelings for the man next door. Given the amount of time most of us invest in our marriages, few regret the additional reflection of an intimacy inventory at home. How can the man you know by heart, who picks his nose, plucks hair from his ears and farts in bed ever compete with the mystery man next door whose personal habits remain hidden from you? At the same time, you may have to ask yourself how sexy you look in those thread-bare flannel pajamas if your husband hasn't been reaching for you lately. Perhaps you too have become a bit too casual with your personal grooming routine. If you want mystery, create it at home.

When the writer of the Song of Solomon in the Bible proclaims, "My beloved is mine, and I am his," we can feel the longing in those words. This may not always match up with our feelings for the guy who sits across the breakfast table from us. Perhaps that farting, weekend warrior with the paunch around the middle sometimes grosses you out. His very familiarity may leave your libido in the deep freeze. But baby, the best thing about your husband is that he belongs to you.

Take your rich fantasy life home to the one who long ago gave over his life to you as you did to him: for better or for worse, in sickness and in health, in plenty and in want, in joy and in sorrow, forsaking all others, including the man next door, until death you do part.

. . .

CHAPTER 12 MALE COUNTERPOINT

DALE ROSENBERGER

Practical wisdom resonates through this realistic call to fidelity, Verlee. No, we are not automatons immune to the heady ambrosia of charming gifts and alluring shapes of men and women out there, teasing and tantalizing us away from the relationship we already have, which maybe bores or annoys us to death. But the truth is we are likely taking our current relationship for granted and cannot see the forest for the trees. For if we were in our fancifully imagined new relationship, it would just be a matter of time before that also became boring or annoying in different, maybe worse, ways. So often the problem we project out there is the obstacle we have not confronted in here, he said, pointing straight to his heart.

Let's be honest, it is not easy to be a couple. Marriage is not for sissies. If we let it, marriage will forge real men and woman of character out of us. With longer human lifespans, and marriages more often lasting sixty years, we face new frontiers in the quest for durability. Couples who understand we are all human and who are unthreatened by the natural pulses of attraction bring a maturity that petty jealous types will never get. Couples who discuss the usually neglected work of prevention and act constructively are miles ahead in their relationship and enjoy greater freedoms. Couples who cultivate a sturdy, strong relationship are able to be more candid to unburden themselves and neutralize temptation's poison into something healing and life-preserving. This completes the circle before it has to begin all over again, as it necessarily will. Here vigilance is key. Here is one place where we cannot be content merely to "let life happen to me."

I like how you emphasize, Verlee, the key moments in which to exercise more caution. It is one thing meeting another couple hundreds of miles away on vacation where one of them absolutely knocks your socks off, and you will never see them again. This is the realm of adolescent crushes. It is something else entirely to commit to conspiratorial plans to see someone already in our social circle knowing that seeing that person in a heady new setting will kick up the likelihood of acting out in a way that cannot be reversed. So often we hear the wandering husband or wife say they don't know how the affair happened. Or powers greater than they recognized took hold and drove the course of events. Or they didn't mean to hurt anyone. I don't want to be rude to these individuals, but I will say, "C'mon. We are all grown-ups here. It is not too much to ask any husband or wife to keep our heads in the game and keep track of the score."

Someone observed that marriage is a reflection of who we really are and romance is a reflection of who we want to be. Trust me, marriage is the truer indication of the reality of our lives than idealized romances spun out of fantasy. In this sense, it's true, the most boring marriage is more interesting and revealing than the most exotic romance could ever be. Can we not take that for granted in the ongoing work and honest efforts of keeping our vows, please?

· 13 ·

INNOCENCE PLUS SENSUALITY
EQUALS HOT MONOGAMY

Dale Rosenberger

My husband wants to experiment with lovemaking in ways new to me. I'm intrigued and hesitant, to be frank. How does a couple travel down this path, remaining faithful to God and each other?

·   ·   ·

Of all the places our painfully modern take on sexuality has missed the boat, the most hidden is the powerful place of innocence within the erotic. It is all but forgotten. Kudos to Rabbi Schmuley Boteach for retrieving innocence as the invisible substratum beneath our most ardent eroticism, the very ground of feeling sexy and seductive. In his fine book *Kosher Sutra* Boteach rhapsodizes in his chapter on innocence: "What makes the innocent person so deeply charming and erotic is the openness of their heart. Because their souls are translucent, you can see right through to their essence. Innocent people disarm us . . . With no agenda other than sharing, openness, and love, the innocent person allows us to lessen our guard as well . . . Innocence is about living honestly, not pretending to be that which we are not; not pretending to be happy or grieved when we are not. It is to be transparent in every situation and act honestly and genuinely."[1] He goes on to ask if we are not honest with ourselves, how can we be honest with our significant other? He is right. Full-blown trust is as rare in a cynical and manipulative world as it is dead sexy.

Boteach contrasts the shifting harmony and mood of Adam and Eve before and after their fall from grace. He rightly insists that soulful transparency with one another as men and women lives and breathes in the same sweet spot as literally getting naked together. At first, because Adam looked to Eve's essence, he first perceived her lovely heart rather than observe to himself "nice hooters," and then hatch a scheme. Because Eve knew Adam loved all of her beyond being "a breast man"—or, or as we say in this book, he loved her from the inside out—she didn't feel judged and opened to him in non-defensive ways. This pure, primeval garden innocence freed them from shame and self-consciousness, from posturing in guarded and contrived ways, and from the pretensions of having to act differently or be better than who they really were. In today's world we easily miss the quiet inner fires that innocence releases. Maybe we only notice it as we find ourselves around the innocent and feel their quiet burn surprisingly released in us.

The spiritual trust that begets innocence functions like the bass line in a finely crafted Motown hit single. You barely notice it as it lays down the foundation for melody, harmony and rhythm, carving out the contagious groove the song moves within, setting the boundaries for the engaging variations that draw us in and win us over. But that bass line, also called "the bottom," and suggesting a bottom line where we are answerable, like innocence, is always there, pulsing, probing and moving. We overlook it, but it is what makes the music possible. This driving beat enlivens our

1. Schmuley Boteach, *The Kosher Sutra* (New York; Harper-Collins, 2009, 64.

feeling for one another such that we smile a lot and others smile who are around us. Would that we spend a lot more time on this sensual dance floor rather than other sordid places.

I am not ignoring your question, I really am not. Instead I mean to suggest that if we seek to fully enjoy our great freedom of sexual intimacy together as couples, this foundation of innocence and trust is where we begin. As you and your husband explore sexually together within marriage, start there. As you go forth and try new things, whatever you decide, don't forget to ask, will this violate the sanctity of our precious trust and tender innocence? As you reflect on what is both loving and also arousing, let innocence be your standard and trust your bellwether. As Adam and Eve learned much too late, once innocence is lost and trust is betrayed, it is extremely difficult to get back. And they are both rooted within our relationship to God.

Your question also correctly implies that through deliberately narrowing our options to live and love with one person alone—forsaking all others—we pass through an opening beyond which many other options present themselves, making possible a freedom we cannot know otherwise. It is paradoxical how this works. We can only say that for reasons deeper than we can grasp, this is why marriage looms so prominently within God's plan and purposes for the intimate sharing of our lives as men and women.

Some people of faith insist if we were pure and loving enough in our sexuality, marriages wouldn't need any erotic enlivening. I don't buy it, and I am not sure such churchy elements are being honest about their own imagination and arousal. We covered this elsewhere in saying we get into trouble as we see ourselves as holier than the God of Genesis who hard-wired us a certain way as women and men and called it good.

Having granola and almond milk daily for breakfast and hummus with fruit and veggies daily for lunch may make for sturdy habits and an excellent diet. But repeating blandness every day in the bedroom can stabilize us right into rigor mortis. Spicing up your marriage need not mean loss of innocence and inevitable descent into feeling degraded. Every couple is an expert who can measure what expanding their boundaries means to them. Every couple differs on the scale of what rates as tame and what rates as bawdy. We articulate and negotiate that as we go.

Lack of variety is a common complaint from couples who successfully manage to stay married for decades. How lovemaking unfolds can become predictable and pro forma: a bit of kissing, or maybe that is long gone; some oral sex for the sake of arousal; he awaits her orgasm and then his follows shortly in a few minutes. We spend the same amount of time and the same amount of energy and rotate among the same moves every time without thinking twice about it. We come to a place where sex more resembles sleepwalking than a stirring and imaginative dance of body, soul, and spirit.

Couples often complain about lack of interest as sparks that once flew between them fizzle and sputter. Couples find themselves having sex much less often and don't know why. And remember, as erotic creativity fails and sensual boundaries constrict, husbands and wives look to variety from without. That much has been proven as long as people have existed upon the face of the earth. So why not tame this dangerous threat with a sexy, enjoyable pinch of prevention better than any remorseful pound of cure afterward?

Sexual therapists refer to the Coolidge Effect, based on an anecdote about Calvin Coolidge, who was not exactly Mr. Bodaciously Sexy. Whether it is apocryphal or actually happened, it is worth recounting. The President and his wife received separate tours of a model government farm. When Mrs. Coolidge first toured the chicken yard, she stopped to admire a rooster busily mating with one hen after another. The First Lady brazenly asked the guide how many times a day the rooster fulfilled his, ahem, conjugal duty. "Dozens of times," the guide replied. "Oh!" said Mrs. Coolidge, visibly impressed. "Would you mind telling that to the President when he comes by?"

When the President's entourage later viewed the same chicken yard, the guide dutifully drew his attention to the rooster's virility, as the First Lady requested. The President took it all in for a moment, then calculatedly asked, "Does the rooster mate with the same hen over and over or with different hens?" The guide said, "Why, different hens, of course." The President smiled, "Kindly convey that to Mrs. Coolidge, would you, please?"

Married couples today assert their freedom to explore their eroticism and enjoy their sensuality with a vigor and fervor probably not seen before. Is it their rebuff to stuffy drabness? Is it defiance of the staid ways in which they might be perceived? Is it their faithful rejoinder to the lie of promiscuous fun? Is it daring to dream that monogamy need not necessarily mean monotony? Is it seizing the sanction God gives us to enjoy the full sweetness of life within our limited days? It doesn't matter, but all of these are at play here. All we can say is let us be grateful, because this is a great time to be alive.

What I want to call the hot monogamy movement first stirred in the 1980s, following a decade of mostly failed sexual experimentation in the 1970s, amid an era where seeking sexual variety from without was killing off whole populations because of the AIDS virus. Wonder of wonders that fidelity of all things could become sexy again. It is striking how what is eternal and true will reassert itself beyond our unruly little protests and rebellions, wandering far afield and swearing we will never return.

In the 1990s hot monogamy meant a newly-discovered, giggly openness to buying sex toys in stores where wholesome couples would never before set foot. It meant a growing interest in erotica as valid print or visual art that couples might share for their enrichment, different from sleazy scenes viewed by furtive men at bachelor parties. In their book *Hot Monogamy*, Patricia Love and Jo Robinson call their hot monogamy program a form of "preventative sex therapy," given how unacknowledged sexual differences painfully widen, drive a wedge between couples and result in divorce.[2] We are familiar with these disturbing patterns. One helpful answer is expanding our intimate and erotic boundaries as couples; in going deeper together, not going wider and apart, as countless divorced couples will attest. In other words, the man who asks his wife to wear a sexy bodice, might truly be telling her, "Please help me stay faithful!"

So what are we really talking about here by way of shared activity? As couples consider expanding their range of intimacy, the first thing that occurs to them is novel positions for lovemaking or making love in unusual places. Something so simple as varying the time and effort we put into our sexual encounters is actually an even more basic place to begin. Perhaps we do well as couples to create a repertoire of styles for lovemaking depending on the mood and the moment. One style might be quick and uninvolved when demands press and schedule impinges and tiredness saps us. Perhaps only one and not both partners reach orgasm in this style. The "quickie" can sustain the more highly sexed of the couple until fewer demands impinge and you can enjoy "banquet" sex, where the table is set and more time is taken. Quickies are under-utilized by most couples and can actually spark enthusiasm if they happen in a new room of the house or unusual venue.

Most couples already have a "garden-variety" style that is their sturdy, go-to way of lovemaking that lasts from a quarter to a half hour. It is comfortable, cozy, reassuring and we know exactly what to expect as we engage in it. Of course, if this is all a couple has, things are likely flat and uninspired, and this might be your favorite chapter in this book.

"Banquet" sex could last up to an hour or more. It often requires planning and scheduling, making the shared secret of anticipation part of the forbidden fun. It may require going to a store for special food or to buy candles, choosing music in advance, digging

---

2. Patricia Love and Jo Robinson, *Hot Monogamy* (New York: Penguin Books, 1995).

hidden lingerie out of drawers, and warming the massage oil just right. Banquet sex happens naturally early in relationships and then trails off over time. Because a little goes a long way, honoring your partner by indulging so elaborately with banquet sex a dozen times a year will make a noticeable difference in the bedroom temperature.

We could also talk about "questing" sex, where something new is attempted and the boundaries of what the couple finds erotic begin to expand. The goal here is to push beyond routine, taking more risk, adding more sizzle, coming to grips with deep desire. Watching or reading erotica, sex toys, ice, sex games, and whipped cream are standbys here. It might also involve teasing, wearing clothes utterly unlike our usual persona, taking us out of character in a way that could seem silly and stupid if it were not also so playful and vulnerable, endearing and erotic. Yes, sex can be funny. Someone once said about romance, "Smart is better than cute, sexy trumps smart, and funny takes them all."

As sex has room for humor, especially at our own expense, the result is not mere frivolity. More than we expect, the result is enduring and cherished bonding that gets recalled years later on cold nights. When sex becomes funny, when we are secure enough to laugh aloud at our quirks—to smile at the absurdity of being spiritual creatures who are so fully earthbound—we are like Adam and Eve in the innocence of God's primeval garden paradise. Of course, that spark requires much vulnerability of us in a bruising world. Many simply will not go there.

I would say two things to couples about what I am calling "questing" sex, pushing the boundaries. To the cautious end of the spectrum, I say if you are not growing your erotic imagination, if you are not willing to stretch what you find pleasurable for each other's sake, you might be less alive and interesting than you were when you met your spouse. Is that doing him or her a favor? Is that really the best you can do? Are we destined to ossify and grow cold as we age? Isn't this an existence where we are either growing or dying with not much in between?

To the more daring end of the spectrum in erotic experimentation, I would say it is possible to get such a taste for the extraordinary that we begin to feel entitled to perpetual novelty as our new baseline. Maybe we feel the need to continually "up the ante" such that we lose appreciation for the ordinariness of the everyday. That is dangerous in terms of lost innocence, in terms of objectified sex replacing soulful sex, in terms of losing the holy love that moves from the inside out, in terms of forgetting that sex is more about souls and spirits than bodies and parts. In sum, this book gladly announces impressive room in our hitherto unexplored sexual freedom for many couples who remain faithful to God and to their partner in marriage.

But as Paul the Apostle traced this freedom, while recalling also our purpose on earth to glorify God, he said, "'All things are lawful,' but not all things are beneficial. 'All things are lawful,' but not all things build up. Do not seek your own advantage, but that of others." (1 Corinthians 10:23–24) As self-absorbed and self-seeking creatures, sex easily, even naturally, becomes selfish rather than edifying the union of our two spirits, putting our beloved first, both of us at the same time. If shared, vulnerable sexual exploration will deepen and not weaken our marriages. But let us keep before us the reality of both strengths and susceptibilities of living out marriage as a spiritual union. For this rare and holy paradigm will not find support out in the world.

As couples feel led to discuss exploring the idea of erotic variety, you can actually find reputable Christian web sites devoted to this purpose. They consist of actual Christian couples sharing real and unblinkingly honest stories they have committed to writing with the purpose of turning up the heat in the bedroom (or out of the bedroom) so all parties can remain faithful. It is striking how the written narratives of real, but anonymous couples next door are sexier than the airbrushed, surgically altered, make-up-with-trowel images of porn stars drearily going through the motions. Ah, the power of wholesome couples whose innocence in marriage as a shared covenant invisibly and inexplicably ratchets up the erotic quotient to downright steamy.

Some sites are from evangelical Christians who have outdistanced us mainline Christians in nurturing this risky but vital conversation around sex and the Spirit. It is funny how we develop tidy stereotypes of how closed-minded "they" are and how open-minded "we" are, only to find that life is more complex than that and reality stands our prejudices on their head as we issue blanket statements about others. This closing story was sent in by a pastor's wife (not from either of the families of this book's authors). I include it because of how it alights upon our themes in a living, breathing and unashamedly erotic fashion. It might change our view of fresh-faced church couples and the startling place of the erotic in the daily walk of remaining both faithful and vitally alive.

I have been happily married for 27 years or so I thought. We certainly lived busy lives with me teaching school and going to college to complete my educational degree and my husband working a full-time secular job as well as pastoring a church. We still found time for each other with occasional dates and sex about four times a week.

I thought life was comfortable, but suddenly my comfort zone was shaken. I was concerned about the amount of time college was taking me away from my husband, and thought he may have felt neglected. He started spending more and more time on Facebook and started contacting old flames. This concerned me greatly, set up all kinds of red flags for me, and I decided it required a confrontation. I called my husband on it, and we sat down to have a serious heart to heart about the situation. I had written some thoughts out on paper, and when my husband came home from work we spent the time in a face to face confrontation. My husband made sure to lock his eyeballs into my eyeballs for the first time in probably years—we've just been so busy.

I made a vow that day that my husband "shall have no need for spoil." (Proverbs 31:11b) I vowed that day that the most important thing to me was my husband. I was going to supply his every need and desire. I was taking the words "no," "headache," "too tired," "don't feel good," and "not tonight" out of my vocabulary. I was going to be what he needed.

This pastor's wife—both sensual and faithful—went on to describe in graphic detail every touch, taste and smell of what she and her husband could only know in private, with bold and clumsy explicitness of how it feels to give and receive all manner of pleasure with her beloved. She told of explosive joy at "mind-blowing sex" made possible by the deep intimacy and safety developing over time between husband and wife. She became daring and vulnerable on both sides of Boteach's Edenic divide—trusting soulful transparency begetting new fearlessness in unselfconsciously sharing their bodies. She somehow took it upon herself to lead their marriage partnership toward this frank, new frontier. Can anyone say hot monogamy?

"It's been nine weeks since I have made that commitment," she concludes the reflection, "and I pray that I will keep the heat hot for the remainder of our marriage." How would it occur to us to link the trusting closeness of our spirits with searing sensuality and playful eroticism? After all, that insight is not out there for the taking in the world of secular sexuality at large. Just another real life, helpful surprise as it occurs to us that sexuality and spirituality might not be as estranged from one another as we were led to believe. Let not man or woman put asunder what God hath joined together from the beginning of time. Let us reconcile the twin sides of our nature—seeking God and seeking one another—until it redeems all our loving commitments, one unto another.

. . .

CHAPTER 13 FEMALE COUNTERPOINT

VERLEE A. COPELAND

The erotic sexuality and sensuality of Song of Solomon opens possibilities for ethical expressions of intimate explorations as you have described. Thank God for this expression of pleasure and delight through the overt sensuality of tasting, touching, smelling, hearing and seeing the Beloved. The innocence you describe flows from the desire to take another into one's self, to enter deeply into the beloved. Every imagined measure of probing with any part of the anatomy can only hint at our longing for completeness in the very being of the one we love.

The innocence of longing embodies every ordinary reach for the one we love. When we love another this deeply, we touch him as he passes in an unspoken moment of gratitude for his very existence. When we climb the stairs to deliver laundry to another floor, we lean over briefly to kiss the top of his brow as if to say, "I miss you already, I'll be back." At day's end, we crawl naked into bed and wrap our arms around one another in tender embrace, knowing that whatever storms rage outside, we now find shelter in his waiting flesh.

Ordinary lovemaking, even without the adventures you describe, creates a baseline for all other experimentation. If we cannot reach for one another safely, lovingly, respectfully, sensually and with regularity, we will not be able to reach for one another dressed in a maid costume bearing a can of whipped cream! Making love first and foremost flows from the shared intimacy of loving and longing relationship. It takes place in the sanctuary of fidelity where no threat exists, real or imagined, and where love finds safe harbor to be authentically oneself, without judgment.

It has been said that two human experiences approximate death: sex and childbirth. In childbirth, a woman can feel as if she is being pulled inside out by the urgent thrust of some Divine and invisible force far greater than herself. Once begun, there is no turning back, no postponing for another day, a better time. The tension builds and mounts until the woman, racked and urgent, delivers her own flesh out into the world. Making love creates an inverse rhythm as each draws the other into their own self with increasing urgency. That which was separate, distinct and apart, begins to move and flow in rhythm until no distinction remains, one from the other, no other now, in scent, sound or form.

As each in turn crashes upon that familiar shore, already a tinge of grief hangs suspended in shared breath at the necessary parting. And then it begins anew, this holy longing, reaching and embracing her sex, his spirit. So this is marriage.

· 14 ·

WHEN NOTHING SEEMS TO MATTER

Verlee A. Copeland

When my wife and I married we seemed to have so much in common, as friends, companions and sexual partners. The friendship and companionship are still there, but sex has become a distant third. What bothers me most is that I don't seem to have passion for anything. Work seems rote and I don't enjoy my friends as much as I once did. What's happening?

· · ·

Sometimes we cry out, "How long O Lord?" What you describe in your question sounds like mild depression. The absence of vitality can feel like the life is sucked out of every waking minute of every endless day. Diminished health, a stagnant relationship, and frustrations with work or economic deprivation can suppress the movement of what might be called the life force. Unexpressed anger or unresolved grief may also rob your passion.

There is a famous quote by Henry David Thoreau in *Walden* that speaks to this sense of a diminished life. "The mass of men lead lives of quiet desperation. What is called resignation is confirmed desperation."[1] This confirmed desperation becomes the barrier to

---

1. Henry David Thoreau, *Walden* (Radford, Va.: Wilder Productions, 2008).

intimacy that kills our sex lives and our joy in all else. Fear is incompatible with joy. Desperation is born in our fear that this is all there is and our sense that if this is all there is, it isn't enough.

Last week I cleaned out the home of my aging parents in preparation to sell it to younger family members. My parents have moved to an assisted living facility, and they are rightly divesting of their worldly goods. A home is not just full of stuff of course. It is full of memories, and mystery. Two things caught my eye as I packed yet one more box of memorabilia, old photos, coins and newspaper clippings. One was a photo taken of my grandmother as a young bride in 1917, and the second was a book called *Sex Force—Our Vital Power,* published in 1913.

I peered at the photo of my grandmother, standing on a farm outside a simple, white clapboard house. She is clothed neck to ankle in cotton, hand sewn to cover her in modest attire. She wears a bonnet to shield her eyes from the summer sun, and lace-up boots for the chores, headed as she is for the chicken yard.

My grandmother lived before electricity, indoor plumbing, telephones or the right to vote for women. My grandfather was the only man she ever had sex with, a fact she disclosed to me before her death. As I beheld this photo with her shaded face turned toward the half-light of a country morning, I wondered what she thought as she read about sex by kerosene lamp on a cloudless summer night.

It turns out that she read the following words, written by a progressive unnamed scientist about the very life force you seek:

> The ideal union, both during the engagement as well as after the marriage, is one of the beautiful manifestations of the great Universal Force; it is the foundation of a useful and happy life, its fruition in beautiful and healthy offspring. But the main purpose of Sex Force is not to propagate the race; it has a higher and nobler purpose; primarily intended to draw the sexes into closer commun-

ion with each other by means of its subtle attraction, this communion is designed to develop the spiritual nature of man, and transform the individual into a higher and nobler being.[2]

At first glance, the photo of my grandmother would indicate to us that she knew nothing of sexual passion and life force. We would be wrong. She found inspiration in this book and in other things we will never know.

The question you pose taps a fundamental issue that faces all of us as men and women. How do we access the power, the vital force, the *chi,* as some would say, that makes more of us than we know how to make of ourselves? What can we do when it seems as if this vibrant energy has dissipated or drained away leaving us with a sense of hopelessness and inability to connect intimately with those who love us?

Studies indicate that close to 70 percent of persons who experience depression also experience some type of sexual dissatisfaction or dysfunction. Causes may be myriad, including unresolved childhood sexual abuse or violence, hormonal changes, erectile dysfunction, etc. Treatment for depression can sometimes make sexual engagement more difficult. Many of the psychotropic drugs to treat depression negatively impact libido, or the physical or emotional capacity to respond sexually. Nevertheless, most mental health professionals agree that depression needs to be addressed prior to addressing any other issues, including sexuality.

This makes sense as depression impacts relationships as well as the capacity of an individual to engage in critical aspects of life such as meaningful work, friendships, marriage, parenthood and contributions to community. It is also true that healthy sex provides an antidote to depression. The endorphins released through

---

2. *Private Lessons in the Cultivation of Sex Force* (Chicago: Advanced Thought Publishing, 1913), 76 77.

orgasm elevate mood and potentially ward off depression. Persons who regularly have sex in the context of a committed relationship report lower incidence of depression.

Our tendency as human persons when we feel blue or depressed is to isolate from other people, the very opposite of the deepest level of intimacy that can occur during sexual expression. When we are unable to experience pleasure and are no longer interested in sex, our partners suffer. This poses a catch-22 doesn't it? Sex positively impacts mood, but a depressed mood decreases desire for sex.

Our brain is our sexiest organ. Sexuality originates in the complicated chemical and neurological workings of the human mind. Neurotransmitters impact blood flow to sexual organs, and the path of signals that link desire with physiological response. Treating sexual and relationship issues sometimes works in conjunction with medical treatment to bring chemical imbalance in the brain and in the adrenal system back into balance. Though this conversation is beyond the scope of both this book and our expertise, it is important to note that God gives us medical tools to help make us well, along with spiritual practices that support our healthy expression as sexual beings. All these work together for good, making possible our full potential for joy.

What we may describe as sexual energy and vitality flows from an essential life force. For whatever reason, God created us with an irrepressible desire to unite with one another spiritually, if not bodily. We were created related. When we successfully unite with another human creature and seek a relationship with God, as we understand God, it seems that we humans tap into a deep well of power that makes us more vibrant and fully alive.

Writers in many faith traditions offer counsel on how best to foster healthy relationships that feed the flowering of this energy or life force. In his letter to a community of new Christians in Ephesus, Paul made a radical departure from the prescribed Greek household tables that determined the relationship between slaves and free, adult men and women, extended family and children. He invited people of The Way, as the early Christians were called, to a radically new way of being with one another when he wrote the following:

> Husbands, love your wives just as Christ loved the church and gave his life for it. He did this to dedicate the church to God by his word, after making it clean by washing it in water, in order to present the church to himself in all its beauty—pure and faultless, without spot or wrinkle or any other imperfection. Men ought to love their wives just as they love their own bodies. A man who loves his wife loves himself. (No one ever hates his own body. Instead, he feeds it and takes care of it, just as Christ does the church; for we are members of his body.) As scripture says, ' For this reason a man will leave his father and mother and unite with his wife, and the two will become one.' There is a deep secret truth revealed in this scripture, which I understand as applying to Christ and the church. But it also applies to you; every husband must love his wife as himself, and every wife must respect her husband. (Ephesians 5:25–33, Good News Bible)

God in God's infinite wisdom and mercy gives us a number of avenues to open to the movement of this life force within us. In another chapter of this book, we explore the movement of the spirit, the life force, through prayer. For some people, intense engagement in music or the arts, sport or meaningful work can also open this same kind of creative energy. The natural endorphins in our chemistry also flow freely when we awaken to love one another, and even a casual observer can almost see the sparks fly when such lovers gaze across the dinner table into one another's eyes.

The road back to the fullness of life has as many paths as the road into the depressed state you describe. To begin, we affirm that we were made for joy. We are wired by God to yearn for deeply intimate connections with one another and with God. We are wired to be satisfied with nothing less. This is the stasis, the natural state of our being. When we drift into a place of not feeling, that numb place, we become spiritually and sexually dis-regulated. Finding our way back takes intentionality; we will not fall into health, though we may grow into it.

The way back to life may require extended conversation with a therapist, Catholic priest, Jewish rabbi, Protestant pastor or Muslim Imam as we try to discern the source of our spiritual malaise. If we have a biochemical imbalance that leads to clinical depression, anti-depressant medication may help to restore us. If we have grown estranged from our partner, couples therapy that addresses the restoration of our sex lives can bring us back to delight in one another's embracing arms and entangled legs. If we have become couch potatoes from too much beer and nachos and not enough sleep, we may also need to draw our attention to restoring our physical health, in order to restore our vitality. Many health issues from hormone and adrenal system imbalance to poor nutrition play a role.

The malaise you describe resembles what it feels like to be stuck in a life pattern that no longer serves you well. To put it simply, you are stuck in a rut. We humans have a tendency to stay in a rut as long as we are stuck in the past, believing that our past experiences were the best they will ever be. When we dream of the football game we're never going to play again we're going to be unhappy.

One church member remarked that: "We do have to change as we grow older. My passion for competitive tennis turned into a passion for social tennis. My passion to teach has turned into a passion to train teachers." Adaptability allows us to grow and change. A willingness to discover and embrace new things can open us to this life force we may be missing. Finding a way to re-engage in relationships, make new friends, explore new interests, and engage in meaningful work, whether vocation or avocation can lead us back to life.

This does not always mean that we will experience intimate relationship and sexuality as we did when we were thirty years old. It will be different now. It can even be better and deeper. One woman compared the renewal of her marriage to the process of recovering as a young person from a near-fatal car accident. "The accident was painful and it changed my life. For a long time I couldn't even walk. I've learned to walk all over again in a different way that has allowed me to slow down and enjoy life more richly."

Here God's grace abounds. When making your way back from the numbness of depression, a simple touch can feel like lightning, or like nothing at all. The connections have gone haywire. Keep trying. Hold hands when you don't feel like kissing. Kiss when you don't feel like caressing. Caress as your body and heart open by stages to life once again.

One couple that came to me for therapy called one day from vacation. They were positively jubilant. "I'm so glad to hear you're having a good time," I said. "You'll never guess what happened," they said. I couldn't quite imagine what might initiate such a call. "What would you like for me to understand?" I inquired in my clinical voice.

I could hear them giggling and jumping up and down in the background. "We had sex and we liked it!" After years of struggle with depression and sexual dysfunction, this was nothing short of a miracle. I couldn't have been happier for them. This happy coupling marked the beginning of their return to a healthy and vibrant marriage and a healthy and vibrant life. God wants that unbounded joy for all of us.

There are many paths to a re-vitalized life. Open communication with your wife can heal you. Spiritual practices can heal you. Improved physical health can heal you. Renewed passion for meaningful work can heal you. Physical intimacy and lovemaking can heal you. These are definitive ways to begin the journey back into a vibrant and energized life. Each pathway is a gift from God. Where do you find inspiration to re-kindle the passion you have lost?

Fortunately, God always gives us a way back to life. This is the promise of the resurrection for Christians. Death is not the end of our story. When we lose our juiciness for life, the spark dims in our eyes, and we shrink back from life rather than leaning into it. It doesn't have to be this way unless we allow it to be so. Even dried bones can dance; our dusty spirits, our dried up relationships can rise again.

. . .

CHAPTER 14 MALE COUNTERPOINT

DALE ROSENBERGER

At first hearing, it might sound like less than cheery, sunny self-fulfillment to say the Christian version of life's pulse is confession and mercy, truthfulness and grace, even death and resurrection. That might sound dark until we are in a place where we must confess that things are no longer as they were; until truths confront us that we had always buried and denied; until we realize that as we let some things die, something like resurrection becomes possible. At that moment, as we feel alone in a dark wood, we realize others have been there before us, a path has been cleared, even that God in Christ has walked that trail before us.

Modern living, dominated by pointless busyness, isolated individuality, and mindless acquisitiveness, can leave us buried beneath the layered and scattered detritus of contemporary life, as a homeless person sleeps under the layers of a newspaper. We rustle underneath those dry sheets wondering if we can find our peace, if we can find a way forward. Of course, many routes lead to melancholy, depression, and the evisceration of our vitality and energy. But as we are stuck there, all that matters is finding one road out, one way back, one exit strategy for feeling like ourselves, and like the life we regained is recognizably ours again.

It shouldn't surprise us that our sexuality can be one of the first casualties in this bleak modern landscape. Our sexual energy is fragile, fleeting, and easily mislaid—if you will pardon the pun. Not only are the terms of life, work and family overbearing sometimes, men are left feeling exploited or manipulated by women just as women often feel abused or subjugated by men. Once burned, twice shy. Twice or thrice burned, we can forfeit the spirit of brimming expectations around a life of companionship, romance, and intimacy, shared with someone beloved.

Verlee has affirmed—as the gospels proclaim—that we turn things around leading with actions, not with feelings. In other words, we can't afford the luxury of waiting to feel differently to live into hopeful expectation. For that waiting could take decades or never happen. Life is too short for waiting to "feel it" before we can "live it authentically."

No, we lead by acting in hope-filled ways, often in defiance of how we feel, as though to say, we trust that feeling down is not the final word, even if we can't access feeling better right now. We step out, act in ways typifying what we want, and live into alternatives until the taste comes back into our mouth, the light and color appear in our field of vision, the scent of a well-lived life perks up again. God always gives us a way back, as you observe, Verlee. Can we see it? And will we take it? It's tempting to stay hidden under newspapers and venture nothing. After all, by not getting out there and risking ourselves again, we will avoid more pain.

All this might sound like a dreary pep-talk. Nobody needs that. But realize this before you dismiss it. Having faced dark nights of the soul, each in our own season, with so many turns in life's confounding sweep, both Verlee and I have spoken words of comfort and challenge to one another as friends, not willing to let the other off the hook of attempting a well-lived life. After all, that is what friends do. We don't let each other give in and give up because we know God wants abundant living for us and for all. And no one should settle for less, despite our circumstances. In my mind, that picture of your grandmother, determined not to settle, shines brightly before me.

· I 5 ·

LOVE, SEX, AGING, AND
THE STIRRING OF PASSION'S FIRE

Dale Rosenberger

Some claim that across the decades, the embers of love, sex and romance must inevitably cool. Some couples give up completely on making love—both literally and metaphorically. I simply don't want to feel that way. Is it realistic to hope to remain sexually alive in all seasons of life?

· · ·

In his book *As for Me and My House*, Walter Wangerin narrates one couple's purgatory of lost passion amid advancing years. We have all seen this scenario before.

> Glance around the restaurant. It's Denny's on a Saturday night, but it could be any place where a couple can sit to eat. There's a low hum of voices. People are talking; waitresses slide by on soft shoes; laughter bubbles up now and again; silverware chinks on dishes . . . But glance around. Do you see the man and woman seated at a single table separated by a low, dividing wall? The

couple by the plastic flowers? Watch them. They do not talk. . . . The waitress sets plates of food in front of them. He stares at his. His wife (she is his wife) smooths and smooths the napkin on her lap while the food is placed. The waitress smiles. The woman smiles. The man does not. They eat. . . . Steadily the man cuts the meat. Efficiently he pokes the pieces in his mouth, his fork upside down. He chews, gazing at his plate. . . . It is curious that the woman should be overweight, because she takes such tiny bites. She fidgets her peas, sips water, darts her eyes around the room, picks chicken with her little finger arched, pats her mouth with the napkin, smooths it on her lap—sighs. Every bite is nibbled to death, as though she chews with her front teeth only. . . . He is done long before she is. So he sits sideways at the table with his thumbs hooked in his belt. Now he stares at nothing, at no one. His eyes are lost in middle distance. When he thinks of it, he blows on his coffee and drinks. But the woman—her nervous gestures have multiplied, intensified. When anyone passes them, she looks up, looks down immediately, smiles too late, then blanks her face. She is an anthill of twitchy motion. Through furious embarrassment, she orders dessert. She attempts a joke about ice cream, cheese, and apple pie; the waitress smiles indulgence. The man clears his throat, gazing away, uncommitted. . . . When they rise to go, the man is not one whit changed from the solemn fellow who first sat down. . . . she checks and rechecks the table to see whether they forgot something, while her husband marches directly toward the cashier. Finally, she follows. This is how they regularly walk together: she follows.[1]

---

1. Walter Wangerin, *As For Me and My House* (Nashville: Thomas Nelson, 1990), 151–52.

This would be painful enough if they were simply having a bad night. But Wangerin describes this as their "date night." The couple "treats themselves" to a café dinner like this every Saturday. So this is their anticipated diversion, the fevered high point of their entire week. This is how they satisfy their marital urge to be together. Imagine what transpires alone between them in the bedroom, if you dare such a gloomy shudder.

The image is upsetting on many fronts. We are disarmed by the man's utter lack of personal presence and attention, never mind anything like emotional investment, to make something worthwhile out of their "date." It is spooky how missing in action he is. More inscrutably, I suspect he likely imagines he is already "doing his part" as the guy, what with being provider, protector and changer of light bulbs. Perhaps he is so absent because he wants sex, doesn't get it, remains clueless, and feels cheated. Resentment could well lurk hidden underneath his distance. After all, he has "done his part," right?

He hasn't figured out it is not about wanting sex. Sex is not the point. It is about wanting another human being as the love of our life, the focus of lifelong devotion, our passion's pulse, our one and only partner, our God-given cherished mate. Find real love together and sex flows ineluctably from what we share. Seek sex while bracketing love—single, married, or whatever—and distance enters in ways that should scare the daylights out of all of us.

It is sad and pathetic how empty, shaken, and uncertain the woman is. Her example clarifies how our outer and inner lives connect. Starved of affection and attraction, she also lives without anything like confidence. Not surprisingly, she fills herself with calories to fill inner emotional and spiritual voids she neglects. She doesn't know if she matters. So she doesn't know who she is. She doesn't know what she wants. She doesn't know which way to turn. She is unsure of whom and what she can count upon. She is lost and unaware of the spectacle she has become. Depression would be no surprise for such a woman, perhaps diagnosed as "a clinical disorder." This is ironic. Rather than "disorder," depression seems the natural consequence of living such a life while having to project it to others as normal, meaningful, and fulfilling.

This snapshot raises bigger questions about aging and intimacy, about loving and the inevitability of life's shining moments receding from us. Must the bright floral accents of brimming, ardent, youthful love necessarily fade as we amass decades together? This question is increasingly important, as we live longer than ever. Must what was once living and vibrant become as brittle and lifeless as the plastic flowers in Denny's? We need to find ways to remain animated and lively together, lest key people and relationships become increasingly disposable, and loneliness gain an upper hand.

Some assume aging necessarily means becoming bigger and heavier, duller and blanker, slower and blander. In the same way, some assume our shared passion as men and women must also inevitably wither, dry, and scatter to the winds. Some expect this outright as established truth of generations past, and then fulfill the prophecy because it is "supposed to happen." And here is another sad truth. Some couples are actually relieved by the falling off of interest in sex, what with passion making relentless demands of mutual interest, engagement, growth, and aliveness. Frankly, some never knew "what the big deal was" about sex and soldiered through the motions, erotically. Aging becomes a convenient excuse to exit that life for tamer and less imposing pastimes—like bingo, bridge, knitting, or watching afternoon television.

God bless the exceptions who refuse to submit to a misplaced sense of destiny. In effect, such couples as these refuse to bow down and worship the glamour idol of youth. They will not submit to the message that sex is—wink, wink, nod, nod—only for the young and the adored, only for the supple and the sensational. Such couples defy tired, misleading elder stereotypes like "the insatiable widow," "the dirty, lecherous old man," "the predatory cougar" or "the burnt-out old fart." The hidden counterculture of their passion contradicts the destructive myth that we naturally must "mature out of sex."

Despite how popular culture mocks the persistence of passion into maturity, such couples as these find ways to witness that aging need not contradict being sensual, and that sexual satisfaction need not decrease with years. In truth, it often *increases* with age. Such beneath-the-radar couples who discover this amaze us as their lifelong passion lends a youthfulness that defies the seeming omnipotence of years, gives them the timeless grace of life's fullness, and radiates a warm glow that naturally attracts us. So much of thinking this through is still new to us. Sex and aging was hardly studied until Masters and Johnson finally got around to it in 1966.

Honestly, I don't believe most couples would enter the promised solidarity of a shared lifetime if they saw the Denny's scenario as a possible outcome in their lives. No, they would turn and flee, men to the labor camps, women to the nunneries. But let's be honest about how common it is. We need not look far to see this sadness. Only just listen to the couple in the next booth, talking past and ignoring one another. How tender and sweet is their lovemaking? How creative and playful? How ardent and satisfying?

So many building blocks assemble to create a relationship and to keep it strong, vibrant, and defiant of the years. We are talking about attentiveness, tenderness, constancy, forgiveness, forbearance, kindness, compassion, whimsy, imagination and then encompassing love to wrap it all into a package. Take each other for granted for more than a season of surviving something, and you both become vulnerable to serious slippage. Fade gently over time into taking each other for granted, letting apathy become the norm, and before you know it, you're toast. Indifference is the silent, cruel neglect that remains invisible as a form of abuse we think we can get away with.

The 2012 film *Hope Springs,* mentioned previously in this work, dynamically expands the Denny's scene by offering up some difficult but real alternatives to living in marital purgatory. Meryl Streep and Tommy Lee Jones excel as Kay and Arnold Soames. As the movie opens, Kay is in the bathroom mirror, nervously fussing over her hair and fixing her modest blue negligee. She wants to make love with Arnold. It has been all of four years since the last time they were intimate. She slips into "his bedroom." His incredulous look says, "Well, what do you want?" Kay stammers, "I want. . . . I want . . ." As Arnold realizes that she beckons him to his conjugal duty as a husband, he dismissively buries his face in the paper. "I'm not feeling well," he mutters. This Nebraska couple is sleepwalking through their marriage.

Kay is not unlike the woman in the opening Denny's scene, lacking in confidence, twitchy and lost, emotionally and sensually starved. But Kay differs in a key regard: she won't accept it anymore. "When did you last touch me when it wasn't for a photo?" she asks him. "I want a marriage again," she calmly declares more than once, implying that the absence of physical intimacy is completely unacceptable. Kay decides to seek intensive marital couples counseling on the coast of Maine. "I'm not going," Arnold responds. "Go by yourself." Much to his surprise, she does. Arnold joins her mostly because he doesn't know what else to do. He complains all of the way there and denies any need for a therapist, or a "quack," like Bernie Feld, credibly played by Steve Carell.

Most of the movie is the couples' interaction with Bernie in therapy and the exercises he assigns for their private time. At one point, Bernie leans in and asks, "Is this the best you can do?" The answer is obvious in the asking: clearly not. Arnold is plodding and truculent. Kay is afraid but heroically determined in the face of discouragement. In a fit of pique, Kay storms away from therapy and plops down in a pub. After Kay's confesses why they are visiting Maine, the barmaid spontaneously asks the gathered patrons, "All right, who in here is not having sex?" Most of the hands go up in a show of widespread, genial, and vexing underachievement. Clearly, they are not alone.

Kay's and Arnold's progress is slow and uneven. Progress is grudging but efforts are made. Sometimes their two steps backward make the three steps forward feel like very hard-earned ground. In the final analysis, they both show up when it matters most, neither gives up on the other again. Breakthroughs begin to dot their landscape. Arnold eventually opens up enough to tell of a daring fantasy: sharing his bed with Kay *and* the neighbor lady who walks her two Welsh Corgis by their house. You find *her* attractive? Kay is taken aback but welcomes Arnold's vulnerability without judging him. After all, it is only a fantasy, a contrivance of forbiddenness, a naughty fiction that might inspire him.

In a humorous moment, back home in Nebraska, that very neighbor lady goes walking by their place the day after they return, this time walking with *three* Corgis, symbolism duly noted. They exchange pleasant greetings and briefly catch up. Kay invites the lady over to hear about the couple's trip to Maine. As soon as she is out of earshot, Kay pivots toward Arnold and smiles, "Don't you even begin to think about it!"

But back in Nebraska, things aren't so good. The two want to implement in their daily routine what they have learned as a couple. This proves no small feat. The inertia of their former divided and dispassionate life again encroaches and envelops them. Seemingly, they are back at square one. Kay packs her suitcase to dog-sit for a work friend as a pretext for getting out of the house, even out of the marriage. She almost picks it up and walks many times. Arnold still lives in his own bedroom. Yet as he walks by Kay's bedroom, he pauses to stare at the doorknob, and imagine the mysteries that lie beyond. He truly wants to open it. Kay resists bailing. Arnold finally grasps the knob and opens the door. It happens before they have reached that point of no return as a couple.

Tender embraces give rise to warm and natural lovemaking, just what they were looking for, just what was eluding them. It is as though the accumulated efforts have suddenly paid off just as all seemed lost. Who knows why it didn't happen sooner? Who knows why it happened then? But the cosmic tumblers suddenly fall into place for them, not coincidentally, after a lot of effort and work. The entire movie we wonder if they will make it as a married couple. The next day, in the simple rituals of breakfast and parting, it is clear they are at a whole new place. And then later, as the credits roll, Kay's fantasy comes true. The daylight they have sought now finally shines on Arnold and Kay at the Maine beach, as they renew marriage vows. In this moment, we see how their promises to be more understanding and considerate feed directly into the rekindled heat they share as a man and a woman.

Summing up the Beatitudes, Jesus said, "Seek first the kingdom of God, and these other things shall be added." The correlate for passion in marriage is, seek first to love in detailed and encompassing ways, and then see if you can't keep your hands off each other. Of course, it is never that simple, is it? To come alive again inwardly, a couple's shared fire must be remembered, respected, nurtured, planned, stoked, restrained, rekindled, rehearsed, and replenished. This is what we mean as we say how much work a marriage is. Such intimacies are daunting to engage, even with those we love. Kay and Arnold's antics remind us that authentic, deep, and carefully nurtured love is the royal road to hot sex, not so much the other way around.

So tell me something, having heard the story of Kay and Arnold. How would you have me respond as pastor to one couple in a church I once served? They were well-to-do, owners of their own business, parents to growing children, and respected leaders in the community. One night the police arrested them for having sex in their car, off in some dark corner of a parking lot. Do I tell them what a bad example they are? What a disappointment to their children? How their irresponsibility reflects badly on their church? Careful, now, about being quick to judge. First listen very closely to their hearts of hearts, and know what they are up against. Or do I congratulate them for not giving up? For pressing against the borders that might hem them in? For striking a blow for liberty just as they needed to break out? Before you answer, consider this also.

I am struck how Paul the Apostle constantly charges the far-flung churches of his epistles, urging them to be controlled, prudent, disciplined, restrained, discreet, sober, and circumspect. While it is good to hear that we are first of God, and not of the world, to learn that we belong to Jesus Christ and not to other idolatrous powers eager to coopt us—thank you, Paul!—we might also be mindful of another fine line we step over.

When fear takes root and we live overly controlled and controlling lives, we can stultify imagination in a way that quenches passion, in a way that quashes footloose joy and gladness. In being good and dutiful, we can drain all of the air, light and festivity from our lives, thinking God blesses what we are doing, all the while. It happens in dozens of little ways. It is how the aforementioned decency brigades form. And it is closer to the goodness of the Pharisees than the goodness of Jesus, as the gospel stories well illustrate who Jesus hung around with and how he responded to them.

Arnold and Kay became prisoners of their unimaginative routine and plodding habits, perhaps imagining that was putting them in good stead with God. It was the same egg every morning, the same bland hellos at work every day, and the same snoring from Arnold in his Barcalounger every night, with ESPN droning. It felt safe to live in a stable, narrow range of choices, a monotonous rut. It is like carbon monoxide to a relationship, invisible and dangerous. Fortunately, Kay modestly but determinedly forced them out of that rut by creating a crisis and throwing them both into the dilemma for which their shared intimacy could be the only answer.

We should note that Paul also means for us to live lives of creative engagement with the Holy Spirit. The Holy Spirit is not about austerity and privation. The Spirit also teems with surprise, breaking boundaries, busting categories, injecting new colors in the tired sepia of selfsame obligation played out within daily routines. The Holy Spirit blows where it will in surprising ways.

So as people of faith, we also ask, where might our passion for our beloved exceed its banks, spill out and over into the rest of our lives, saturate our respectable work clothes, drench us with erotic wetness that shakes us loose and undresses us for a spontaneous skinny-dipping with our beloved? Funny, isn't it, how no one has to commend such impulses in our exploratory youth. They naturally occur to us. Funny how sometimes we need to find permission again to become who we once were, and then forgot. This is the renewing nature of the Holy Spirit, with power to tamp us down in one moment and also to explode artificial barriers, holding us back, in the next moment.

In other words, the third person of the Trinity is surprising, enigmatic, and paradoxical in its holiness. The same Holy Spirit that offers us secure foundations also bids us to risk breaking the mold as life becomes utterly prepackaged. The same Holy Spirit that Paul commends to Corinth to button them down in their disturbing excesses can then come back around when we least expect it to unbutton our stark austerity, to commend youthful playfulness, to fan our playful exuberance and exploration.

The message is clear. Sharing bland, routinized, mechanical sex is not pleasing to God. Refraining from sex is not necessarily a holier way to live. And breaking outside the box to live playfully and without fetters like Adam and Eve in the garden is not displeasing to God. God created that garden and it was all God ever wanted for us. God wants it for us still. Let's be careful not to stereotype God, put God in a box, make God predictable and boring, and then call that Christianity and morality. Do not do that or you will have to liberate yourself from the prison where you have placed God and yourself.

CHAPTER 15 FEMALE COUNTERPOINT

Verlee A. Copeland

Contentment is not the same thing as complacency, is it? It's so hard, when gazing upon the behaviors of other people, to imagine what goes on in their hidden lives. It seems fair, however, to assume that the couple in the opening illustration has grown distant and bored with one another, if not with life. It saddens us to watch their empty interaction when we know what they have forgotten, how much more dynamic and fulfilling life can be. They have perhaps lost sight of the rich possibility of enjoying the love of one's life.

On the other hand, when a seasoned couple enjoy deep contentment with one another, their silences become neither empty nor sad. Deep silence then resonates all manner of unspoken intimacies and the sweet comfort of certain familiarity and routine. Unfortunately, we do not see that here. You observe that the wife fills herself with calories to feed a hidden emotional and spiritual void. Our tendency as human creatures is to reach for all manner of temporary satisfactions to fill a God-shaped hole that can only be satisfied by the Holy One. As early church theologian Augustine once famously said, "There is no rest until we rest in Thee." Whether we fill our sadness with calories or alcohol or sport or hobby or even a pretty good relationship, anything can become a false god. The emptiness that we experience can be satisfied by God alone. The loves of our lives can only hint at that for which we pray: "Thy Kingdom come, thy will be done, on earth as it is in heaven. Give us this day, our daily bread."

The road back from the dull co-existence that passes here for marriage may begin with the call to faith renewal. You invite us to refrain from putting God in a box as if that were our decision to make. We don't shape God, but rather God shapes us, and reforms our tired relationships for good when we're open to it. As often as not, the re-vitalization of life and love begins in the church pew in worship or on our knees in prayer as well as in the bedroom. Blessed by God, any ordinary place can become the holy ground on which God resurrects our weary and wounded relationship to new life.

· 16 ·

MAKING LOVE LAST

Verlee A. Copeland

Remind me please about what we promised as Christians when we said "I will" and "I do" on the occasion of our wedding? What difference does the context of marriage make in our sex life?

· · ·

When I meet a couple for the first time who want be married in the church, I ask them to tell me their love story. This usually puts the nervous couple at ease. A few generations ago, their nervousness might have come from wondering whether they were making the right decision, or what it might feel like to have sex for the first time on their wedding night. More often than not, couples already live together today. At first they are nervous, wondering if I will agree to preside at their wedding when I find out about it.

Great sex starts with a great love story, every time. For Christians, the fleeting love stories of tabloid stars bear little resemblance to the deep and abiding love of people of faith. That love can be grounded more deeply in the love of God for God's people. When a love story starts in such a place as this, hot sex takes on new dimensions. It is no longer a sprint to the end of a date, but a marathon of perfect delight over the course of a long and fruitful marriage.

Both love and our sexuality change over time. One woman described married sex in this way. "When you're young and full of lust, sex is like a hot fire burning, burning. As you mature in your love, the fire becomes burning coals, and then to embers, more rich as the years go by."

Every love story has to start somewhere. Jesus' affair with the world started at a wedding at Cana in Galilee, where his mother provoked him to take the next step in God's work for him. At first he resisted, as sons do, saying, "Woman, what concern is that to you and to me that the host is out of wine?"

After he thought about it, he knew what we have come to believe through him. Every time we gather as the people of God and seek God's blessing on our work, our love, or our service, we have the opportunity to point toward higher ground. Jesus turned water into wine late in the wedding feast, as a sign of three things: that God's unmerited grace pours out upon us without end; that God's fierce mercy grows stronger over time; and that God's peace is a gift not only for us, but for all people.

You may well ask what that has to do with us on such a joyous occasion as a wedding, in marriage, and in the bedroom that follows. From this miracle—Jesus turning water into wine at a wedding at Cana in Galilee—the answer is: everything.

First, God's gift of marriage is more than a fantastically orchestrated social event called a wedding. Rather, this day for people of faith becomes a sign of God's unmerited grace poured out upon us without end. Many of us have known great love in our lives and bitter disappointments. Most often we are not eighteen-year-old star-struck lovers who entered this day unadvisedly, as perhaps our grandparents did, who may have been too young to know what they were getting into (as if any of us ever do). If there is not fear and trembling involved, there should be. We marry as Christians because we have come to know the ecstasies of a growing and beautiful love between us, yet we know that love is fragile. The wine does not always last to the end of the party. Despite our best efforts and most earnest intentions, we do not know how to make love come or stay, and when our loves become broken, we do not always know what to do to make things right. The high divorce rate in this country testifies to that.

According to the McKinley-Irvin Law firm, an average of 50 percent of marriages end in divorce: 41 percent of first marriages, 60 percent of second marriages, and 73 percent of third marriages. The average age of divorce for first-time marriages is thirty, and the average length of marriage for the first-time divorce is eight years.[1]

You may have heard it said that Christians divorce at the same rate as non-believers. Research does not bear out this myth. While it is true that those who simply identify themselves as Christian do get divorced at roughly the same rate as those who do not, those of either Jewish or Christian identity who regularly practice their faith have a significantly higher commitment to marriage and report significantly greater marital satisfaction than those who do not. Faith practices such as regular attendance at worship services, participation in a faith community and disciplines of faith—such as scripture reading and prayer—make marriages last.

When we stay married and deeply committed, we become more confident that we are loved and cherished. We humans have a tendency to express greater satisfaction in our sex life when we feel loved and cherished. Therefore, it is worth pausing to consider what we learn from our faith that can inform our life together as marital partners.

How fitting it is that Jesus' ministry was revealed at the wedding at Cana in Galilee. Jesus went to that party, turning water into wine, as an act of God's boundless generosity in preparing for us all good things, as a wedding host prepares for every detail of the wedding.

---

1. McKinley Irvin Law Firm, "32 Shocking Divorce Statistics," www.mckinley irvin.com/blog/divorce/32-shocking-divorce-statistics/.

What do we learn from the fact that Jesus came to this wedding party and chose to reveal himself in this context? Through Jesus we have come to know God's love given to us, and for us, as free gift. We trust that God will reveal to us what will be needed to love one another fully, deeply and intimately as husband and wife. As God has loved us unconditionally, so we practice loving one another unconditionally. God helps us to do this faithfully, not only for our own sakes, but also as a sign to the world of God's intention for human life.

In that sense, though our weddings are for us, our marriage is not just about us. As much as our relationship brings us perfect delight, a passionate, joy-filled miracle, it is not about us, our personal happiness, or even our mutual satisfaction. God gifts us with marriage for the sake of the world, so that others may look to us with hope that what God has done for us, God may do for us all. Whether married, single or widowed, God reveals to us the ways of love and satisfies the deepest longings of our sacred hearts.

Second, God's fierce mercy grows stronger over time. We humans have a remarkable capacity to act as if we do not need God when the bloom is on the vine. We're at the top of our game; everything is going well and according to plan, our plans. There's humility and a vulnerability that can grow as we mature. We know our knees and our backs won't last forever. We understand that there will come a time when the party will be over. But we pray, "Please God, not yet." We do not know what the end game will be, which partner will die first, whether we will remain healthy or end our years with illness or injury. When we marry, we pledge ourselves to stand by one another, regardless.

Surely the love we find in one another is a sign of God's fierce mercy, that when we seek first God's kingdom and God's righteousness, all things really will be added unto us. Perhaps this mercy is never sweeter than when we receive the gift of marrying again. When a spouse dies, we may grieve and discover by the grace of God the capacity to love again. When a marriage covenant ends through circumstances that irrevocably break vows and culminate in divorce, God graciously forgives us and allows us to begin life anew as forgiven people. God's loving kindness and fierce mercy may include the formation of a new love, a new bond and a new covenant.

Sometimes the best and sweetest wine really does come last. How great is that? At whatever stage of life we marry, God reveals to us the path to passionate friendship, faith partnership and deep intimacy expressed in part through our sexuality. The world may think the best happens only for the young, but God's ways are not our ways. Through God's mercy, we can discover in one another a passionate friendship and partnership that will bring us joy all the days of our life.

For people of faith, God's peace through this sign of God's love given to us comes as a gift not only for us as couples, but also for all God's people. We don't know how to do this for ourselves. In fact, we're more than capable as human creatures of messing things up. This may be hard to imagine on the day we wed. One writer remarked that on our wedding day, we are perfect specimens of earthly beauty, with one, long downhill slide to death thereafter. Whoever said this was not very happily married, I suspect.

A happy marriage is not always a prerequisite for a happy sex life, but it helps. For example, one couple I know had quite a contentious marriage. He was an active alcoholic who lost first one job and then another. She was insecure and more closely tied to her mother and siblings than to her husband. When asked after 50 years of marriage what kept them together, the wife remarked unabashedly, "The sex was great!"

Most of us want more from marriage than this. We want great sex, however that is not enough. We want to know the love of God and to serve God in meaningful ways. We want to cherish another human being and love them to the best of our capacity. And we want to be known and loved by another for who we are, and for what we can yet become.

The story of Jesus' love affair with humankind began as a cautionary tale. Just because the wedding wine lasted with abundance, we know that we need to resist squandering the gifts of God just because God promises that more will be provided. All the gifts needed for our marriage to grow, deepen and endure have been given to us, but we humans have the capacity to spoil even the greatest of God's gifts. When we neglect, bruise, crush, or squander those gifts, the greatest of loves can be damaged if we insist upon it. We all have times when we think we're more important than our relationships. It doesn't have to be that way.

Therefore, if you want a great marriage, trust God in all your ways. Hold lightly as a treasure all that you have been given. Receive the deep and abiding contentment you have come to know through your love one for the other, and God's love for you. For all these things are signs that God alone can and does bring us perfect peace. We may not know how to keep the party going. Fortunately, God always keeps the party going when we utterly rely on the Holy One. God turns all water into wine, every time, not only sometimes, but always, for us all.

That said, if you want a hotter sex life, you might want to consider putting down the sex chronicles from the newsstand, and pray with your partner instead. There is nothing sexier or more deeply intimate than prayer. Whenever we open in love to the God who uttered us, and allow God's sweet grace, mercy and peace to flow through us all the days of our lives, anything is possible.

Let the love story between us as men and women then begin in the love of God for us. Let our vows create a safe, enduring and faithful context for mutual intimacy to grow. If you haven't said your vows lately, you may also wish to renew them with words of devotion like these from the United Church of Christ book of worship:

I take you _____, to by my husband (wife)
I promise to love and sustain you

In the covenant of marriage
From this day forward
In sickness and in health
In plenty and in want
In joy and in sorrow
Forsaking all others
As long as we both shall live.[2]

Doesn't that sound sexier, a whole lot sexier than "Hey baby, want to come up for a drink?" Or, "How about hooking up tonight, no strings attached?" This type of negotiation is contract, not covenant, an agreed-upon exchange of goods or services for personal benefit. That's why it's called "friends with benefits." This kind of benefit is always about "me" and "mine." There is no "us" or "ours." Such couplings are transient and always incomplete. They hold out an empty promise they cannot keep. The fruit of such couplings is most often regret, often lingering. What has been given cannot be taken back.

Unlike what happens in this type of human coupling, God makes love last. As we seek to keep the covenant promises we make in the context of marriage, God promises to remain present to us, to love us unconditionally, to forgive us, and always to respect us in the morning.

---

2. *Book of Worship, United Church of Christ* (Cleveland: Local Church Ministries, Worship and Education Ministry Team, 2009), 334.

CHAPTER 16 MALE COUNTERPOINT

DALE ROSENBERGER

"That's the story of, that's the glory of, love . . ." goes the elegant old refrain, as rendered by a great like Ella Fitzgerald. I like how you have injected the notion of shared story into satisfying sex, Verlee. I like it because it is not an idea found in the mainstream of our secular pop culture, yammering about sex. Yes, sex—like every worthy, magnificent thing in life—is contextual and not some hovering idealized abstraction. The fascinating thing about the wedding at Cana of Galilee is how much detail it gives about this first great, miraculous outpouring of divine love at the outset of Jesus' ministry and new inbreaking of God's reign. True and deep love, the kind that nurtures our spirits and never dies, happens in real time and real life between real people with a shared history. That is what makes us explode with joy as the flirting of body parts becomes a springboard to propel us into the deep end of the 160 gallons of wine Jesus fermented from water.

Of course, the sex industry shears sex of its context, featuring anonymous couples who have just met moments before filming their eight minutes of grinding bodily contact. They share no past and want no future together. All they can see is the surface landscape of each other's bodies. In all likelihood they avoid deep and lingering looks into each other's eyes—yes, the very eyes that thoughtful observers dub the window unto the soul. To look into each other's eyes would embarrass them both because, while their act is intimate, they really share no intimacy. Because they lack any context or common story, their plunging merger lacks soul, which is why porn snippets aren't very sexy. They are slaking the most superficial craving or thirst, like scratching the itch of poison ivy, or unwrapping the cellophane from a piece of hard candy.

They clearly do not drink from the same wine bowl that Jesus dramatically replenished at a neighbor's nuptials in Cana of Galilee.

So much of the spiritual genius behind the deep, soulful sexuality we lift up resides in the unfolding of slow, patient details. I mean, who knew that standing by our beloved when his or her mother suddenly died would charge the moment as we later found each other in our nakedness? Who knew the painstaking years of sacrifice for another, allowing the finish of an education, could physically meld and fuse our pleasure as one? Who knew that standing by a life partner when he or she was ridiculed or attacked would morph quietly into a hidden aphrodisiac?

Sex is not the silly splish-splash in the shallows of a pond, as pop culture has it. Real sex is rather the majestic surging of a mighty sea, where Jesus can make all of those waters holy into wine. All we need to do is want more than silly frolicking to let God lead us out into ocean depths where currents hidden beneath the surface transport us to places we hardly dreamt existed. Of course, it takes a lot of trust, a lot of faith, in God and each other. But it is worth it. Thank you for lifting this up and celebrating it, Verlee.

· 17 ·

PUZZLING OVER THE PULLS, TUGS, AND QUIRKS OF ATTRACTION

Dale Rosenberger

Why is it women are attracted to bad boys they want to turn toward the good, and men are attracted to good girls they want to make a little bad, both with very mixed results?

· · ·

If we can agree that both our spiritual and sensual selves are shot through with unfathomable mystery, it would be hard to find labyrinths more inscrutable to our conscious choosing and more removed from our control than the sexy other we find ourselves attracted to. So much of our sexuality is involuntary—how we look, our level of desire, even the fantasies we harbor. They are simply part and parcel of how we are put together. They vary with each individual. Our attraction to the opposite sex feels, at first blush, like the first fragrant warm breeze of spring that made us feel fully alive. Then retrospectively, right after everything was so wonderful, the same attraction can loom like a witch's brew of unseemly and contradictory ingredients some malevolent force gleefully assembled expressly for our undoing. We incredulously look back on romances, relationships, and marriages only to scratch our heads. What was I thinking?

Of course, in the endorphin rush of the first inward tug toward our beloved, it made all the sense in the world. It was self-evident to any but the most opaque. We openly ridicule those who dare call it into question. We rationalize why the relationship was meant to be, why it simply had to be, down to such impressive evidence as the two of us sharing the same favorite brand of toothpaste. Oh boy. Perhaps the dynamics of attraction are why the saying "Love is blind" was first coined about romance in general.

In truth, seldom are we more subject to unrecognized and unacknowledged forces than in that magical, breathtaking moment as we first see Mr. or Ms. Right. Indeed our eyes seem wide open, as we abound with rational-sounding explanations for why we felt it was right to go out with somebody. But our eyes are more shut than we acknowledge. Lacking any explanation on the surface of things, clueless about how attraction works, the ancient Romans invented a happy, reckless cherub named Cupid randomly shooting capricious arrows to land wherever they might. I have not yet found the civilization since then that has coined a superior or more apt symbol.

Despite this sight-impaired state of attraction, the opposite sex will often tell us—directly or indirectly—the downside of who they really are. Call it truth in advertising, if you like. Or perhaps at some level we all want to be loved not at our best, but even despite the worst of who we are, way down deep. So we pull back the curtain and give a sneak preview of what should set red lights blinking and alarms sounding. What is amazing is how we blithely wave off these exposed relationship trip-wires as silly and immaterial, at least for us. We all act like experts in love in that we assume we know precisely what we are doing and why we are doing it. *Caveat emptor.* Let the buyer, or rather the chooser, beware! Choices are being made for us that we cannot even see.

We could throw up our hands and despair of cutting through the thicket growing up around sexual attraction, because even when we manage to identify exactly who attracts us—what he or she sounds, looks and acts like—we can't do much about it. But your twinned question points to a specific scenario of our strange behavior as we are attracted to the opposite sex. We have seen this "I love you, you're perfect, now change" phenomenon before. Seeking some answers, or at least some better questions, we look to tools like endocrinology, biological anthropology, and Christian theology to cut through the knotty and naughty mysteries of attraction.

Let's begin with basic biology. We hear smug laughter about how testosterone-driven men are, how we think with parts of our anatomy not known for deep cognition. Doubtless that is true enough. But women are also deeply shaped by hormones, relative to where a woman is in her fertility cycle upon meeting a man, as she considers and responds to his overtures. For example, when a woman is ovulating, research has shown she is much more likely to choose a "bad boy" (meaning, a sexy, charming, rebellious George Clooney or Tatum Channing type) to become her mate, even father for her children.[1] Even more dramatically, an ovulating woman often perceives a bad boy rebel as an involved and supportive father for her future children, even over men who are clearly more steady and dependable. Over and over, a woman at this peak in her cycle will pick a bad boy over a steady guy. It transcends sexiness and even colors her view of his likelihood to contribute to child-care, household chores, and shopping for food. In other words, as female hormones surge, Mr. Wrong looks exactly like Mr. Right.

---

1. Kristina M. Durante, Vladas Griskevicius, Jeffry A. Simpson, Stephanie M. Cantú, and Norman P. Li, "Ovulation leads women to perceive sexy cads as good dads," *Journal of Personality and Social Psychology*, vol. 103(2) (Aug 2012): 292–305.

What's more, further research showed highly fertile women perceiving the sexy cad as becoming the reliable dad to her children, but only for her and not for any other woman. When asked about the sexy cad's likelihood for successful relationships with other women, the women typically recounted in detail how they were doomed to failure because of evident sensitivity and relationship deficits on his part. When asked about that same bad boy's propensity as *her* helpful homemaker and supporter of *her* life cause, an ovulating woman quickly waved away the same deficits, making herself the exception to the rule she saw for every other woman. She saw the charismatic and precarious cad as becoming a tremendous father to their children in spite of his natural disinclination. Seemingly, the testosterone/adrenaline cocktail that makes men clueless in the dynamics of attraction has a female counterpart. Though still unnamed, science has described the female equivalent of guys thinking with their Johnson.

How do these relationships turn out? Anecdotally, we would have to say poorly. Let's just say that for every woman who smiles vindicated and satisfied about stepping out beyond her reasonable doubt to reel in and reform a Jack Sparrow as her fetching mate, another nine women likely feel their high-wire relationship reach of derring-do was probably some form of death wish. They feel in their relationship less like a sexy woman to a dashing rogue than a mother to some pathetic, inept boy who refuses to grow up.

Of course, why bright and discerning women seek bad boys is more complex than the hydraulics of female endocrinology. Maybe women as young girls had fathers with roguish and wild styles only to be deeply imprinted by this definition of manhood as normative. Maybe their sturdy mothering instinct makes them feel called and confident in their ability to salvage and save wayward men. Maybe after a staid childhood, to rebut restrictive limits, they crave the varieties of adventure that popular culture everywhere peddles as the romantic dream come true. Or maybe, loosely in the words of Cyndi Lauper, good girls want to have a little naughty fun.

Or, get this, maybe a "no gamble/no glory" risk ratio is unconsciously at work in the fleeting sparks of these internal computations matching otherwise clear-seeing women to rebels without a cause. Could it be the clear downside of risky cads might be offset by their higher ceiling for glorious achievement and making a singular difference in the world by virtue of their daring after "the path not taken," if only these bad boys had the right influence to channel their passions in the right direction? Women attracted to bad boys often perceive themselves alone as the missing ingredient to polish these masculine diamonds in the rough into shining crown jewels. Conversely, while solid dads lack the scary downside of roguish cads, their plodding, risk-aversive, flat-footed and pedestrian approach to life may also radiate absolutely zero chance for transformation into that shining, bravura man among men who takes the world by storm.

Suggestions like this might sound more plausible if we more fully appreciated the degree to which our behavior is rooted in the DNA of advancing and preserving human beings as a species as opposed to making carefully deliberated choices as individuals. Yes, much more than we realize, we take it upon ourselves in our dating and romance moves to ensure that *homo sapiens* will survive in perpetuity. This is true from pimply adolescence through autumn years. And we cannot much help this trend because most often we are not aware of it. Let me explain.

Much is made, for example, over how society in general and men in particular judgmentally loom over women, in their infinite variety of shapes, holding to a narrow balance of slender and curvy in deciding and dictating which women are desirable. Is this unthinking discrimination, dismissing sometimes a majority of women as less than attractive, merely the boorish superficiality of men? Perhaps. Is it the greed of Madison Avenue merchandising goods by seizing upon an elite and unrealistic range of female bodies to promote goods and products through advertising? Maybe. Is it the random standard of one society existing in one epoch as opposed to another where much slimmer or much more robust women might have been more popular? We know this happens, comparing the women promoted as attractive in the 1950s versus, say, the 1980s. But before we get too excited over these social explanations, let's sift through the biology of our cultural anthropology and see what other clues we can find.

What if scanning for what physiologists call body/fat ratio is hard-wired into us as a device for selecting the hardiest women most likely to carry to full-term the children of the men who impregnate these women? What if they are chosen because they look like they are worth the investment of our seed, versus the other women who will only squander it by miscarrying before they are due? What if it all our va-va-va-voom begins there, with the likelihood of our female partner bearing us a strong and durable child, ensuring our DNA will show up well with other male competitors, and our contribution to life's gene pool will continue forever as a biological equivalent to immortality? What if something so primally true of the human herd is at the heart of what we call "sexy"? No few bright people see this as foundational to our attraction to others and their attraction to us.

Men seek healthy female specimens who are good bets to keep alive in children the distinctive qualities of our chromosomes in the highly competitive natural selection of survival. The weak get crushed; only the strong survive. Nature is a brutal scheme. Of course, men also unconsciously seek women who will make good mothers. But delivering a trophy-like healthy child unto us comes first and foremost. How does that begin but with a physical inspection, a visual once-over, of potential mates, focusing on every available clue in her shape, scent, complexion, fitness, hair, stamina and general vitality? The body/fat ratio gets quickly computed as a key indicator of desirable female fertility in preliminary forays to locate the right partner.

What's more, I believe women also make these same assessments of other women. Why would this be true? We are better served as we can assess our own ceiling with regard to who else is out there competing for the same pool of opposite sex partners. If you doubt this, watch the very brief scans of turning heads following an attractive woman as she walks across the floor of a restaurant on a Saturday night. Decisions are made about her attractiveness within milliseconds—thumbs up or thumbs down. And the heads that turn are as often women as men—in different ways for different reasons, but still assessing the same visual cues. In my experience, women are harder judging the bodies of other competing women, and much more critical of their own bodies than men are. So often, men are just, well, grateful, if I may say so.

In sum, if our mutual attraction as women and men feels like some wondrous and cruel lottery, know that all manner of risks—longshots and sure things—are calculated, brokered, and pursued in the milliseconds of eye-to-eye contact and blushing smiles. We have no idea what powers and influences lurk beneath the surface as a lady drops her perfumed handkerchief and a shining gallant retrieves it, returns it, and kisses her gloved hand. As the carnival barker chants, "You pay your money and you take your chances!" Some deeply primal forces are at work as we imagine ourselves carefully attentive and warily deliberate over life decisions as basic and essential as these.

Why are women attracted to bad boys they then want to turn back toward good? The bad boy could well do a relationship face-plant that lasts decades. He often does. Then the woman tries to make a decent human being out of him, to make him a good person. Why take this risk? The very few men genuinely ahead of the curve who see something truly different and radically new in the mix of life often rebel by refusing to be herd animals. But at first blush it is hard to tell a gifted genius rebel from a mooching bum. It is a higher stakes game women face. It is high negatives and high positives, no gamble and no glory, and a high wire act with few safety net assurances in between.

Why are men attracted to good girls they want to make a little bad? Beyond the physical suitability of women for bearing men's seed and carrying a healthy child to term, a man needs a woman to shape that child into a respectable human being of substance. He cannot do that by himself, especially with our many busy journeys out to kill the woolly mammoth. But beyond the humdrum of the wife who gets his child to the math tutor on time, shows him which fork to use at table, and teaches him how to properly greet newcomers like a gentleman, men also seek excitement in women.

Exciting women often lack instincts for or interest in showing a child how to become someone other than a slob. Society often calls women disinclined toward motherhood as bad, exotic or dangerous. They are not the girls you take home to meet mother. They are the other kind. Occupying a space beyond the vagaries of poopy diapers, runny-noses and visits to the children's museum, these women pique men's natural curiosity. They evoke alternative realities. Men prefer strong and healthy mothers who are also not entirely devoid of this capacity. But the two types do not easily blend, do they? Too many find themselves in circumstances where they feel they must choose one or the other. God bless the man who has found both in one woman.

Back in the 1970s, as psychology and the human potential movement were ascendant, one very bright professor of theology liked to say, "Way down deep we are all very shallow." This upset no few, but we see his point in this arena of romantic and sexual attraction. Women say no less about men dumping wives who have grown more interesting with years only to run off with the big-breasted, ditzy blonde secretary nearly a generation younger. Actually, women say much more and positively fume over this. Men are animals! Men are pigs! It has become a caricature and a stereotype of men, but it must have a foothold in reality, because we hear it all the time. Way down deep we men are all very shallow, seeking mere receptacles for our seed when we could have had a fascinating human, if we could only see beneath the surface of things.

At the risk of offending everyone, maybe women are equally shallow in a different way, more subtle, more hidden, and acted out less because women have had less power, although this is changing. We men notice how many women are attracted to power, influence, and money even when the suitor man is unattractive, dumpy, unintelligent, and often much older. Yes, this is the proverbial squat, bald, narcissistically rude and boorishly oblivious shaker-and-mover of society, driving his convertible with some sweet young thing fawning over him in the passenger seat.

Let me cast this in my own experience to get us beyond generalizations and stereotypes. Having recently been single for nine years, I had dated gifted professional women. Invariably, a telling pattern unfolds. The women are often rebounding from relationships with businessmen who had more money, status, and influence than charm, sensitivity, and creativity. So they greet me as a pastor, someone with far less money and social status, as a breath of fresh air. Because I can focus intently as a listener, I can be savvy in relationships, and since I deal inwardly in matters of life's meaning, I seem like a rare and exotic find. Groups of accomplished women have told me how interesting and "evolved" (ugh, I hate that word!) I am. Frankly, I don't see myself that way. Who but a boor would fawn over himself like that? The point is they insist that a vast pool of desirable women is out there waiting for someone like me, while lamenting that women have many fewer choices in men. I have learned, to be honest, it ain't necessarily so.

Once the glamour of dating a man who reads Kierkegaard wears off and these women realize that I actually do spend time with the poor and dispossessed, cannot call the shots like a CEO, and do not draw from the same deep wells in my spending habits, they find that they begin to miss the shallow, boorish businessman a lot more than they expected. Anyway, I am surprised to find myself suddenly evaluated on those terms: "Why don't you spend more freely like I do?" "Why don't you just blow those people off and tell them where to go?" We pastors do not act recklessly in that way—that is, if we wish to remain pastors for long.

These same women will complain of men, "Why do they seek a young, busty, ditzy sex kitten, when they could have a bright, complex woman with rich experience, who is their equal?" But according to my experience, in a very different direction, women do something very similar. Women are attracted to power, money, and social status more than they realize, and vulnerable to their own brand of silliness in their attraction. Why? Our evolutionary history, constantly speaking through us when we realize it the least, says that a conventionally powerful and prosperous man is better able to guard them and their progeny. Maybe way down deep we are all—men and women—pretty shallow.

I write of this only to accentuate how much of mutual attraction plays out in fields we never even notice. And we fancy ourselves such deliberate shapers and choosers in our own destiny! Afterward, we wonder what happened as things went wrong. Can anyone say *Oedipus Rex*? Then, more often than not, we repeat our mistake: those previously divorced will divorce their new spouse more often than they did first time around. Ouch.

Paul the Apostle wrote, "I do not do the thing I want, but the very thing I hate." (Romans 7:15) Maybe Christianity and the church can help us acknowledge and persevere in areas where our own choosing has fallen far short and we find ourselves amazed at what we have missed. Bigger forces are at work beneath the surface than we reckon in the romance between men and women, in God's romance of heaven and earth. As we fall down in the adventure of loving, what if the church were the place to help us back to our feet, give us a fresh start, and point us in directions God would have us go? Why knows, maybe even discernment groups in the church could help us realize when we blindly stumble into "the very thing I hate," and when a prospective union is heaven-sent in ways to which we might be equally obtuse?

A little redemption in the painful politics of attraction could go a long way to soothe a great many hurting souls. Clearly, we all need help seeing our future as couples. Clearly, grace is ready and waiting to be mediated in the marketplace of desire.

· · ·

CHAPTER 17 FEMALE COUNTERPOINT

VERLEE A. COPELAND

I confess that I want to poke fun at you for all manner of characterizations, not the least of which that men and women can be shallow when it comes to attractions. I want to protest with righteous indignation at your description of hormone-driven desires, as if we human creatures are incapable of emotional intelligence and rational thought. It's tempting to object to your tongue in cheek portrayal of men as shallow cads and women as seekers of the wealthy and powerful. You would be an easy mark, but it would be unfair, as I know that you regard and respect women and appreciate their virtues beyond the ever-mysterious girls hiding beneath their sweaters. But mostly I won't push back too hard because women sometimes want what you want, someone hot who adores us.

Like you, I notice the attraction of some accomplished women towards bad boys that they want to make good and of some otherwise capable men towards good girls they want to make bad. However, we may disagree on what comes next. It seems to me that you have described initial attraction of some dating relationships, but not the enduring attachments that lead most people to marriage. Unless a woman has grown up in an abusive household or among those suffering from addiction, she is unlikely to remain attracted to men as fixer-up projects for the long-term. Unless a woman marries a man she has known only briefly, his true character will emerge over time.

Recent studies indicate that what women find most attractive in a man is neither his bad boy charm, nor money and power. The number one thing that mature women seek today is a man with no debt. He doesn't need to be rich. He just needs to be able to hold his own as a responsible partner. When a mature woman discovers that beyond his good looks and charm there is no there, there, she will likely walk away. Increasingly, men want the same as we have discussed. Mature men want a true partner with interests and a sense of life purpose and meaning of her own, not just another pretty face.

Anthropologist Margaret Mead recommended that people consider a marriage contract for a period of years in order to raise healthy children. She assumed that men and women would choose partners with the emotional maturity to go the distance. Though she did not say so, I can imagine her voice encouraging women to look beyond initial attraction and pick a grown-up to marry. In our secret fantasies we may want a hunk to adore us, but we also want him to stay up all night with the sick kids when it's his turn. Is that too much to ask?

The Christian marriage covenant is intended to last a lifetime. Whatever initial attraction we may experience, we eventually turn to deeper sources of guidance to discern a good match. People of faith pray for discernment regarding their potential partner. When we listen deeply to those who know us best, we discover their wisdom as they encourage a potentially healthy union or advise us to steer clear of the bad boy whose true character we may not yet see. Christians may ask God to reveal the one with whom we might find enduring love and faithful partnership, as well as a colleague, lover and friend. Bad boys may seem attractive to be sure, with their self-confident swagger and mega-dose of testosterone. Beyond our shallow and star-lit initial attractions, God directs us towards gifts that endure.

· 18 ·

DISTANT MEMORY OR FUTURE HOPE

Verlee A. Copeland

Popular culture obsesses over sex to the point of worshipping it as the only way to make living worthwhile. We are made to feel inadequate and less than alive if we're not having sex. This seems so empty to me. Isn't life more than romantic and sexual pursuit?

· · ·

Right about now it might seem as if everybody in the world is having wild and raucous sex, and if not, that we should be. In this book we have made the case after all that God created us to live in relationship with one another, and that we are hard-wired with the deepest of longings to be united with the one we love. Many find such desire a compelling reality. When we love someone, we desire to take him or her into our own self. The very sight, smell, taste of our beloved can be unbearably sweet, raw, bitter or bright.

Such moments of exquisite longing belong to the couple gazing into one another's eyes on a hazy summer's night. We can observe the lingering touch, the graze of a shoulder, the trace of fingers upon the brow, brushing a stray hair out of the face of the beloved. We can imagine the tingling sensations that ensue from the smallest, even casual touch of our beloved on the nape of the neck.

In truth, many who read this book already enjoy sex and want to enhance their experience. Others want to know more about God's promises and how to fulfill them without guilt or shame. Some people may read this book simply because they are curious about what two pastors have to say. It sounds as if you may be among those who dream of such deeply intimate couplings but who have never experienced such a thing, or at least not for a very long time. If that is the case, this chapter is for you.

This book is about living the passionate life. By that we mean both our spirituality and our sensuality. As Christians we know that passion comes in many forms and sex is only one way to express it. We're not writing this book to peddle sex. We lift up healthy sexuality as a good gift from God and hold it among other passions, a theme running throughout this conversation.

At a couples' retreat held in the Rocky Mountains of Colorado, a group facilitator separated the men and women for a discussion about sexual frequency and marital satisfaction. The men lamented that it had been a long time since they had sex as often as they like. They rolled their eyes and commiserated with one another about how hard they had to work to get their partner's attention. Unsurprisingly, the women said the same thing. "Since the kids were born, we rarely have sex."

You too may be reading and thinking about these matters from the perspective of distant memory. If so, you are clearly not alone. Lots of people are not getting any, as the saying goes. And lots more of us are not happy with what we are getting in the bedroom. Even more among us who are actually having sex with our partner on a regular basis find that we may be sexually content some of the time, but certainly not all of the time. We sigh quietly, as if in resignation that sexual satisfaction is for the very young and exuberant, as if we've moved on to some higher form of meaning in life, some deeper joy than the fevered couplings of young lovers.

While sex is a good thing, even a great thing as fulfillment and expression of love and affection between committed persons, it is clearly not the only way to love and serve one another as God's beloved own. There are lots of reasons that we don't have sex, make love or engage in intercourse. And there are many ways to enjoy a vibrant, vital, passionate life without a human lover.

The Bible encourages fasting from sexual relations for religious purposes or to devote oneself to prayer. Orthodox Jews refrain from sexual intercourse during menstruation until after a ritual cleansing, giving the body and the relationship a season to naturally build sexual tension before fulfilling it. Sometimes we withhold having sex in order to wait for it until the right time. Not everybody thinks it's particularly sexy to come to bed, for the third time in the middle of the night, after little Lucy Jane throws up on us with the flu. Perhaps sex can wait after all. There are many such practical reasons to refrain from having sex.

Roman Catholic couples of childbearing age who practice the rhythm method of birth control may abstain during anticipated dates of fertility. Couples who have difficulty becoming pregnant sometimes follow elaborate rituals to determine the right time to have sex, to increase the likelihood of conception.

During most long-term relationships, there are times when one or the other person in a couple is sick or injured, or exhausted and unable or unwilling to engage sexually. Medications, alcohol, and general health, as well as life stage and age can impact desire for sexual intimacy.

You may then wonder that if God made sex, and if sex is a good thing, what happens when we're not getting any? Have we somehow failed to fulfill God's intention for us if sex is on the back burner, or not on the burner at all? If sex is so great, how come it is so hard to come by, and relationships so complicated to maintain?

These are all good questions. God made us as sexual creatures, and God called creation good. We therefore believe sex is a good thing. But sex isn't the only thing, or even the most important thing. Professor of Theological Ethics Stanley Hauerwas has said that people hold out for orgasm as the highest hope or example of self-transcendence.[1] It burdens sex, however, when it has to become too much, an overburdened ritual. It's too much to expect from our partner what only God can give us. This is true in sex, but also in every other part of our relationship. Popular culture says sex is salvation. Sex is a great thing, but it won't save you. Only God can do that.

Sexual intimacy is not essential to fulfillment as a human being or to sustain life. We need to breathe, to eat, to sleep and to drink more water than we imagine. These practices are essential to life in a way that sex is not, at least not for most people.

From a psychological point of view, researcher Abraham Maslow developed a hierarchy of needs with physiological needs as most essential, followed by safety needs. In the middle of the continuum he described the human need for love and belonging that includes sexual intimacy.[2] However, Maslow knows what anyone who ever visits the hospital understands. If you want to get out of the hospital, you have to have a good bowel movement. Maslow therefore is saying that the need to excrete trumps the basic need to have sex. There have actually been studies done that men in their sixties prefer a good bowel movement to having sex!

Sex is a great gift from God that points us towards something more. The unity we experience sexually with one another points us beyond ourselves to shared longing for unity with God. However mundane or exquisite, the desire for unity is common to all of us. Quite simply, we are wired by God, and for God. We long for intimacy with God. Our desire for one another can only hint at the deeper yearning we share to fully experience a relationship with God.

1. Stanley Hauerwas, keynote speech at Conversations: A Gathering of Clergy of Large Member Churches, Orlando, Florida, 1993.
2. Abraham H. Maslow, "A Theory of Human Motivation," *Psychological Review* 50 (1943): 370–96.

That's why as a pastor I sometimes tell parishioners that a good Bible study and nourishing prayer life or engagement on a mission trip can be better than sex. It's true. When we develop practices that root and ground us deeply in the love of God, we can experience the sweet gift of God's grace, that is, God's love for us unmerited.

Knowing this can take the pressure off all this conversation about sex. Intimacy with God is available to everyone. Such intimacy does not require the capacity for sexual intercourse, the companionship of a human partner, or a relationship to sustain it. It does however require opening the heart to God. This is no small thing. Yet when healthy sexuality is a part of our life experience, it may open our emotional life and our capacity to connect with others, even God. Said another way, sexuality can open us to the holy. Spirituality can open us up sexually, and faithful sexuality can open us spiritually. The two are intricately linked.

Our sexuality and our spirituality are woven together. Early studies in large orphanages indicated that infants who were not regularly held and embraced became still, lifeless and depressed. They developed a failure to thrive and were more prone to the development of illness, even death. Physical touch is directly related to spiritual connection. While we may not all have a spouse or a lover, we experience a common human need for the warmth of human touch and companionship. We have a tendency to become dry and brittle when we do not. Widows and widowers who live alone often express that one reason they come to church on Sunday is to hold the hand of another during the passing of the peace, and to receive their weekly hug from their pastor and friends.

While not all people desire or are in a position to express their love through a sexually intimate relationship, every human creature can draw closer to the ultimate beloved, God, who searches for us tirelessly until we are found. Whether or not we are sexually active, we all crave and benefit from an active prayer life, alone as well as in community with others. Regular prayer and meditation keeps the physical and spiritual juices, the vitality of life, flowing. The power of prayer to energize us can be evident in certain members of religious orders who practice celibacy. For those who are practicing Christians, their true joy is complete through spiritual intimacy with Christ.

For those who do experience a deeply intimate and committed relationship with another human being, and who express that relationship sexually, the bonds of love strengthen when rooted in active prayer and devotional reading. Sexuality and spirituality feed one another. If you want to grow closer to your partner and enjoy more fulfilling sex, you can buy sex toys and watch porn together, and/or you can develop a more consistent, richly nourishing prayer life. Together we also can harvest the fruit of shared spiritual experiences and practices such as worship or common service toward humankind.

I understand that you may find this conversation too religious, out of reach or out of touch for the average person of faith. Perhaps this is so for you. Nevertheless, if you want to enjoy life as a fully embodied, joyful human creature, I commend you to prayer. There you will learn to listen more deeply to the voice of the Beloved who relentlessly seeks you, who will not forsake or abandon you, and who will never let you go. There is no human lover who will ever match the power of God to cherish you whom God has beautifully and wonderfully made.

Make no mistake. Sex is fantastic. Yet it is liberating to know that all of our belovedness does not hinge on how many orgasms we've had in a given week. Rather, we all can know our deepest belovedness in the arms and embrace of our true and living God whether we have a human lover or not. When sex is one path to vitality among others, it removes a great deal of pressure to experience unconditional love in the bedroom that ultimately can only be given to us by the grace of God alone.

Insofar as the Song of Solomon in the Hebrew Scriptures serves as both a love song and an allegory of our longing for God, we hear this constant refrain of desire for unity with the beloved. "On my bed night after night I sought him whom my soul loves. . . ." (Song of Solomon 3:1)

The writer of Song of Solomon rises from bed and wanders about the city searching for the beloved until she finds him, and then she holds him and will not let him go. We hear this same longing for intimacy with God through the writing of St. Augustine.

> Great are you, O Lord, and exceedingly worthy of praise: your power is immense, and your wisdom beyond reckoning. And we, who are a due part of your creation, long to praise you . . . You arouse us so that praising you may bring us joy because you have made us and drawn us to yourself, and our heart is unquiet until it rests in you.[3]

All this is to say that if our culture were to have its way with us; it would make us believe that there is something wrong with us if we're not regularly enjoying a romp in the hay. In fact, much of this book is about how to more fully experience ourselves as sexual creatures, made in God's own image, a God who created sex and everything else and called it good.

This chapter, however, is for the rest of us. Here we offer a word of hope and encouragement for those who desire intimacy with God and a vibrant, faithful life, but for whom sex is not in the picture, at least not now. Awaken your desire to intimacy with God, and intimacy with others may follow. When we draw near to God, what becomes of us for dwelling there may waken us to the ecstatic mystery of unity with Christ. Even the best sex between the most ardent of lovers can only hint at the glory that awaits us through our relationship with the Holy One.

---

3. Augustine, *The Confessions of St. Augustine of Hippo*, 2nd rev. ed., book 1, chapter 1 (Indianapolis: Hackett, 2007).

• • •

CHAPTER 18 MALE COUNTERPOINT

DALE ROSENBERGER

As a boy and youth, I hung out with a neighbor friend named Grant. We found mischief together, mostly harmless, as we explored the edges of growing up and found the boundaries of life, fueled by testosterone and adrenaline. Every time Grant did something enjoyable and edgy, he felt self-conscious until I chimed in and did whatever with him. Sometimes I did and we laughed and enjoyed it. Many times I did not because I couldn't see the sense of it, for me personally. The point is Grant felt threatened until he could coax, cajole, or counteract my resistance into compliance with what he had done. He would recruit others to convince me to take the leap—whatever it was—so he could feel vindicated. A bit insecure, his fragile sense of self didn't allow for the dissonance he felt when close friends did not act uniformly. The splendid Jungian therapist Marie Louise von Franz observed, "The surest sign of neurosis is the inability to agree to disagree."

Sometimes it feels like people with active sex lives do something like this to those who don't see what the big deal is with sex or who don't have a love in their lives as a sexual partner. "What is wrong with you? Boy, your existence must be awfully barren. How could you skip the best part of life!" Sometimes it feels like our hyper-sexualized society at large enforces this mindless conformity, perhaps insecure because sex might not be the transcendent be all and end all of human existence. And that threatens those obsessively stuck in their dead end, refusing the intimacy of entering a relationship with the true and living God.

Verlee and I have written this book because we believe the beautiful, healthy and blessed place of sex within God's greater purposes has gotten lost within the larger life of the church and wider Christian faith. Clearly, we believe that sex is a great gift from God and we unabashedly tout it as such for all who feel this gift has been scuttled, for whatever reason. But let us be clear: sex is merely a reflection and portent of a greater union and romance—between heaven and earth—with the Lord God who is busy attempting to win back all that was lost by our rebellion in the Garden of Eden.

If we sneer at others who are not as enthralled by a Hefner-esque gospel of sex trumpeted by a secular popular culture, we have gotten the two romances confused. And we have lost our way as to which is essential and which is merely important. God remaking us in God's own image until we are at peace in God's presence is a worthy life purpose. Remaking others in our own image because our love life is conflated and confused, elevating human love over defining divine love, is a pretty neurotic variety of human sinfulness. This book is about resting easy within ourselves as God's beloved children, male and female, not enforcing as *de rigueur* upon others who we are and what we do. And so, yes, friends, there are varieties of gifts, but one Spirit, to which all return and in which we live, move, and have our being.

· 19 ·

THE MIND OF MEN
IN THE DANCE OF SEX

Dale Rosenberger

Sometimes I wonder what is going through my hus-
band's head as we make love. He seems far away and
preoccupied . . . . But maybe I don't want to know, if
you get my meaning. Then again, it could bring us
closer. What would he like to tell me as a woman about
his sexuality as a man?

· · ·

What an exquisitely phrased question, full of love and concern,
the honest desire to keep your marriage vibrant and growing,
rather than merely taking things for granted. You are wise to get
outside yourself, reaching out to understand him from where he
lives, especially if you hope for the same from him. It is a redemptive posture not only in marriage and sex, but in all of life.

Your husband might also welcome this question because,
frankly, we are used to women not being interested in knowing
what makes us tick. Or even worse, women tell us how shallow
and immature we are. In the same way women might not get why

men find the Three Stooges funny, they don't care to know the mind of man in the dance of sex. Of course, I have not met the woman who doesn't expect her husband to strive after a deeper grasp of who she is inwardly, how her mind works, what her needs are, even if she cares not to reciprocate in kind toward him.

And this divide between the sexes sets up early in life. A friend related to me the story of watching a sex education film in public school when he was an adolescent. Boys and girls were in the same room for the viewing of a movie spelling out the facts of life. As the narrative of the transmission of sperm swimming toward the ovum set up, the animated production represented the male sperm cells as something like paratroopers gnashing their way behind enemy lines to set up a stronghold. We all know how the urge for uncontrolled, unbridled hilarity sets up in solemn settings. Anyway, my friend and his cohorts muffled their mirth for so long before they erupted in gales of laughter. None of the girls even snickered. They only glared at the inappropriateness of the boys, and how they would typically "ruin things for everyone." It was a shaming moment.

The only problem with the stereotypes grinding away in this scenario, said my friend, is what they viewed was actually funny. Is it more mature not to laugh at the comedic proportions of sex? Are we deeper people if we deny what should be obvious and will not stay suppressed? The overarching humor at stake here, constantly hovering over us as sexual beings, is the patent absurdity of being symbolic creatures capable of lofty aspiration made in God's image who also dwell in the animalistic biology of urges and actions that leave us emitting all manner of moans and gasps. Wisely, couples therapist Ester Perel observes about the irrationality of our sexuality, "Most of us get turned on at night by the very things that we will demonstrate against during the day."[1] Anyway,

---

1. Esther Perel, "The Egalitarian Marriage Conundrum," *New York Times Magazine*, 9 February 2014, 29.

if we have forgotten the sheer incongruity involved in this collision of the lofty and the earthbound within our nature, as revealed by sex, it is not lost upon the average adolescent.

Actually, when they staged the sex education session for my class at the same age, the girls were invited to attend and the boys were sent out to recess on the playground. Maybe they also feared we would laugh out loud rather than solemnly hush up what was genuinely comical.

Suffice it to say, more is going on beneath the jocular surface of things within men, for those with eyes to see, for those who do not peg men as superficial pleasure hounds, interested only in conquering women. Men and women experience and perceive sex differently, and this is not unacceptable. For example, apart from our hormonal differences, men do not carry the hefty responsibility of providing progeny to society. Neither are we venerated as fathers in the same way motherhood gets revered in society at large. Nor are we as likely to be the Queen Bee of the relationship, forever busy taking the temperature of our mutual rapport at any particular moment.

We observe elsewhere in this book how women are more vulnerable, with more to lose as sexuality gets transacted in our daily lives. If this means our bearing as males toward sex can be lighter, it might also means the absurdity of being at once heavenly and earthbound creatures in our sexuality is move evident before us. Maybe that is why it is often male comedians saying things like, "Do you believe there is sex in heaven? . . . No, but I'm taking a change of underwear just in case." Men traffic in how funny these absurdities are. The humor of this is not lost upon us. And they are the fodder not only for our jokes but even our outlook toward sex.

So thank you for your interest in the mind of man around sex—rare as it is. But bring him along slowly in asking, for he might be shy. As the sex ed story reminds us, we get punished for our honesty. Typically, as we are asked something like this, we wonder: "Is this a trick question? How can I get in trouble here, meaning well, without even knowing it?" For a parody of this, see Will Farrell in therapy with his estranged wife in the film *Old School*. After gentle reassurances about therapy as a safe place, where one can speak any truth without any fear of being judged— "a nest in the tree of trust and understanding"—Farrell takes what is said at face value. He rambles on, speculating about the panties of their waitress at the Olive Garden the night before, whether they were white or pink, cotton or silk. In the awkward upset of that overly honest moment, he quickly learns that complete honesty is rarely the straightforward invitation it might seem to be.

Frankly, you would be bored or perplexed to know what your husband thinks during sex more often than you would be scandalized by it. So let's sprinkle sample thoughts any husband could entertain to line out what goes on within us guys, lying within your loving embrace, to put an accent on the absurdity of what is happening. But hold on to your hats, for this chapter gives permission to laugh at ourselves, knowing we are at our best when vulnerable enough to be self-deprecatory, and that our unwillingness to poke fun at ourselves makes us grim and sanctimonious.

> *Wow. I still can't believe she said yes, on a Monday! Maybe if I leave myself a mental bread crumb trail remembering how this unfolded, I'll have a reliable system, so she'll say yes again.*

Men generally have a more durable, persistent, and less fragile sex drive than women. Of course, exceptions are not unusual, where the wife consistently experiences more desire than her husband. And there is likely, for example, greater variety in desire among all men or among all women than there is inherently between men and women. All of this is true. But let's face it, if we are honest, many more women get annoyed over men "wanting sex all of the time," hoping this trend will slack off, than the other way around. For most men, this "phase" is never over. Men generally cease expecting sex when they are gravely ill or deceased, and not always then. That mostly summarizes the tenacity of what you are dealing with, ladies, in case no one warned you.

It can be truly difficult for women to grasp how powerful the average man's sex drive is. Know that the average male is more interested in sex than the average female. Males fantasize roughly twice as much and twice as often as females. And women can count on this much: men feel extremely unhappy and disaffected with life when we do not have regular sex with the partner promised as our lifelong lover. And these shadows of disappointment and distress will deeply affect how men view the entirety of the relationship. Does that mean for men the relationship is only about sex? No way. We get typecast this way, but it is an extremely superficial analysis.

I summarize it like this: for men, feeling cared for in our sexuality with our one and only lover is the gateway to thrive into the relationship; for women, a secure and close relationship is the gateway to discover and enjoy exciting and satisfying sex. Consider this carefully. For this inherent difference has much to say about our starting points in approaching one another. If both men and women continually held this truth before us it would mean fewer angry unproductive showdowns where he hears, "All you ever want from me is sex!" or where she hears, "You have grown cold, lost the passion of our youth, lack desire, and never want to make love anymore."

Anyway, assume your husband thinks about sex more often than you do, and wants it more often than you do. Assume the romancing of getting candlelight and mood just right is ancillary to the agenda of actually making love, for he acts out of a deep biological imperative to leave his seed within you. Yes, this may sound crude, even unspiritual, but it is true. Of course, many men become faithful husbands, sensitive partners, and matchless advocates for their wives. But know that the male drive toward intercourse is involuntary and deep in our ancient biology of propagating the species for many, many millennia. Men are foundationally programmed this way. And we learn the subtle nuance of courtship and romance as secondary to this potent drive.

This means two things. When you smile upon him by making love to him even as you do not completely feel it, doing more than merely going through the motions, he should bless you and never forget to be grateful, if he is a real man. For it means you have profoundly understood him, and not begrudged who he is and how he is put together. If that seems like too much to ask, remember, it is a lot like the lofty love you seek as a woman, being accepted for who you are.

All of this also means rejection looms as a larger reality for men. And remember, even simple rejection is never easy for anyone. That is the part about the bread crumbs. We wonder what manner of romancing, friendship, and support we might offer so she might feel attracted to us and respond to our erotic overtures. And we have no idea how to write that formula for once and for all. We think we know what it takes, but the woman draws a line in the sand, called expectations. And that line keeps shifting faster than we can adjust, because relationships are dynamic and not static. So we become magical or superstitious or start believing in aphrodisiacs just because of this lost feeling we have in attempting to conjure up a sexy night of closeness and pleasure. This side of men is at once pathetic, clueless, riotously funny and sometimes endearing.

> *I wonder what my friends are doing now. Is Louie going to clean his attic, like he said? Or is he with Helen this very minute. Boy, I can only imagine, she must get wild. He doesn't deserve her. Is he over his hamstring injury yet? Will he suit up for the softball game tomorrow night?*

Because we men ask for sex more often than she does, we are not always prepared when she says yes. We may not even be feeling aroused, but we ask anyway because we know we will feel aroused the next day, when she might say no again, so we ask today as an insurance policy. Does that sound complicated? Maybe we are not so simple as we are made out to be. Similarly, feeling deprived, men sometimes exaggerate beyond any sensible expectation the power of sex to fulfill us and make life worth living. Walking around semi-aroused and unsatisfied much of the time is oppressive. As a result, men can idealize sex as our salvation, as the one thing we lack for happiness. Yes, absence can make the heart grow too fond until we overstate the importance of the orgasm, freighting it with too much expectation to give our life meaning, aggrandizing it as our only shot at self-transcendence. But burdening our sexual release with such vast existential expectation places too much weight upon our carnality as human beings. Sex is not sin, this book gladly reports, in contrast to the church's darker messages across the ages. But contrary to the constant marketing bombardment of pop culture's consumerism, sex is not our salvation either.

So sometimes, having wanted sex so badly for days, we are not prepared when it finally happens. We might be unable to be fully present and emotionally available in the tender erotic serendipity of the moment. Maybe that is why you sometimes wonder what we are thinking. If our mind wanders and we lack focus, we spice up the immediacy of what is happening now with fantasies we carry with us to fuel the flame of our arousal as a bridge between times of sexual intimacy. Perhaps because women start from the relationship, women are better equipped at bringing full emotional care and presence to the sharing of sex in the moment. More often than you think, we feel empty or distracted, and fantasies help us "get our head back into the game."

Also, men are competitive and comparative. Without even wanting to, we look at other men and "how well they did" in securing a mate, to see how we stack up. This is not once and for all, but lifelong. Without even meaning to, we evaluate both our desirability and yours over against other male friends and how "well they did" with their lifelong mate. Much like animal behavior, the primal pattern of where-am-I-in-the-pecking-order? plays itself out across our days. So your attractiveness helps us peg where we fit in the male jostling for status. As you take the time to make yourself attractive, you are actually making us feel good about ourselves as well.

Let me reissue an earlier qualifier here again. Just as it is ignorant and unhealthy to be unaware of our sexual differences as men and women, we can also make too much of our differences and forget the essential shared humanity at our core. Several studies show, for example, that the top three reasons sexually motivating both men and women are the same: love, commitment, and physical gratification. Of course, that is not always reflected in the wandering particularities within the male stream of consciousness, and that was actually your question.

So much is layered within us as sexual beings. Psychological, social, anthropological, biological, moral and faith dimensions are all at stake and playing themselves out with regularity. They intricately blend and interweave until we can no longer tell where the warp of one ends and the weave of the other begins. This is the rich, complex fabric of our sexuality. It is complex, majestic and mysterious in one moment. But as we fail to understand each other in the next moment, it can be a giant empty plea for help, echoing within the impasse between the sexes.

> *All right, Lois Griffin on Family Guy is just a cartoon. But she is sexy. She seems wholesome, but her curves tell another story. She's hot and I know it. I bet she was a gymnast as a teen. She's shaped like a Smurfette combined with my third grade teacher, Miss Kish.*

Neither side talks much about this, but guys know women think about other guys in the act of making love, and we men do as well. In divinity school, my pastoral counseling professor called this "running filmstrips in our heads," conscious streams of sexual stimuli from recent and long-term memory that arrest and focus our erotic attention, making for arousal and climax. All right, the filmstrip technology dates me, but you get the point. It hasn't changed in the decades since then, and it won't change over the next millennia. In truth, we are all not only individual sexual creatures but also social ones. This asserts itself and invades our bedrooms without our creating or inviting this dynamic. That we are made this way is apart from what we might wish or want for ourselves. We could hide it to seem "more spiritual." But we write in the hope of Jesus' gentle promise, "You will know the truth and the truth shall set you free." (John 8:32)

In some measure, as we make love to our beloved one and only, we make love to all of womankind or mankind. Again, we might want to deny this feature or suppress it as promiscuous and unholy. But this tendency is not self-created by demented selves. It is how we find ourselves hard-wired because our sexuality also has social dimensions. Wise couples neither fight nor deny the truth of who we are, knowing that as God has fashioned us as male and female, it is good. At the same time, we must be responsible stewards of our sexuality as God's gift, careful about how we handle it, responsible in what we say, for wrong impressions might endure with our beloved.

For example, a very common fantasy among men is sexually having one's wife and the wife's female best friend. I am not inventing this. Why? Who knows why we are wired this way? Again, this fantasy is not something we consciously choose so much as something that can choose us. I am not sure that much is to be gained by talking this out with a wife or girlfriend. It could well affect how the friendships play out, creating distance, fear, suspicion, alienation and jealousy, if broached poorly. Yes, we men could easily do a Will Farrell face-plant here.

Still, the more couples can disarm this daring but real side of attraction by talking about it openly in healthy ways that do not drive us apart, the more a couple will move forward with the helpful agenda your question brings: mutual understanding leading to deeper consideration of the other, and creative new ways to share pleasure. How a couple does this could be as different as every couple. After all, some couples seem immune to jealousy and would laugh to hear we find "the best friend" sexy. Other couples are reflexively jealous and might blame the best friend for making imaginary advances to steal the beloved, leading to the end of a very special friendship.

A story explains why finding constructive ways to share fantasies is better than burying them with embarrassment and shame. I knew a man who found himself in trouble because his fantasies got the better of him, purchasing explicit sexual materials. It almost derailed his life and ruined his career. The saving grace here was his wife, who bravely said, in so many words, "There is nothing wrong with fantasy, even all kinds of fantasy. Yes, everybody fantasizes. What is wrong is failing to creatively channel sexy dreams back into our marriage." She has an excellent point. For as sexual fantasies are outside looking in, the secrets divide us. When fantasies are inside looking out, such daring intimate honesty can bond us. It amazed me how he related this simple story, looking fully forgiven and loved, as she acted so wisely, with healing.

> She seems to like what we have been doing for the past nine minutes. But I am out of shape and not sure if I can sustain it. I don't want to feel humiliated, like the advanced yoga class where I couldn't keep up. Oh well, I didn't think I could get though basic training either. Just keep on.

Performance anxiety can be an issue for men in a way that surprises women. Remember, male sexuality is outward and overt; female sexuality is more inward and veiled. Just imagine, as we men are aroused we have a swollen exclamation point projecting on our front for everyone to notice; when a woman is aroused, it remains private, with her natural self-lubrication as her own secret. Just imagine, when a woman reaches orgasm, it can be hidden with no outward indicator. When a man reaches orgasm, faking is less of an option, as the stream of our seed, numbering in the millions, issues forth. Men have more performance anxiety because of our anatomy, and also because of our special role as initiator in the romantic courtship of our beloved.

It is less true today, but still true that men are expected to initiate and get out there to put the relationship in play. Anyway, beyond gender equality, women generally don't respect a man refusing this role. Because we are cast in the role of responsible party for making it happen, this subjects the charm and skillfulness of our overtures to scrutiny and ridicule. Of course, despite our arrogance, bluster, and bravado, we usually have few detailed ideas and no overarching plan for making the "you-and-me thing" happen. We typically fly by the seat of our pants, whether we soar gloriously and brag about it, or crash and burn, never to mention it again, if we can help it.

Are wallabies mammals or marsupials? Hmm. Was John Tyler the ninth or tenth president?

Across the years I have heard from women about how selfish we men can be in attending to our pleasure and neglecting yours. Some truth must attend this, or I wouldn't hear it so often. Still, I wonder if that rap falls more heavily on younger or more inexperienced men. Remember, men mature more slowly, and such as these could suffer tunnel vision, distracted by the heady cocktail of endorphins massaging our conscious self at the explosive moment of orgasm, even to the detriment of fulfilling her desire. Truth be told, I don't hear this critique of men so much during the second half of life. What I hear directly from veteran men is an almost competitive desire and commitment to pleasing our woman, and taking pride in that. In our delusions of grandeur, we believe we have moves no other man has even attempted to bring his beloved to heart-stopping paroxysms of pleasure. Kindly allow our male egos a little room, please. It might be good!

That may be the bluster of showboating male bravado, as opposed to the reality women would describe after lovemaking, but it does reflect an orientation and attitude. As men become true men, we take pride in satisfying our wife and lover. What I hear from experienced men is a willingness to organize our pleasure around yours, not only in terms of who reaches orgasm first, but also in the more subtle and exquisite intimacies surrounding timing. If timing is everything, as we tend to hear, that is never more true than as wonderfully passionate lovemaking unfolds.

That means in the same way we men use fantasy to bring ourselves up to speed with our lover as we lag in arousal, we also sometimes find that we must distract and neutralize ourselves to slow ourselves down and let her catch up. After all, men typically orgasm within three minutes as opposed to the more than ten minute average for women, depending on which study we read. What goes through our heads in moments of staying involved while waiting for you? Let's see, how about the biological taxonomy of the Australian subcontinent or where we last left the car keys or who played centerfielder for the Milwaukee Braves in 1954. (Hank Aaron, by the way.)

We are keenly aware that female orgasms can be as complex and fragile as a NASA launch ("Wait, call it off, a small cloud has appeared on the horizon. This is going to be a scrub"). That certainly must be a lot of pressure for you women, but remember, it is also pressure for us. So when things get hot and heavy, when we are getting close to our release, random things help us delay and allow you to catch up. But too much of thinking about the Postal Service or who played Greg Brady on *The Brady Bunch*, and we will lose our erection, and that is not good. So this is an exquisite tipping point for us, a delicate balance. Maybe we are not the insensitive cads—sexually speaking—we are made out to be, at least among men truly deserving to be called men.

Much of this book has been full of reassurance that sex is God's good and natural gift. To be honest, that will console some, but leave others—who cannot feel and experience that—more alienated. Why? The candor of this stream of consciousness gets at that: the sheer incongruity of being at once primal sexual animals while also being lofty children of God disturbs and unsettles us. One seems to negate the other. For such as these, I hope this level of directness can reassure.

Some have trouble being this honest to acknowledge how strange, odd, and outside of the mainstream sex really is. Such as these might dismiss others who insist upon full disclosure as demented or perverted. I believe these denouncers are dangerous. The alternative I here advance is laughing at ourselves, taking ourselves less seriously, and enjoying how God made us. That is all any good stand-up comic does, reveling in the absurdity of all this, with more time probably spent in their routine recounting the sexual oddities within our humanity than any other subject. Maybe the most seriously helpful thing we could do is walk on the lighter side of being human as men and women. If nothing else, it might keep the sin of pride from judging and condemning us as we already feel a little lost in our dilemma of being human.

So thank you for asking what makes us men tick. Simple questions can lead to surprising depths, I suppose.

. . .

CHAPTER 19 FEMALE COUNTERPOINT

VERLEE A. COPELAND

Thank you for your forthright conversation about what goes on inside the male mind while having sex. While we appreciate the response, there are perhaps ways in which we don't want to know. That is to say, we would like to imagine as women, that when men hold us in tender embrace, they think of nothing but how much they love us and want to come into our very being, as the deepest expression of commitment and affection for us.

Don't let me bust your chops here, Dale. Women think of all kinds of stuff while making love that might surprise you. "Let's get on with it. I have a nail appointment . . . I wonder if my assistant got that project out the door on time . . . That feels fantastic, how can I ask you to go slower without ruining the mood?"

We like to talk sometimes while making love, even laugh. We're not laughing at you. We're just having a good time. We're less focused than you are. Since we build slowly and stay physically aroused longer, we can laugh, whisper a story, or change directions or positions without losing momentum. We never have to worry about how to maintain an erection, though oral sex remains a mystery. You don't always tell women what you like in that department and trust me, this isn't a skill our mothers teach us. It's an apprenticeship. Talk to us in sweet low tones. "Oh baby, I love it when you touch me like that. I get so excited when you move faster and just a little harder. You make me feel so good." Better yet, "I can't wait until it's my turn to touch you like this. I want to make you feel this good baby, I want you to want me as much as I want you right now."

We hope that the one human being to whom we have pledged ourselves in particular desires us as no other. Even if our partner has more sexual experience than we do, nobody wants to win second prize. I suspect you feel the same way. In the moment of ecstatic embrace, we all want to believe that we are the most fantastic of lovers, and that any other love would pale by comparison.

We know the difference between being loved, wanted and cherished in particular, and being the object of self-ejaculatory fantasy. When men and women covenant with one another for life, grounded in a mutual desire to please God in all things, our sexuality becomes something different than the endless search for perfectly timed orgasm. Between married couples, there becomes less need for performance anxiety, because frankly, making love is less about performance than about expressing gratitude and cherishing the other for the other's sake. Seen in this light, both partners may forego orgasm on any given occasion in order to please the other, knowing that their turn may come, if not today, maybe tomorrow. There's more room for patience and less need for fear when love prevails.

We want you and we want you to want us. When you engage in thoughts and fantasies that keep you in the present moment, filled with deep appreciation and rich gratitude for us, we can feel it. You will be rewarded with a heightened and intensified sexual experience. Not only will lovemaking take flight, but the relationship itself will soar. She knows by how you move and how you touch her whether you are with her or not. There's nothing sexier than being deeply desired and knowing it.

Women describe to me their thoughts during lovemaking quite differently than you have described it in the minds of many men. This may be a function of differences in the sexes or something else entirely. Many women focus more on how it feels to taste and touch their man than on what he looks like visually, real or imagined. There are exceptions to this, although it seems that fewer women than men get erotically charged through visualization.

Safety trumps visual stimulation for many women. Since one out of five women have been sexually abused or raped, many women articulate their need to feel safe and cherished. This increases the chance that they will release themselves to give and receive pleasure at every level: spiritually, sexually and emotionally. You may think that we'd prefer to fantasize about the six-pack on the pizza deliver guy or the pecs on the arms of our favorite sports hero than ponder your pudgy mid-line. To be fair we do fantasize about other people from time to time. We have been known to swoon when some well-muscled guy looks up from his occupations to lock eyes with us, give us the once-over, or smile at us appreciatively. But our hottest sex is when we merge into you and you into us in a mutual and unitive experience unlike any other. All other loves or imaginings pale by comparison. In that moment, we don't actually think about anything at all.

We do love your body. Your erection is stunning. But we don't care as much whether you can sustain an erection as you do. We aren't that invested in having an orgasm every time. We hope you find this reassuring. This isn't an Olympic event whereby our goal is to land a perfect ten. Women want deep intimacy, and we want to believe that you want deep intimacy with us too. We long, not to be with someone else or to become someone else so much as to become fully ourselves. Whether gentle lover or unfettered wild thing, we secretly desire to become utterly lost with you, in this passionate romance between heaven and earth.

· 20 ·

A LOVER WORTH WAITING FOR

Verlee A. Copeland

I love my wife so much, and want to keep my marriage. The surgery I had several years ago made it impossible for us to engage in a physically intimate way again. I still see my wife as really sexy and I respond to her in my heart in ways that I can't with my body. How can I love her as a man in ways that will keep her satisfied?

·   ·   ·

What a tender struggle you share. It is so clear from your words how much you love your wife and want to be husband to her in every way. The situation you describe is not as rare as you might imagine. I am sure she is deeply moved by your intentions to put not only her pleasure but also even her happiness before your own.

I confess that it is tempting to avoid addressing this issue, however urgent the importance to do so. Just asking the question seems to stir general anxiety among those who struggle with issues of sexual intimacy and disability or sexual dysfunction. However, this question is indeed an issue of sex and the spirit. Sexy in the brain and sexy in the heart are inexplicably linked to sexy in the body. Passionate, faithful, erotic sex happens in the brain and the heart as well as the genitals, and is therefore worthy of the exploration your question provokes.

Let me share a story with you about how another couple worked this through. I sat with a man and woman, married for fifteen years who asked a similar question. Both young and vibrant, Tom had developed a debilitating disease that left him unable to engage in sexual intercourse without excruciating pain. Medication to control other manifestations of his disease significantly reduced his libido, though he continued to love his soul mate and wife Janie, passionately.

Were it not for the anguished conversations shared with this couple, I might never have thought to ask this question. His eagerness to provide sexual satisfaction for his healthy and vivacious wife pressed me to reflect theologically on their situation, one I now know other couples share.

When they came to see me, they expressed their deep and abiding love for one another. Clearly they were happily married. Yet this man was tormented that he was not fulfilling what he saw as his marital obligation to sexually satisfy his wife. He would be in good company. In Colonial America it was a crime to fail to meet the "due benevolence" or physical needs of one's spouse. And so it was that they struggled to express intimacy in non-sexual ways as a couple, and with some measure of success. Though they share deep intimacy through shared conversation, satisfying meals prepared in their common kitchen, and regular home movies, he remembered the urgency of sexual desire, and did not wish to leave his wife wanting. He imagined that she did in fact desire the physicality of sexual expression common to human creatures, and yet out of her love for him she would not say so. He feared that she remained silent out of fear that his masculinity would be threatened if he were to learn that she had such desires, or that he would feel diminished in some way, as if she felt less than adequately loved when their intimacy could not be physically expressed.

Out of great love for his wife, Tom thought about releasing her to a sexual relationship with another man. He felt deeply that it was unfair to her to cut off sexual intimacy just because he was unable to meet her as a lover in this way. She was quick to respond that she was devoted to Tom. It was not the act itself that she missed, but the intimacy with her husband. She wasn't looking for a substitute for what she considered the real deal. Was it painful for her that they could not enjoy the pleasure of making love in the familiar language that couples share? The answer was a resounding "yes." Both his question and her honest response required tremendous courage.

Eventually, he took the risk of becoming her lover through oral sex and the use of sex toys to pleasure her. His love for her and his desire to please her, his emotional commitment to her and relationship presence, made it possible for her to take risks physically. They eagerly discovered new avenues of physical and emotional delight, as he treated her sexuality as if it were a thrilling wilderness to be explored. Pleasing her pleased him and restored his sense of lost manhood. Allowing him to please her without feeling selfish about it increased their intimacy. He in turn, helped her understand ways that she could touch him and care for his body without causing pain. Regular massages helped satisfy her desire to touch and caress her beloved without causing him emotional or physical distress.

As a pastor, I have listened to other sexual frustrations and struggles of those who find the covenant of marriage significantly changed from what they imagined life would be like when they pledged themselves to one another. In addition to the situation I have described, some people struggle with a libido gap that widens over time, leaving one partner deeply desirous of sexual intimacy and the other indifferent or even unwilling to engage sexually. Further, reduced libido remains a common if unwelcome side effect of many essential and life-giving medications.

Men and women may feel guilty when they continue to desire sexual intimacy after a partner becomes unable to have sex due to accident, illness or surgery. Expressed anger and a sense of potential betrayal may further challenge a couple. One soldier returning home disabled after military service expressed that the thought of his wife sleeping with someone else was his worst nightmare. He worried that she would do so since he was unable to engage in intercourse with her. Prostate cancer, treatment, and or surgery can significantly change the capacity for some men to have an erection or have sexual intercourse.

Though I have not discovered a study to substantiate this, anecdotal evidence would indicate that many if not most couples prefer to express their love for one another in non-physically intimate ways when one of them become unable to do so, rather that express sexuality outside of marriage. Affairs seem to be less common when one partner is unable to engage in sexual intercourse rather than more common. This at first seems counterintuitive. Yet anecdotal observation would indicate that at least for women, affairs are more common when a husband fails to be emotionally present than when he is unable to be physically engaged.

Deep listening reveals that many couples share a profound sexual intimacy even when it cannot be expressed in overtly sexual ways. Many couples find this intimacy deeply satisfying, whether they are able to have intercourse or not. Their love and commitment to their partner trumps their "need" to have sex.

As we have said elsewhere, what we want most as human beings is to love and be loved. Everyone wants to be loved by someone who makes her feel like she fills up the room. What man doesn't want to be held and cherished by someone who treats him as if he were the best thing since sliced bread? What could be more compelling than to connect with someone across a crowded room who looks at you as if no one else were present, or mattered, but only you? Whether or not a couple engage physically with one another, virtually everyone who discussed this question wanted to be that one, that cherished man, that beloved woman.

There are those persons however, who burn with desire and find themselves unable to go forward in marriage without the full meal deal. If you are one of those persons, you could of course get a divorce. But what if you actually love your partner and find so much common ground, not to mention the complicating matters of life and work and children that you wish to remain in the marriage? I have heard the argument as a pastor from both women and men that having sex outside of marriage actually contributed to their marriage by taking pressure off of their partner to "deliver the goods" when they were unwilling or unable to do so.

Many people share this ethic in our culture today. We may say to a willing friend to whom we are not married, "My spouse cannot have sex with me or is unwilling to have sex with me, so why don't we periodically have sex?" I would assert that this is outside the boundaries of Christian marriage. Does it happen? Yes it does. Is it forgivable? Yes it is forgivable. Does it impact our marriages in some way if we choose to be in an intimate relationship with another? Always, and in ways that we may not see clearly at the time.

I suspect that as some of you read this you are arguing with me, that in fact the extra-marital sex you enjoy has made your otherwise untenable marriage possible. You might say that it made it possible for you to stay in the marriage without anger and resentment for what you did not have.

Who has not heard some guy try to explain away sexual infidelity with the words, "It was only sex." What woman has not known someone who had sex with a guy, hoping to secure the relationship or draw him deeper into an emotional bond, only to watch him walk away in the morning, because emotionally he finds that he can. Statistically, men are better able to compartmentalize in this way than women, but should we?

While many attempt to justify extra-marital sex for a particular purpose, and while it may in fact accomplish the goal of taking pressure off of the spouse to "perform," it is still unfaithful.

For Christians, being emotionally and physically intimate with someone with whom one is not married violates the marriage covenant: in sickness and in health, forsaking all others.

The flip side is when a man releases his wife to have sex with someone else. Is it still adultery if you choose to resolve this dilemma together by essentially forming a new marriage that makes room for extra marital sex? Instead of a secret affair, this then becomes a new covenant, a new agreement between husband and wife under the guise of being for the sake of the marriage. One could pose the argument that if the two agree to extra-marital sex then it isn't an affair because it isn't theft. It isn't taking something that belongs to another and absconding with it if it's freely given, or so the argument might go.

While some couples expressed a willingness to release their partner to have sex with someone else, everyone said the same thing. "I don't want my partner to form an emotional bond with someone besides me." Ah, now there's the rub, so to speak. While some men and women can compartmentalize sex from other aspects of relationship, many cannot. Even if we can, is it really a good thing to cut off such an essential aspect of our experience and shelve it quite apart from the rest of our life?

People of faith believe that God is good and wants all good things for us. When we cut sexuality off from the bonds of deeply committed and intimate relationship it becomes a partial good at best. God wants the whole deal for us, more than a one night stand, better than hooking up, more nourishing than what might otherwise amount to mutual masturbation.

There is nothing new under the sun, or so the saying goes. You may recall that this attempt at compartmentalization is exactly what happened several thousand years ago between Abraham, the founding father of our faith, and his wife Sarah. God had promised Abraham a child, and that his progeny would be more numerous than the stars. However, Abram and Sarai, as they were called then, had not borne any children. Remembering that at that time it was believed that women were the fertile ground, and the seed resided only in the male, Sarai devised a plan for Abram to plant the seed where it could grow. She said to her husband Abram: "'You see that the Lord has prevented me from bearing children; go in to my slave-girl; it may be that I shall obtain children by her.' And Abram listened to the voice of Sarai. So, after Abram lived ten years in the land of Canaan, Sarai, Abram's wife, took Hagar, the Egyptian, her slave-girl, and gave her to her husband Abram as a wife. He went in to Hagar, and she conceived; and when she saw that she conceived, she looked with contempt on her mistress." (Genesis 16:2–4)

At this point, the consequences of what seemed like a good idea to preserve both the future and the marriage go awry. Sarai became angry that this arrangement was now about more than sex. If we haven't figured this out by now, let me just say, relationships are complicated. Perhaps her husband enjoyed himself a little too much. Perhaps Sarai grew jealous of the fact that Hagar was pregnant. In any case, Hagar exceeded the boundaries of her role as surrogate mother and looked with disdain at Sarai. This turned out to be a devastating idea.

Sarai expressed her anger to Abram, saying, "'May the wrong done to me be on you! I gave my slave-girl to your embrace, and when she saw that she had conceived, she looked on me with contempt. May the Lord judge between you and me!' But Abram said to Sarai, 'Your slave-girl is in your power; do to her as you please.' Then Sarai dealt harshly with her, and she ran away from her." (Genesis 16:5–6)

Our marriages as people of faith rest in a context and purpose that is grander than our own particular desires and needs. For that reason, things can turn out rather badly when we take matters into our own hands. This doesn't mean we are helpless bystanders in the course of our lives. But it does mean that when we make covenant vows in marriage, we promise to explore fully our sexuality within that relationship, whatever the future may hold.

The most important question is always: "What does God think of all this?" When we make our marital vows, they are between the two of us as a couple, the gathered community and God. It matters profoundly what God thinks about how we love one another. We cannot faithfully have this conversation without bringing God into it. God is the source of all that is good, including our sexuality. The 139th Psalm is clear that there is no place we can go apart from God's spirit, the God who loved us into being and knit us together in our mother's womb.

If you are both married and burning with desire because your partner can't or won't be sexually intimate with you, please talk with one another. This is a difficult issue needing much mercy, forgiveness and grace. Insofar as you are able, take the emotional, spiritual and physical risks necessary to draw you closer in fulfillment of your marital vows. Remember that this is not work you have to do alone. Your concerns matter to God. There is nothing we cannot bring before the Holy One who made heaven and earth and you and me and yes, sex: that wondrous, mysterious and delicious gift of God for the people of God.

.   .   .

CHAPTER 20 MALE COUNTERPOINT

DALE ROSENBERGER

As resident ethicist for their congregation, every pastor finds him or herself confronted with and discerning exceptions to deep and historic moral imperatives of faith that seemed straightforward and unimpeachable. Life is decidedly untidy. Complex circumstances teach us that ordering human existence in godly ways is more complicated than lists of do's and don'ts, that ethics is more fluid than hard and fast rules. Jesus kept reminding anyone who would listen that the laws of the Torah were meant to serve humankind, not the other way around. He meant it.

Beyond this, time has taught us that things considered scandalous or even blasphemous in one generation can easily become commonplace in one brief lifetime. When I was a boy, the thought of a European-American woman in the arms of an African-American man made a majority of upstanding citizens—north and south—physically ill. Today the thought of denouncing two persons of different ethnicities deeply in love, eager to hallow their affections in sacred vows, is enough to make most everyone physically ill. In the words of the old hymn, "New occasions teach new duties, time makes ancient truth uncouth; they must upward still and onward who would keep abreast of truth."[1]

Moreover, while I hold that sex is most beautiful and belongs in marriage in the same way an eyeball belongs in our socket, this ideal is inaccessible for a shocking number of people, for reasons such as you list. Brokenness is very real in the world. We cannot blithely wave it away with chapter and verse because it doesn't fit any of our preexisting categories of thinking. While I never forget the narrative of Scripture and the scaffolding of Christian ethics as a minister of the Gospel, I hope to God that I listen to couples from my heart of hearts when they sit in my study and open their hearts with troubles of a scope previously unknown to me, with abiding hurts I scarcely imagined could possibly exist. We cannot do ethics unless we are first capable of this broken heart. For we will do no good.

Generally, couples who approach me vexed by life and marriage like this, do so in the humblest way, fearing God's judgment will be rained down on them. How can we not reciprocate with humility as they seek a way? In a word, deep humility before

---

1. "Once to Every Man and Nation," *Pilgrim Hymnal* (Boston: Pilgrim Press, 1958) 441.

God—for all parties involved—must remain the keynote here. This is especially so, thinking of Tom and Janie, a real life circumstance where people of faith are asking hard questions, only putting first the interests of their beloved.

Some ministers wield something called "the biblical standard on sexuality" like the Securities and Exchange Commission going after insider trading. Not so fast. Where do Solomon's 1,000 wives fit as part of this moral standard? How might we to respond to the wives of the twelve apostles forced to forego any semblance of a marriage after their holy men of God traveled to the earth's four corners? What options were acceptable for these women? You have already mentioned, Verlee, how Sarai loaned Abraham a surrogate wife for the purpose of securing progeny. But what about when Abraham loaned Sarai to Pharaoh out of self-interest? She lived with Pharaoh and nearly entered his permanent harem. (Genesis 12:10–16)

I am not of the "all cats are grey in the darkness of night" school of moral relativism. I am saying life is untidy. The Bible is untidy. Large doses of humility are in order around both our interpretations and judgments. It is well and good to have fixed values from which to shape, order, and live life. A moral compass is a fine thing as we make our journey and navigate rocky shoals. But we had best be prepared for adjustments as we go. For the older I get the more I realize the joys and struggles, the hope and despair of real people are bigger than I am. God in Christ can and will encompass all of them in his redemption of heaven and earth.

· 21 ·

DARING TO DISCUSS EVEN
THE SEXUALITY OF JESUS

Dale Rosenberger

Besides being fully divine, we are told Jesus was also fully human. So what was his sexuality like? It's a disturbing question, yes, I know. But if Jesus is a sexual being and that was good in God's eyes, maybe my own sexuality can become something good and godly. What do you think?

· · · ·

If the sexuality of Jesus seems vague and amorphous, it has been by design. By keeping sexuality and spirituality as separate as oil and water, it hasn't occurred to the Church to respond to your query in any detail, except in recent years, and then only out of necessity. Let me explain.

While the church has not embraced the question, popular culture willingly fills the void with novels and films. After all, Jesus the Person remains wildly popular at large, especially if we can reinvent him in our own image or conjure the Savior as we imagine he should have been according to our human understanding. What makes Jesus tick still piques our curiosity two millennia later, even as his friends (the Church) get dismissed as backward and uninteresting. So it should surprise no one that this ancient simmering pot waiting on the back burner gets uncovered and stirred by films and books like *Jesus Christ, Superstar, The Last Temptation of Christ,* or *The Da Vinci Code.* They toy with this theme using artistic license to supply a small but sturdy titillating social niche. Of course, it is not lost on writers and producers that these works earn money hand over fist. So pointless embellishment or silly conjecture shouldn't surprise us.

As everyone knows by now, *The Da Vinci Code* trumps up an ecclesiological conspiracy to keep secret the "historical fact" of Jesus and Mary Magdalene sharing passion, liaison and progeny. If you recall, *Jesus Christ Superstar* describes a following of devoted, faithful women eager to caress him and who "don't know how to love him." That song from the rock opera, featuring the writhing and moaning of ecstatic women, is perhaps the anthem of this quest. As we finalize this volume, a film called *Son of God* is in theaters with a studly Jesus sporting six-pack abs, and this has people buzzing, which is the intended consequence, of course. So this question will persist until we answer it. This question will persist until we answer it. Whether the mention of Jesus' sexuality offends us as sacrilege or intrigues us as a humanizing consolation might depend on whether we affirm Jesus as the Christ. Or it might not.

In essence, the Gospels remain relatively silent about Jesus' sexuality in the same way we don't know his favorite dish for dinner and preferred hobbies, how much sleep he needed nightly and whether or not he teased his brothers. The Gospels are not objectively written biographies governed by historical data, a version of truth that has only existed for two centuries. Gospel—a literary genre that didn't exist until Matthew, Mark, Luke, and John—proclaims Jesus' messiahship by looking backward over his life, re-narrating his story from the perspective of his culminating death and resurrection, and seeing God uniquely at work through these events to reconcile heaven and earth.

Just as the Gospels eagerly focus on details of Jesus' life, teaching and ministry that attest to and describe the nature of his messiahship, they are pretty casual about the rest of his life, including curious incidentals shedding no light upon his God-given mission. The Gospels care nothing about our modern proclivity for what "inquiring minds want to know" in waiting room magazines like *People*. The Gospels count on our trust that they concisely share the essentials and that no series of volumes could contain all of the anecdotes and angles we crave about Jesus' person. John's Gospel actually says this as it closes, "This is the disciple who is testifying to these things and has written them, and we know that his testimony is true. But there are also many other things that Jesus did; if every one of them were written down, I suppose that the world itself could not contain the books that would be written." (John 21:24–25)

In the popular consciousness of our age, sexuality is everywhere, so why not Jesus too? It is hard to decide whether to roll our eyes at popular culture for occasioning a distracting and salacious conversation or instead to be grateful to these outsiders for surfacing a long overdue and sorely neglected core consideration of Jesus' being. Perhaps it depends on the spirit we bring to this conversation. Perhaps it depends on whether we are coopted by a sex-saturated, sex-obsessed, sex-worshipping society convinced that our sexual self and behavior is the most distinctive and defining mark of our personhood. Or perhaps it depends on whether as people of faith we can see the rightful and healthy place our sexuality plays within the whole of our existence: a telling and essential part of our aliveness as humans that we can unashamedly consider alongside other vital human earmarks such as our creativity, perseverance and loyalty.

Jesus' struggle to channel his desires to advance God's reign while remaining celibate might fascinate us. But to think Jesus was without sexual desire runs afoul of him being fully human, completely knowing our existence, and giving himself utterly for God's redeeming purpose. The sexual part of our being human is wonderful, yes. But it is also a difficult part of our humanity to come to terms with. To imagine that God took on our human flesh in Jesus Christ only to skip our human dilemma as sexual creatures undermines core suppositions of the incarnation. You see, it wasn't enough for us that God told us he understood us, and did in fact understand us. God further decided to become us, in every way except sin, to end all doubt about whether God cared, and to close all loopholes. It was God's defining act of self-giving, selfless love in Jesus. Why would God dodge the magical and yet perplexing sexual part of our existence? I don't believe God would. I do believe that Jesus was fully God incarnate in our human flesh, sexuality and all. Your question correctly traces this trail and begins to play out the implications. People of faith best not be silent any longer on this, lest sensationalists and opportunists carry the day and define what they truly do not understand.

It is striking how many eagerly advance the idea that Jesus had romantic and sexual love interests, or that he married and fathered children based on the widely shared assumption that he was "a regular Joe." Actually, I don't dispute this impression of Jesus. It is spot on. Clearly, he was someone with whom we might easily strike up a conversation at the next restaurant table or while studying maps along a highway. That much is clear. What this version of Jesus forgets, placing him in a warm human range of approachability, however, is his vocation. Jesus' unique, consuming, and holy calling splits him off, separates him, and elevates him squarely within the range of the phenomenal, both in its scope and its sweep. I am not sure how anyone singularly called by God to save the world, even before his birth, could be described as "a regular Joe."

A raft of questions present themselves at this juncture: what was Jesus' mind churning with as he woke up every day as a fourteen-year old? Was Jesus tempted to self-pleasure? How exactly does that work from one who observed that anyone who even looked on a woman with lust was guilty of adultery, even if he did say that to help all people—especially those convinced of their utter righteousness—to know their own imperfection? Was Jesus' "love life" different during his thirty years of relatively normal life as carpenter/tinkerer than the last three intense years of his world-transforming ministry, wandering the countryside? How could that switch have been fair to an earlier love interest, to put her aside as push came to shove at his full-blown pursuit of his ministry?

Would Jesus have subjected any woman, never mind one he loved, to the terrible rigors of condemnation by authorities, complete social rejection, and painful death by crucifixion? How could Jesus possibly have prepared her for that when even his core followers could not grasp the implications of traveling the way of the cross? Would he destabilize her life like this only to abandon her and exit heavenward to enter his glory? Wouldn't that have been a supreme act of selfish personal expedience by one who announced a way higher and more exalted than raw desire, God's new way of self-giving love, which considers first the happiness of the other? And if Jesus bristled every time someone like Peter interposed himself between Jesus and the cross, between Jesus and the will of God, would Jesus have taken on another intimate fated to not understand him and to attempt to deflect the destiny for which he came to earth?

This much is clear. We cannot talk about Jesus' personhood and his needs as a man apart from his calling and the uncompromising purposefulness with which he lived it out. The two are finally indivisible and one. It is a very modern prejudice to believe we best understand a person by splitting him or her off from key relationships and commitments, peeling back the internal personal layers after we isolate them, like peeling an onion. Neither the form of the Gospels nor the mystery of Jesus the Christ will yield to these prejudices of modernism. To believe otherwise is arrogance.

So let's review the bidding on Jesus' sexuality and assert the basics before we move on to entertain the fanciful. Christian tradition, including the testimony of the early Gospels, almost unanimously portrays Jesus without a wife or children. Other sayings raise the possibility he was a sexual ascetic, like John the Baptizer, a non-participant in the dance of the sexes (Matthew 19:10–12, Mark 12:18–27). But ascetics like the Essenes also rejected the use of oil for anointing, enforced extreme physical modesty, and were very moderate in their diet, for example. That doesn't sound like Jesus. He was more known for feasting than fasting. And ascetics like the Nazirites avoided all contact with grapes and grape products like wine as well as avoiding all physical contact with the dead. That doesn't sound much like Jesus either. Jesus touched the dead to raise them and his first miracle was the creation of over a hundred gallons of a very exquisite wine.

Jesus clearly doesn't fit into any known form of Jewish self-renunciation back in his day. Surprise of surprises, we have more information that he rejected the structure of the ancient family and household (Mark 3:31–35) than that he rejected the legitimacy of sexuality and desire. Also, it is curious that we never mention how odd it is that when the early church made its appeals for celibate living, it never points to Jesus as the model, but always to Mary, whom we know was not celibate, at least not after her firstborn. The imitation of Christ might make us vulnerable to various sufferings—lowliness, endurance, abandonment, even martyrdom—but it never sets us up for the deprivation of sexual passion and desire. Historically, Mary is invoked as the Virgin for this purpose.

All of these considerations are important. But none of them truly get at your question. So how can we get beyond this Jesus of vague, uncertain, and ambiguous sexuality? Perhaps it is time to drill down into Holy Scripture and to get more specific:

> One of the Pharisees asked Jesus to eat with him, and he went into the Pharisee's house and took his place at the table. And a woman in the city, who was a sinner, having learned that he was eating in the Pharisee's house, brought an alabaster jar of ointment. She stood behind

him at his feet, weeping, and began to bathe his feet with her tears and to dry them with her hair. Then she continued kissing his feet and anointing them with the ointment. Now when the Pharisee who had invited him saw it, he said to himself, "If this man were a prophet, he would have known who and what kind of woman this is who is touching him—that she is a sinner." Jesus spoke up and said to him, "Simon, I have something to say to you." "Teacher," he replied, "speak." "A certain creditor had two debtors; one owed five hundred denarii, and the other fifty. When they could not pay, he cancelled the debts for both of them. Now which of them will love him more?" Simon answered, "I suppose the one for whom he cancelled the greater debt." And Jesus said to him, "You have judged rightly." Then turning towards the woman, he said to Simon, "Do you see this woman? I entered your house; you gave me no water for my feet, but she has bathed my feet with her tears and dried them with her hair. You gave me no kiss, but from the time I came in she has not stopped kissing my feet. You did not anoint my head with oil, but she has anointed my feet with ointment. Therefore, I tell you, her sins, which were many, have been forgiven; hence she has shown great love. But the one to whom little is forgiven, loves little." Then he said to her, "Your sins are forgiven." But those who were at the table with him began to say among themselves, "Who is this who even forgives sins?" And he said to the woman, "Your faith has saved you; go in peace." (Luke 7:36–50)

The Roman Catholic bishop who joked about Jesus, "He liked to eat good food with bad people," must have had this Gospel story squarely in his sights. After all, while this story might be the most telling about Jesus' comfort level as a man around women, and his unconcern with what opinion-makers thought about his "appropriateness," scenes like this repeat themselves throughout the Gospels. Clearly, Jesus brought one standard of judgment and grace to what some call the "warm-hearted sins" and another standard to what get called the "cold-hearted sins." Of course, it was the "cold-hearted sins" of pride and power from the Roman rulers and the temple authorities that crucified Jesus. We almost get the feeling from the "warm-hearted sinners" that they saw Jesus as one of them, outsiders looking in who are living for the moment, albeit badly. Jesus almost always tells them, "sin no more," but he never denounces them as "white-washed tombs" either, as he does the powers coming after his mission and his very life.

Just verses before the above text, Jesus was typified by his "eating and drinking" in contrast to the grizzled ascetic John the Baptizer, who wore an animal skin and ate insects. Is this instructive? Frankly, I have seldom met the person who adored exquisite food and didn't also appreciate the wonder of sex. Nor have I known many who cared nothing for fine dining but who thought sex was something wonderful. These gustatory delights are related. So Jesus is clearly not an anti-pleasure, party-pooper, kind of guy.

In this text from Luke we learn why Jesus was called "a friend of tax collectors and sinners" (Luke 7:34) immediately before this sequence of events begins. An anonymous harlot woman from the gathered public outside the home of a prominent Pharisee named Simon enters Jesus' dinner banquet. This was not so unusual in Jesus' time and place of open-air Palestinian architecture as it would be for us today. She weeps with gratitude that a woman like herself is allowed to approach the likes of Jesus. When her tears fall on Jesus' feet—who leans on his left arm, so he can eat with his right, his feet splayed out and away from the food and table—she lets down her hair to wipe away her tears. But that she has brought a jar of ointment with her shows premeditation in her plan to anoint Jesus as a sign of her love, beyond the spontaneity of her tears. After washing Jesus' feet with her tears, she anoints them with the jar of perfume to the seeming shock and dismay of everyone in the room—except Jesus.

The scene is rife with sensuality and eroticism. For an unfamiliar known prostitute to spontaneously touch and caress Jesus' feet was replete with sexual overtones that defied the social conventions of Jesus' day or any day. In Hebrew, the word for feet is also the word for genitals and the wordplays of double entendre (especially in Song of Solomon) are common. Of course, that this woman was not only a sinner but also ritually unclean would have also rendered Jesus unclean by dint of her lavish touch upon him. The scene is set for Jesus' interactions with both the Pharisee and the harlot. The harlot has created quite a scene and the host is duly scandalized.

If Jesus were a true prophet, Simon says, he would know what kind of woman he was dealing with, and wouldn't have allowed her physical fawning over him. That accusation is ironic because this tale is situated in a series of stories from Luke intended to reveal that Jesus was more than a prophet, not less. Exactly no one is surprised as Simon the Pharisee takes offence and Jesus vindicates the tearful harlot. Was the woman so loving toward Jesus because she had been forgiven earlier? Or was she forgiven because she was so loving toward Jesus in moments here and now? The beauty of the story is we cannot decide.

But getting back to your question, Jesus is clearly someone comfortable in his own skin, at ease with the genuine but also sensual attentions of a woman given over to sexual pleasure, and no above-the-fray, shrinking violet when it came to being touched. Jesus' approach to righteousness is not distancing himself from sinners but moving toward them to bless with forgiveness and peace. We see no flinching on Jesus' part toward her vice and no reluctance to associate with the shady, fearing for his reputation.

Let us not forget the most intense eroticism can be found in self-denial, as any sexually experienced person can verify. Intimacy, flirtation, proximity, fantasy, teasing and even the lines between friends and lovers can blur within the overarching truth of God's embracing love, as Jesus declared it. Not only that, this inner world can be much sexier than a perfunctory and obligatory performance of intercourse between indifferent parties. If sex is more about heart and mind and soul even more than body, we can say Jesus was all over it—in this limited sense. We need not begrudge him his humanity and the pulses of attractions to maintain his holiness and affirm him as Christ, just as we need not begrudge ourselves this same reality, made as men and women in God's image.

Can it make sense to describe Jesus as a red-blooded, erotic, and sexual man, even if it seems unlikely he ever had sex with a woman? The idea is worth considering. We need not think of Jesus as "having sex" to appreciate the sensuality of his humanity, and the humanity of his sensuality. That is written all over this encounter in Luke chapter 7. Above all, Jesus was a man of passion who held faith in God's reign as life's highest passion. But these passions—from setting his gaze resolutely to face Jerusalem to the pleasing deliciousness of fine foods—will seamlessly connect if we can remove our binary categories of good versus bad and us versus God, and simply let God's reign in its completeness carry the day with tender judgment and embracing grace. Yours is a question we must allow to come to us a little more because, frankly, we can only talk around the edges rather than play out grand detailed scenarios.

If we find this answer unsatisfying to our modern prejudices and proclivities, maybe we need to reevaluate ourselves, what we expect, and how we approach God. After all, we affirm God has given us everything we need as Creator of male and female, and Redeemer of our brokenness around sexuality, and every other aching divide haunting our existence. Finally, it comes down to this: God is good. Sex is good. And they don't intersect in Jesus' life like a made for TV movie. Next question, please.

. . .

CHAPTER 21 FEMALE COUNTERPOINT

VERLEE A. COPELAND

The Christian church asserts that Jesus was both fully human and fully divine. As a fully human man, we would expect that he had sexual feelings. He clearly expressed his passion through faith in God, as expressed in his teachings and healings. He desired to please God in all things. Jesus was a man well acquainted with physicality, at home in his own skin. He touched the sick, the blind and the outcast. He dined with those perceived at that time to be sinners.

There are those, as you have said, who imagine that Jesus could have been married, or at least desired to be married to Mary Magdalene. Clearly their relationship was at least that of beloved teacher and disciple, if not friend. She was the first to come to him in one version of the resurrection, and the first appointed Apostle whom he sent to proclaim to the others the good news that he was not in the tomb, but had risen. His plea to Mary to refrain from touching him in the garden would indicate that she had in fact embraced him in the past but could not do so now. We can almost feel the tension and sorrow in Mary, as portrayed in the gospel of John. Jesus says to her, "Do not cling to me." She draws back from him at his request, knowing that the man she loves will be unable to touch her in the flesh this side of heaven, again.

If we believe that Jesus was both fully human and fully divine then I clearly agree that he may have had sexual thoughts and feelings, but it would be inconsistent with his nature to have acted on them. His primary purpose as demonstrated through the gospels was to proclaim that the Kingdom of God is at hand. Once he made visible a sign of God's abundant provision for all God's people through the miracle of water to wine at the wedding at Cana in Galilee, after he humbled himself at the hands of his cousin John to be baptized in the waters of the Jordan River, his heart and life course were secured toward heaven.

I believe Jesus' relationship with God and with God's people trumped any personal desire for sexual fulfillment he may have experienced. Given the laws regarding sex outside of marriage, it seems inconceivable that he would have jeopardized the reputation and well-being of another for the sake of personal pleasure or even mutual relationship. There was no provision in Hebraic law for faithful sexual relations outside the bonds of marriage. While it is possible that he married prior to starting his ministry, it seems that there would have been mention of it in the gospels. Such personal details of the disciples' lives were frequently included, such as their profession (fisherman and tax collector), and marital status (Peter's mother-in-law). While Christians confess that Jesus is both fully human and fully divine, the writers of the gospel did not see overt expression of genital sexuality as a central question to his life and work.

We make the claim in our writing that as humans we can love and serve God and live fully and faithfully as sexual creatures. Yet it seems that God and God's call and claim upon Jesus' life required his complete devotion and utter commitment to the work that claimed him after but a few brief years. Whatever his sexual feelings or experience, Jesus clearly embodied the intention of this book. He celebrated the unity of sexuality and spirituality as a man hopelessly in love, if not with only one person, then also with all God's people to God's glory.

· 22 ·

CELIBACY, SEX, AND THE
YUMMINESS OF GOD

Verlee A. Copeland

I am a passionate, single person with a deep and abiding faith. What I yearn for in life is a deeper intimacy with God. How can I more fully express my passion for God as a sexual being who chooses not to be sexually intimate with a partner?

· · ·

Your question points toward the very reason that the Apostle Paul encouraged singleness. You are free to love God passionately with an undivided heart. What a great gift! God created us for joy as human creatures, fully embodied, sexually and spiritually alive. When Jesus exhorted his disciples to love God with their heart, mind, soul and strength, he was encouraging them to love fully with their body, not just their brain. There's nothing in our sacred texts that points us toward loving God only from the neck up, yet many of us act as if we must cut ourselves off from our sexuality in order to be devoted and faithful to God.

This prevailing understanding has complex origins which we will explore, but let me begin by saying that your question is grounded in a long tradition of religious persons, both men and women, who identify themselves in mystical ways as the bride of Christ. The language of Roman Catholic orders resemble the vows of couples that marry. Years ago a local Catholic church was desecrated by vandalism. The hands of a statue of Mary were shattered, windows broken, urine marking the pews. What devastated the priest though was that the tabernacle had been broken, the receptacle that housed the communion bread. He wept as he told me that he felt as if his bride had been raped. He felt he had failed as a priest to protect his beloved. The union of husband and wife is but a symbol of the greater union between Christ and the Curch.

While most of this book addresses faith issues in sexual practice between a husband and a wife, many people have chosen not to marry or have lost their partner, and yet wish to live as fully alive, sexual creatures. For much of history, including the earliest years of the church, celibacy and singleness have been lifted up as the ideal state for devotion. Celibacy does not mean sexless or passionless. Those who view celibacy as a synonym for asexuality have misunderstood its gift. Celibacy is the state of remaining unmarried, a choice historically preferred in order to free the man or woman for greater devotion to God. Celibacy was not intended to be the consolation prize for those who don't have a mate. Further, the call to celibacy by the Apostle Paul took place in the context of a belief that Christ would come again at the close of the Age. This was anticipated in his lifetime, at any moment. This belief created a heightened sense of urgency to devote oneself to sharing Christ with a world imminently expected to end.

When this didn't happen, celibacy was still held up as ideal, even as allowance was made for those called to what became known as the vocation of marriage. The convention of marriage as the normative state for life has a relatively recent history. Martin Luther, in his work on the estate of marriage, addressed the challenges of erotic desire in singleness, and encouraged marriage as an antidote for making vows as religious men and women that they could not keep. Chicago Theological Seminary Professor Scott Haldeman reflected on Luther's work in this way. "His honesty about human frailty, about the power of our sexual drives, and about the grace of a secure and stable relationship life into which such drives could be channeled in order that one might contribute to a productive and faithful household makes this a remarkable pastoral document. Yet his questions are not our own. We contend not so much against a view of marriage as a distant second behind celibacy in terms of the shape of a faithful Christian life, but as the be all and end all of Christian life itself."[1]

In Western culture and in recent times, we have come to worship marriage. We have made an idol of it and sentimentalized family life. We have denigrated the covenant of marriage between a couple by creating a wedding industry that makes mockery of sacred vows and reduces such occasions to an opportunity for overindulgence in food and drink, not to mention the draining of the bank account of whoever pays for the whole thing.

The Apostle Paul in the early Christian church, far from seeing marriage as normative, offered marriage as a concession to the problem of burning passion so great as to interfere with service and devotion to God. In 1 Corinthians 7, Paul rather endorses celibacy for those capable of it, writing to those yet unmarried and to the widows: "I say that it is well for them to remain single as I am. But if they cannot exercise self-control, they should marry. For it is better for them to marry than to be aflame with passion." (7:8–9) Of his allowance for marriage, he writes, "I say this by way of concession, not of command. I wish that all were as I myself am. But each has his own special gift from God, one of one kind and one of another." (7:6–7) Again, Paul expected that Jesus would return any day.

---

1. Scott Haldeman, "A Queer Fidelity: Reinventing Christian Marriage," *Theology and Sexuality* 13/2 (January 2007): 137–52.

He goes on to make the case for celibacy, that is, for remaining unmarried. "Those who marry have worldly troubles, and I would spare you that . . . The unmarried man is anxious about the affairs of the Lord, how to please the Lord; but the married man is anxious about worldly affairs, how to please his wife, and his interests are divided. And the unmarried woman or girl is anxious about the affairs of the Lord, how to be holy in body and spirit; but the married woman is anxious about worldly affairs, how to please her husband." (7:27–34)

Notice that not only is marriage not considered normative but is to be engaged with great caution. The text also does not say that in singleness all passion is dead. Can you imagine anyone more passionate than Paul? It simply allows those who are overwhelmed and distracted by passion to marry so that they are freed to serve God. The point is not whether it is more desirable to marry or not, whether to express passion or not, but rather what state allows the greater freedom to serve God.

It distresses us greatly as pastors that the church has largely ignored the issue of healthy sexuality and Godly passion among single and widowed men and women of faith. Our silence has abdicated responsibility for this conversation, relegating all counsel to the pages of public opinion and cultural myth. People of faith can far more readily obtain advice on how to live the passionate life as single men and women on the Internet or pages of *Cosmopolitan* or *GQ* than in church. We apologize! We've let you down!

There remain a few bright lights in our time, illuminating the relationship between sexuality and spirituality. One such beacon shines through the work of Benedictine brother Father Thomas Keating, who delivered a lecture series at Yale Divinity School in the late 1980s. It seemed shocking to me at the time to witness this aging priest compare the courtship of young lovers to a dating relationship we have with God. He described in detail the movement from hanging around with Jesus, to steady dating. He spoke of the intimacy of shared commitment and of the "yumminess of God." These words fail to adequately convey the sparkle in his eyes or the brightness and passion in his voice as he spoke. Clearly, here was a man in love with God. No one could ever say he was the poorer for his singleness, or that his sexuality was repressed. Father Keating shone.

Celibacy is a spiritual gift that directs spiritual and sexual passion toward the service of God alone. Celibacy does not mean that we are asexual creatures, without sexuality or desire. Rather, celibacy is the state of holy devotion to God and union with God in such a way that human sexual desire is taken up in love of God. This is what celibacy at its best is intended to be: freedom to love God and neighbor rightly and fully without the preoccupations of marriage.

Father Keating's teaching is not without precedent in the church. Mystic writers such as Hildegard of Bingen wrote passionately in the 11th century about their relationship with God. While Hildegard rejected the temptations of fleshly desire and wrote against adultery, she eloquently described female orgasm. How she knew of it, whether from personal experience or counseling other women, remains unclear.

"When a woman is making love with a man, a sense of heat in her brain, which brings with it sensual delight, communicates the taste of that delight during the act and summons forth the emission of the man's seed. And when the seed has fallen into its place, that vehement heat descending from her brain draws the seed to itself and holds it, and soon the woman's sexual organs contract, and all the parts that are ready to open up during the time of menstruation now close, in the same way as a strong man can hold something enclosed in his fist."[2]

---

2. Hildegard of Bingen, *Book of Divine Works*, edited by Matthew Fox (Santa Fe: Bear and Company, 1987).

You may wonder why I include this quote about the expression of sexual passion between a man and woman in your question about passion for God as a single person. Hildegard turned her own passion toward God, rejecting a physical relationship in the flesh with a male partner. Instead, much of her sensuality and passionate writing appear in relationship to her understanding of the Holy Spirit. Her intimacy was with God, not man.

> O fire of the Holy Spirit,
> life of the life of every creature,
> Holy are you in giving life to forms . . .
> O boldest path,
> Penetrating into all places,
> In the heights, on earth,
> And in every abyss,
> You bring and bind all together.
> From you clouds flow, air flies,
> Rocks have their humors,
> Rivers spring forth from the waters
> And earth sweats her green vigor. (*O ignis Spiritus Paracliti*)

Does this sound spiritual? This writing is profoundly spiritual. Does this sound sexual? This writing is also profoundly sexual. What God has joined together in the unity of sexuality and spirituality, let no one put asunder. Let's appreciate what's been said here and what it means to us.

A case can be made that the exquisite desire of human persons for God can only be hinted at, tasted briefly in the intimate context of human relationships. We often reach for one another, but God alone can ultimately satisfy our deepest longing. Prayer really is more intimate than sex, and the ecstasy of a unitive moment with the Divine cannot be touched by the most satisfying orgasm on earth.

Many years ago, a woman came to me in the midst of a discernment process regarding her future vocation as a Christian. She had been praying for God to open her understanding about the course of her future. She had been meeting regularly with her spiritual director, who listened deeply to her questions, helped her form better questions, and to open herself to the movement of the Holy in and through her.

She wanted her pastor to know about an experience that she had shared with no one else. In the course of her discernment process and prayer, she saw Jesus walking towards her, long white robes flowing, gazing at her with the deepest of love in his eyes. To her great surprise, he continued gazing upon her, opening his robe to reveal a fully erect penis. In that moment she experienced a wave of desire for unity with Christ that was at once profoundly sexual, and deeply spiritual. At first she felt the impulse to resist, perhaps out of a perceived inappropriateness. But then she heard him say, "You are mine. You belong to me. I claim you for myself. I will come into you. I will reside in you, and embrace you as my own beloved."

As Christ approached her, she removed her jeans and panties and lay down to receive him. He entered her, face to face, embracing and enfolding her being, such that she experienced a turning inside out, as it were. Though she struggled to find words for it, she understood that Christ had come to her as "yes" to life, inviting her to be taken up by him and through him in an entirely sexual and spiritual way. It was unity. It was ecstasy. It was communion. She had become the bride of Christ.

Does such a story scandalize us? Perhaps no few people feel this way. But the simple truth of God's redemptive power is that there is nothing that God can't use for God to bring us into closer relationship, so that we might be used for God's glory. Though it might seem so in the hearing, there was nothing lewd, prurient nor salacious in her description. Her articulation of the vision was more akin to prayer. Though unwitting and nearly unwilling, this woman was transformed. This is redemption.

Yet we know that we do not all have such mystical experiences, not today, not as a medieval mystic like Hildegard of Bingen. We may not have had a mystical experience of the Holy. We may not know what it is like to enter into Holy union as the bride of Christ. In like manner, we may not have engaged intimately with another human being, male or female. We may never have experienced an orgasm that rocks the universe. We may not even want that.

If what you most want is ever-deepening intimacy with God, there is no other way but to open fully—body, mind and spirit—to the workings of God. In an entirely sexual and spiritual way, we can let God have God's way with us: with our lives, with our thoughts, with our bodies, with our hearts. That's what it means to pray, "Thy will be done." We are confessing that what we most want is not what we prefer but what God wants. We do so through prayer and also through openhearted embrace of the world God has made. Sometimes such engagement is utterly un-selfconscious. It is an awakening, a noticing of life, of breath in movement, of beauty in the world. Passionate engagement with God, as voiced by Father Keating, means hanging out with what God made and loves. To do so is to place us in a position to be awakened by the spirit, to open in the innermost regions to the movement of God in our lives. Now that's sexy.

Whether married or single, this kind of erotic participation in the life of the spirit is available to all. We were made in God's image for such as this.

. . .

CHAPTER 22 MALE COUNTERPOINT

DALE ROSENBERGER

This surprising direction and meaning of this chapter was not already out there and available at large. While this notion of passionate union with our God runs deep and long within Christian tradition, these ideas are counterintuitive to those who filter everything through popular culture and even unsettling among those for whom sexuality and spirituality have existed in permanent divorce.

A couple of thoughts immediately occur to me, Verlee, in light of your time-honored but still radical discussion of intimate union with the Divine supplanting earthly marriage. First, we have observed elsewhere in this book that there is far too much burden placed upon the orgasm to make up for the empty places in life.

Maybe that happens because the orgasm travels too much alone and in isolation when it wasn't meant to. Maybe the passion for God which is called faith best connects with other passions like sex, learning, beauty and justice to round them out and give life a completeness that wells up together into something deserving of words like fulfillment and satisfaction. Maybe all of these passions taken together and lived in concert form a magnificent suspension bridge between heaven and earth, a bridge on which we witness far too little traffic in these secular times. And maybe compared to isolating sex from all these other momentous passions, the orgasm becomes a lonely rope footbridge dangling over a steep and severe chasm, where it feels inadequate. This theme has repeated itself throughout our book.

Second, I remember attending divinity school back in the seventies, a day of aggrieved and militant feminism, where even praying, "Our Father, who art in heaven . . ." in worship was enough to send a pew of angry women to a righteous exit from Marquand

SEX AND THE SPIRIT

Chapel. The objection was that because Jesus is both man and Son of God, women were being neglected, women were being dismissed as inferior, women were being excluded from the power transactions like mercy and grace and salvation. So in the Bible and historic hymns, every mention of Jesus' maleness (pronouns like "he" and "his") were stricken and dismissed as exclusive at best and oppressive at worst.

I asked the question whether at least in one sense the maleness of Jesus was more exclusive of heterosexual men than women. That is, if Freud was even half-right and sexual attraction has much to say about the dynamics surrounding attraction, the guys only attracted to women are the ones left out in the cold with natural attraction as a "starter." Of course, in the seventies that argument fell on deaf ears and was dismissed. But you, Verlee, have just helped revive it. That is my roundabout way of saying that you have spoken truly in this surprising chapter and I have discovered the same from the other side of the gender divide.

23

HOW WE FINALLY RECONCILE BEING SPIRITUAL AND SEXUAL CREATURES

Dale Rosenberger

I grew up as a Christian, and yet I cannot also help but live and breathe as a fully sexual creature. The tension between them feels impossible at times. So how do the two get reconciled?

• • •

First, let's say that if the church sends mixed messages about sex, God does not. Sex is God's good gift. Period. It is finer than the taste of fresh raspberries, dappled sunlight on a cool summer morning, the scent of a newborn baby's fragrant tender scalp, or robins singing outside your window after a long frozen winter. Sex was God's idea, not ours. We are incapable of creating anything so lovely, even if we are fully capable of ruining it. If we believe in the God of Genesis, who created us male and female and gladly declared that plan good, then we know God is enthusiastically in favor of sex. So what throws us off the rails as we live, traveling simultaneously down the twin tracks of spirituality and sexuality?

The problem is sex, like all powerful and precious gifts, is vulnerable to abuse. The Latin *corruptio optimi pessima* means that in the corruption of the very best things, we find the very worst things. So as unfaithfulness and regret enter the picture of our sexuality, they cast a long shadow. Still, blaming all of that on sex is like vilifying pizza as unhealthy when the real issue is eating five heaping pieces instead of two with salad.

We can't blame God either. Sex is one more magnificent God-given gift we clumsily botch. Think of it: our sexuality tenderly and bracingly connects us with each other; its dynamic pull and creative tension are the yin and yang of our being, propelling us through our day. Its ecstasies suggest heavenly and eternal bliss beyond this mortal life, about as close as anywhere in this earthly lifetime. Made as sexual creatures, the challenge is how to live out of that dynamic polarity with more celebration than shame, and with more happiness than remorse. The challenge is to live out the radiance of being made in God's image.

I don't mean to blithely wave sunshine at the all-too-real anxiety of your question. For our sexuality presents a fearful dilemma and real burden for many. Sex is a big stage where we feel alone, on exhibit, and challenged by the character assigned to us. All of this begins in adolescence. Sex can make some feel farther from, not more connected to partner, to self, and to God. Sex can drive wedges into relations with significant others and the Significant Other—God. For starters that is because for some of us, merely having deep, strong, abiding sexual energy means feeling simply wrong or even corrupt for being made that way. How can we make peace with who we truly are, with how God made us? Really, this book is written for unspoken queries like this.

Some people aren't as deeply sexual as others, and that is o.k.—unless our sex-saturated society shames us for preferring needlepoint or watching the NBA. Others have clearly known themselves as deeply sexual beings since they were small children. It was not something they chose so much as something that mysteriously chose them. Such as these might gather at a party, for example, and feel deep wellsprings of attraction involuntarily stirring toward other couples, friends, and guests behind all of the polite, civilly appropriate facades. All of this just kicks in without throwing a switch. Their lifelong secret passion remains undetected as they maintain a wholesome domestic façade over the churning cauldron that is their loins. That reminds me of how Christian author Frederick Buechner described himself, for example, as a "secret sensualist and a would be-believer."[1]

As this gravitational pull constantly exerts itself—new every day—we can feel like something is seriously wrong with us, like we are less faithful, even for feelings not acted upon. We can get appalled at ourselves and begin to dislike our natural sexual essence and energy as a burden. Can such as these be convinced that our sexuality is God's good gift? That's not always easy, even though it somehow remains true. The gift of sex is like every other spiritual gift. If God gifts us in a certain way, and that gift doesn't find adequate and rightful expression in our living, that gift will make us unhappy. It is true for our sexuality, true for intelligence or athleticism, true for every good gift that God gives us.

As humans made in God's image, we don't stop having and being flesh just because we give God the final word over our destiny. And God doesn't want us to do so. We may be heaven bound, but for now we are decidedly earthbound. Let's face it, wherever we gather, sparks are going to fly. And that's just the point, isn't it? In many ways the church has missed it, getting co-opted by self-appointed "decent" elements of society content to pretend sexuality can be ignored and suppressed, or that it is by nature inglorious. The example of the Pharisees in the Gospels in contrast with the person and presence of Jesus teaches us that as we attempt to become even more "decent" than God is, human beings do unto oth-

1. Frederick Buechner, *The Alphabet of Grace* (San Francisco: Harper and Row, 1970), 14, 45.

ers negative things that displease God. And we sadly miss out on positive things for ourselves that we end up regretting later.

I recall summer Bible camp where the sexual interaction between girls and boys was real, but ever so mild, especially by today's standards. After a few days of infatuated teens holding hands, one day at lunch we were subjected to a stern lecture about "pairing off." We were told that the boys and girls noticing each other, stealing a furtive good night kiss or touching a girl's budding breast, were "ruining things" for everyone. As though this could be otherwise among healthy boys and girls who had waited all year to see one another, set amid the splendor of Lake Michigan beaches and forests, beholding the unfolding glory of bodies developing in swimsuits, pushing each other off the raft, going off into the deep water, then gasping to the surface, watching sensual magic precede us up the ladder for it all to repeat and play itself out over again. Was this really so unhealthy and displeasing to God? Had God set us all up for naught with the charming differences in our bodies and heart-pounding parallels in our desire?

That midday scold didn't increase our respect for the church as knowing the score and fearlessly telling the truth in delicately vulnerable parts of our lives. It did not increase the church's credibility. It made the church into what Camille Paglia calls a "sky cult," removed from, unacquainted with and fearful of the human earthen temple within which we live. The church still "didn't get" what we gawky, gangly adolescents already imperfectly apprehended about being human. They imagined they could hide it from us. The church was stuck in the childish Sunday School faith Paul commented on: "When I was a child, I spoke like a child, I thought like a child, I reasoned like a child; when I became an adult, I put an end to childish ways." (1 Corinthians 13:11)

Sometimes we feel unease or fear within us when the real problem lies beyond us, outside of us. And it is hard to know the difference. It is distressing to feel wrong about who we most truly and essentially are as men and women, about how we were made, most especially when God placed this desire within us. This is one of those cases. A first response to your question is you should not be put in a position of having to choose between your spirituality as God's beloved child and your sensuality as a human being. While acknowledging we do need careful help in boundaries with a gift so powerful as our sexuality, still the church might repent of this sin as a false choice.

I recall what helped turn this all around for me as a young person. When I was in high school, I took a course in the Bible as literature. I became friends with two young women who were glamorous, shapely, attractive and brimming with passion. But our relationship was hatched as and always remained one of genuine platonic friendship. With no "pursuer" and "pursued," we were freed up for candid learning about things sensual and erotic from the view of the opposite sex in a way not otherwise possible. Lana was a year older than I and went off to a Protestant college on the west coast. Ellen was more effervescently blue-collar Roman Catholic, but the bravest of us three about her passion and desire, with a hilarious candor and flip attitude.

We would have what we called "sex and body talks," standing in the hall outside the lunchroom beholding the full variety of young women and men parading by us, or in the classroom after reading about the Pentateuch or the parables of Jesus. We felt safe to ask each other what we found attractive, what struck us as sexy, what turned us on, what everyone else seemed to hold as standards, and what kind of lover we yearned for and hoped to become. This was high school in another era and we were barely sexually active. But the funny, insightful, and sexy sharing of us three, learning about the sultry mysteries of what the opposite sex thought and why, propelled us into dating more self-possessed and with a greater sense of confidence. Our regular talks were funny and naughty sometimes, as honest and idiosyncratic as we were. They were human and helpful. They seemed forbidden and wrong, but besides being groundbreaking for our

likes, they were helpful, chaste, and modest, and doubtless holy
in the eyes of God.

I remember how special those relationships felt in assisting
each other to find our way. I also remember as a Christian feeling
like I was doing something terribly wrong by being so honest about
sexuality and eroticism with the opposite sex, when that sort of
conversation—even being friends as male and females—found so
little sanction anywhere in society. What seemed steamy and forbidden then now seems like a minor miracle in that we looked each
other in the eye, dared honesty about our inmost selves, and got
over our blushing to share something vulnerable and precious
about ourselves. At a time when we barely knew who we were sexually, we were able to see things from the perspective of the opposite sex. That was a bigger gift than it seemed at the time.

I believe that, with few exceptions, the church falls way short
in helping us in ways like this, in leading us to be the male and female sexual creatures God intended. The life of the church has
suffered demonstrably for it. This is not to condemn or reject the
church as God's chosen vehicle of salvation. Rather it is to say,
even like the best and most loving mothers, all have serious and
abiding flaws. The Christian faith has truly not done well here.
We have shared this dialogue within this volume in the hope that
the church can and will do better.

Really, what's amazing is that some—apparently, like yourself—manage to preserve both identities, sexual and spiritual, despite the church treating the two natures as irreconcilable, pushing
sex to the sideline, and forcing you to choose. "What if they find
out?" you wonder. Frankly, if they found out who you really are,
the church might learn something vital to being alive and essential
to the task of Christian ministry. In posing the dilemma as you
have, the church should be the one interviewing you, to grasp how
you have managed to cope and flourish, probably imperfectly like
the rest of us, balancing these two natures of sex and spirit without
giving up either one.

"So how did you manage to keep both sensuality and spirituality alive?" we might ask you. My guess is it has something to do with your ability to draw a line between sexual attraction and fantasy, on one side, and sexual advances and initiative on the other. Christianity has given the impression that as soon as we feel sexual feelings or entertain sexual images of another who fires our imagination, the wall has been breached, the invader has entered, the battle is over, and the war is lost. I am not sure that is the message we want to bring forward as people of faith. If it is, we are in deep trouble.

First, much of this borders on involuntary, as in DNA. We can find ourselves steamed almost before we realize it, almost like we find ourselves feeling fearful or lonely before we know it. Second, if we know where sexual fantasy ends and actual overtures begin, fantasy can embellish our sensuality without delivering us over to circumstances where we are compromised. Frankly, this awareness is how people have coped anyway, whether the church acknowledges it or not. Our sexual tensions get reconciled and recycled like this every day, everywhere we go, year in and year out.

I find something heroic in your struggle to be true to both your spiritual and sensual selves without compromise, almost like Galileo insisting on a heliocentric solar system despite the church. Your struggle to reconcile sensual and spiritual selves pains you, as it does us all. But how you endure the tension reminds me of Huck Finn helping the slave Jim escape down the Mississippi, despite social sanctions. Well, Huck figures, I guess I'm forever lost now. It's settled, on with it, come what may. This comes close to what Augustine, no stranger to carnality himself, meant in saying, "Sin boldly." Here in the courage of our nature and convictions, daring what "decent society" dubs wrong, in utter truthfulness we can end up justified in God's eyes. I hear this daring in your struggle.

How did the church muddle into this division? It has nothing to do with Jesus. When we perceive Jesus in the Gospels, apart from our preconceived childish celestial images of him, he rests easy both in his humanness and his maleness. Jesus, for example, was actually more at ease around women—even loose women, like the Syrophoenician woman or the adulterous woman caught in the act—than he was around the overwrought power-broker males in the temple establishment. Jesus hung around with fishermen, for goodness' sake, noted for salty language and chippy jokes. As the wedding reception at Cana of Galilee crashed to a halt, he revived it by changing large jars of water into wine such as they had never tasted. Bring on the last course! Let the dancing and merriment continue! Let celebration carry the day! Jesus was unafraid of passion, because for him, faith in God was not a dry set of rules. For Jesus, faith was life's highest and most daring passion. And faith relates to every other passion.

So where did Christ's church go wrong? This is a complex history. But in a nutshell, instead of turning back toward our Jewish roots during our first embryonic centuries of theological clarification in our spiritual identity, we turned toward Greek philosophy for the sake of respectability, moving out into the world. Judaism is delightfully and unabashedly earthy in its outlook toward sexuality. To be faithful, rabbis encourage Jews to make love to their spouses on the Sabbath. Sexual intercourse makes that holy Sabbath day even holier, they insist. The Christian church has not been as bold in pointing out the obvious.

Greek philosophy, even before Plato, was marked by rigorous division between body and spirit, flesh and soul, tactile and theoretical. The physical realm (like bodies) was tainted; the world of ideas (like theology) was pure. For the Greeks, material things were inferior to lofty spirit. In this, our two natures were set in opposition as never before, and the division still haunts the church.

Never mind that by taking on our flesh, arriving in the body of Jesus, God confronted this division and abolished this painful chasm at the heart of being human for all time. What God had joined together, theologians and church authorities put asunder. Why did we take this alien turn rather than moving back toward our Jewish roots? Judaism and Christianity squabbled like rival cousins during the first centuries as the newer faith unfolded. We imagined that to make our own mark of respectability in the world, we had to scaffold the faith with larger and fancier ideologies. It was a big mistake—at least in our theology of sexuality.

All I know is that for too long the church has created and endorsed deeply divided selves, and we cannot afford that neglect anymore. In a day when authentic faithfulness is eclipsed by encroaching secularity, we must equip the people of God better than this. In a word, we are sorry. We can do better. And I believe that we will.

· · ·

CHAPTER 23 FEMALE COUNTERPOINT

VERLEE A. COPELAND

You have said that the church sends mixed messages about sex. Let me respond that I disagree. What message? The church neglects to send any message at all, even a church as progressive as the one we serve. We don't talk about sex, teach about sex or preach about sex. Socially, we talk about everything else: yesterday's golf game, the Blackhawk's Stanley Cup victory, and losses from our retirement account. We're willing to describe in intimate detail our latest health crisis, down to the bloody details of our dripping sinuses. But move the conversation south of the navel, and conversation stops altogether.

I recently experienced this phenomenon at a men's club meeting at church. Sitting at the table with a half dozen men I know well, they discussed the greatest joys in retirement. One gentleman expounded on his improving bridge game, another remarked on the travels he enjoyed with his wife. A third had taken up tennis. Everyone joined the conversation with tales of their own best card game, recent trips to see the kids out west, or the impact of their knee replacement.

Finally I turned to one gentleman who had been very quiet, and asked him how he had been devoting his retirement years. "Sex," he said levelly. "And how's that going for you?" I asked. "Very well, thank you," he said. That was it. Then it was as if the man had disappeared. No one acknowledged him or contributed to the conversation. Everybody froze, wildly searching for a graceful way to change the topic.

The silence of the church sends a clear and compelling message that sex is not o.k. Here you and I profoundly agree, Dale. The church has brought shame on itself for failing to equip the people of God to live faithfully and wholly as sexual and passionate men and women. No wonder so many people think church is boring. We have failed on our end of the bargain by talking much about things that are important but not essential. If we can't talk about sex, then we can't talk about the God who created our sexuality and called it good. Yes, we can do better. It's never too late to do the right thing. For God's sake and our own, let's give one another permission to discuss all manner of things hot and holy. Let the conversation begin.

· 24 ·

THE ROMANCE OF
HEAVEN AND EARTH

Verlee A. Copeland

Sometimes it seems like we're supposed to have wild and crazy sex when we're young and single, and get it out of our system, settling into good but not as interesting sex when we're married. What's the difference between making love in the context of the covenant of marriage and just having sex?

· · ·

Do you still remember that first real kiss? It happened for Anna at an overnight slumber party at her best friend Diane's house. After the usual popcorn and movies, giggles and gossip, there was a knock at the door. John stood outside, halfway through puberty at the age of fourteen, whispering in his newly changed baritone voice, "Anybody wanna go steal a watermelon?" Anna and Diane looked at each other, Diane rolling her eyes in reticence that her Mom would kill her if she got caught as Anna slipped out the door.

Halfway down the block John slipped his hand around hers and she held her breath. By the end of the street he turned toward her and put his arms around her drawing her into his chest. He reached down gently and cupped her chin between his thumb and forefinger, tipping her face up towards him as he leaned down to brush her lips against his. To her shock it felt as if she had been mildly electrocuted. An indescribable energy in unfamiliar places rendered her immobile, and then he kissed her again.

They never made it to the grocery store where he had suggested they make off with a melon. Instead, they stood glued in the half shadow of a streetlight no more than a block from home, tasting and experiencing the delicious mystery of budding sexuality.

That innocent experience took place more than fifty years ago. Today's adolescents more frequently negotiate oral sex by the age of fourteen, with the hook up, or casual intercourse between mere acquaintances considered a not uncommon if accepted practice. When one mother caught her eighth grade daughter having sex in the basement, the daughter said, "Don't worry, Mom," we're not dating." These parents thought her too young to date and had not allowed her to go out for the evening unless in a group of friends, supervised by a parent. It never occurred to them that their daughter would sexually engage in such a way as this, not only outside of marriage, but also outside the context of a serious relationship.

Fast forward to one experience of this author in her twenties. Raised in a Christian home, I had always believed that sex was intended for marriage. Most of my friends that had pre-marital sex did so with young men they believed to be their future husbands. Whether or not it worked out that way, there remained the expectation that fourth base and a home run were intended for marriage. Good girls didn't sleep around, and we didn't hang out with girls who did.

It was therefore a great surprise to me at an early morning study session when one of the group members showed up slightly disheveled and clearly sleep-deprived. "What happened to you?" I asked. "I met this most amazing guy at a party last night and we had mind-blowing sex all night long."

"You had sex all night long?" I couldn't imagine such a thing. "What do you mean?" I asked.

"You know," she said. "We had sex for a couple of hours and then we slept a little bit, and then we woke up and had sex again, and then we slept a little more, and then when it started to get light we woke up and had sex one last time just as the sun rose. It was unbelievable!"

She could say that again! It wasn't that I had trouble imagining such intensity of desire or such physical endurance. It was that I couldn't imagine opening to that much vulnerability with a virtual stranger. To be honest, I still can't. Yet I've lived long enough to know that people do report having "mind-blowing sex" with people they've just met. Some pay for it, for the illusion of having someone pretend that they are special or beautiful or handsome or gifted in the love department or particularly well-endowed. More often these days, this illusion is created for free by willing participants who perhaps have not fully considered the consequences of their behavior.

We might think of this as fast food sex. Theologian Anthony B. Robinson writes about this in his work *Common Grace*. "Recently I heard someone use the phrase the McDonaldization of sex. What was meant by that phrase I think, is that sex, like so much else, has come to be seen as accessible, convenient, and immediate. Why wait? 'You deserve a break today!'"[1] When we read the statistics on obesity in America, it is clear that a growing number of folks settle for fast food as a diet staple. It's quick, it's easy, it doesn't require much social interaction, and it's temporarily satisfying.

Many people settle for mind-blowing pre-marital, extra-marital and what I will call "stranger" sex. It appears to have benefits if you consider sex to be a benefit contract. "I'll touch you if you touch me, I'll bring you to pleasure if you'll bring me pleasure." There's a

---

1. Anthony B. Robinson, *Common Grace: How to Be a Person and Other Spiritual Matters* (Seattle: Sasquatch Books, 2006).

freedom that comes from not knowing or carrying any relationship burden or baggage or any future obligation. There's also a kind of thrill when engaging in behavior that is slightly dangerous: riding fast on a motorcycle, bungee jumping, sky diving, even stepping onto a decrepit roller coaster at the local amusement park.

While fast food sex might be exhilarating in the present moment, the satisfaction is short-lived. It sets us up for expecting that our marriages will be or should be mutually beneficial all the time in order to be satisfying. There have been many times through the years when a couple has come to me for marital counseling with the complaint, "I'm just not that satisfied with the relationship anymore," or "I'm not in love with her as I once was," or "My needs aren't being met." I'm always so tempted to say, "And your point is . . . ?" This would be more polite I suppose than what I really want to say which is: "So what?"

Stay with me here. I'm really a pretty good pastoral counselor, or so I'm told. The point I'm making is that marriage is not a mutual benefit contract that promises satisfaction in every moment. In fact, when talking with couples who have been married fifty years or more, they often say they've had forty good years and they are ecstatic about that. I have never known a person who proclaims that they get exactly what they want every moment of life, unless they have narcissistic personality disorder. In that case, they may think they are happy but everyone around them is miserable because that person's happiness has exacted a dear price from everyone else!

Marriage is different than this. Marriage between two persons of faith who love one another creates a context for deepening intimacy over time. Mind-blowing sex happens sometimes for married couples, but that is just the beginning. Making love with the one to whom you have pledged your love, your life and your mutual devotion to God provides nourishment that lingers far longer than one night.

The marriage covenant creates a sacred space for sexuality that can be explored intimately and deeply over time. A shared commitment to faithfulness with our spiritual partner, lover and friend makes possible the fullest expression of erotic sensuality, or Song of Solomon sexuality as God created it to be.

Some people mistakenly believe that married sex is good girl sex. Conversing one afternoon with a hairdresser who grew up in what she described as a traditional, Roman Catholic family from Eastern Europe, she remarked that her mother told her that sex was only for marriage, and that the church told her that sex was only for making babies. "I haven't had any babies for twenty-five years. So I feel guilty every time I have sex with my husband."

This conversation reminds me of a slightly scandalous hit song of 2013 called "Blurred Lines." Robin Thicke sings: "You're such a good girl . . . you know you want it."[2] Though the song attracted controversy, Thicke has been with his wife, actress Paula Patton, since they were teenagers. The song was her idea, according to an Internet interview. Thicke comments that his wife has always been a good girl, but that the longer they are married the more he gets her to be a bad girl. While we can't speak for Robin Thicke and his wife, they make a great point.

As ministers of the United Church of Christ, we clearly assert that it's o.k. to be a bad girl/bad boy, a little bit naughty, with your partner and within your marriage. For all the prohibitions against sex before marriage, whether those prohibitions are followed or not, marriage creates a faithful no-holds-barred arena for experiencing your heart's deepest desire and fulfilling your greatest sexual fantasies. We know that some religious communities will not agree. Yet we believe that if God made us sexy and sexual and called creation good, then marriage is the place and now is the time.

If what you want is fast food sex with your wife, get some take out and eat in. Have a great time. A quick frolic in the hay before work, right before dinner or at half time during the big

2. Robin Thicke and Pharell Williams, "Blurred Lines," on *Blurred Lines* 2013 © Star Track Recordings.

game sounds great. But there's much more. The thrill of instant gratification between groping lovers has nothing on the lingering touch of an older couple scarred by the wounding experiences of shared life. Let me recount one such recent observation.

Walking along a crowded boardwalk near the beach town where I live, I heard the strains of a German polka band playing from the ocean park gazebo. This is hardly considered sexy music by anybody's taste. Internally I made a bit of fun at the music and the couple of hundred old folks planted in folding chairs on the lawn, listening. But then I noticed something. In the center of the boardwalk an aged German couple, plump, wrinkled and folded in all the usual places, twirled one another in a most elegant dance. In his adoration for this eighty-something woman, he seemed to be seeing her, not only as she once was when first they danced sixty years ago, but adoringly as she is now. She in turn captured his gaze with a look of joy undiminished by the cane she left propped against the bench in order to swirl gingerly into his arms. Their practiced turns and dips reflected the years of shared joy and misery common to any life, clearly made bearable by their love for one another. Couples holding hands stopped to gaze at them. Children held sand toys, teenagers pocketed cell phones, gaping. This couple bore witness in a few moments to what is possible between two people who love one another for a lifetime.

In the movie *When Harry Met Sally* you may recall the restaurant scene where Meg Ryan fakes an orgasm and the woman at the next table says to the waitress, "I'll have what she's having." Meg was imitating sex while the elderly German couple were making love, right there in plain view. I don't know about you, but wouldn't it be great to have what they're having?

Making love, sharing intimacy, experiencing an erotic sensuality and sexuality that matures over time, does not happen automatically or for every married couple. Many couples grow distanced over time, by unhealed woundedness or outright neglect. When they stay together, it is sometimes to lead parallel lives held together by love of family, religious conviction, or fear that there isn't a better way.

There are couples however, who do the real, transformative work of growing an authentic relationship, grounded in love of God and mutual friendship. They learn the secrets of compassion, acceptance and forgiveness. They stand the test of time together, coming up beneath one another, each in turn, supporting the other through the inevitable hard stuff of life. Whether we are married or single we become familiar with disappointment, discouragement and grief if we are blessed with the number of years. When we live in covenant as a married couple, we don't get to skip the hard stuff, we simply find our way through it together. That's sexy.

It has been said that for men, sex is the glue that binds the relationship together and expresses the love that makes ordinary things possible. While for women, being loved in the ordinary things makes sex possible. I don't know if this is true or not, certainly not for all men, nor for all women. But I do know this. Making love with your husband, your wife, can be as accessible and nourishing as daily bread.

Song of Solomon sexuality invites us to love-making as feast. God sets the table by creating us whole and beautiful and perfect in God's sight, lumps, bumps and all. God gives us one another to taste, touch, lick, explore with the tenderest of ecstasy and purest delight.

There's something about a certain smell that carries with it the memory of love: the smell of soap on wet skin when your man gets out of the shower, or the scent of his neck in that hollow place where you rest your head. As you make love he turns toward you and your eyes meet. He pauses for a moment to gaze into your eyes. He realizes how lucky he is to have you, and whispers this into your skin as the intimate dance continues.

When a couple deeply committed through the years in such a way as this make love to one another, the world becomes still. With the breathlessness of the adolescent girl experiencing her first kiss, we can experience the abandoned joy of being relished, savored, and enjoyed. What greater joy can there be than to bring intense pleasure and delight to someone we love?

God gives us healthy marriage as a safe place to be wholly vulnerable, naked and without guile. While the world judges and finds us wanting, a faithful love embraces the lover in a way that overlooks every perceived flaw. Like other spiritual gifts, lovemaking builds up the other. Here in the intimacy of this sacred space we can do no wrong. There is no need to hold back, or save something for later. It isn't as if by using up all our passion there will be nothing left. An ever-flowing stream of expressed desire refills our passion like a living well. Making love with our lover and friend involves whatever brings us to the peak of ecstasy, the "Oh my moment of O."

Some people think church ladies a stuffy lot who pooh pooh sexuality and wear their knickers to bed. That image blew apart for good when the women from my discipleship group threw a surprise shower for my wedding as their young pastor. I thought they might get a little risqué and give me massage oil along with tickets to the theater, new bath towels and a coupon for a nice local restaurant. Instead they pitched in and bought a white feather boa, see-through negligee and edible undies. It was a surprise party all right! I first learned from them what I later came to learn from countless stories over time: strong faith and steamy sex go together.

One of the most faithful Christian women I know exudes sexuality, well into her seventies. Years ago on an outing with other women from the church, we stood by the shore recounting the riches of the day. Sharing a snack of fresh fruit, she remarked that she could tie a cherry stem into a knot in her mouth. We looked at her incredulous, waiting. After a few moments of concentration, out it popped, a perfect knot. "I bet your husband loves that," another women exclaimed aloud. "Oh he does," she replied, grinning, a decided twinkle in her eye. What they do at home in bed can be left to the imagination, but this story confirms once again what we all need to hear. When sex and the spirit become the romance of Heaven and earth, it is God's good and perfect gift. Always!

. . .

CHAPTER 24 MALE COUNTERPOINT

DALE ROSENBERGER

Who knew? The hottest sex is not about envying the imagined paroxysms of idealized supple and slender celebrity bodies, bought and sold as icons of pop culture's highest and most desirable forms of pleasure. No, the hottest sex also happens to be the holiest sex in that it is about getting caught up in each other's common life purpose and shared sacrifice through thick and thin. And when that couple's shared connection further becomes caught up in God's ultimate dreams for humankind, with God showing the way forward together through sacrificial love before us and after us through thick and thin, well, the quotient for incendiary sex goes ballistically off the chart. We are talking about Cape Canaveral blasts here.

Who knew? The vapors of details like standing by and silently enduring together through the good and the bad, and the mists of living life in the sacred presence of a transcendent God occasion the most potent volatility for explosive and satisfying sex. Perhaps at some level we suspect this is true. Perhaps that is why our most common exclamation upon our orgasmic release is, "Oh God, oh God, oh God!" Let's face it, this is the highest court in the universe for whatever transpires in life, especially something so universally esteemed as our sexuality.

Remember, Verlee is talking about the difference between having sex and making love. Lauren Winner has helpfully likened this difference to going to the Epcot Center for French food on plastic plates versus visiting Burgundy to partake of a seven-course dinner in a French household where the family knows the names of the purveyors who aged the cheese, fermented the wine, caught the fish, raised the cattle, and lovingly tended the garden-fresh produce. It is just no contest.

Years after her divorce, my wife started dating only because a good friend practically forced her to assemble a profile—she wrote it for her—and pushed her to get back out there. When my profile started talking to her profile in the way of online dating, and when my future wife first saw that I had served as a Christian pastor for decades, she dismissively lamented, "Yeah, right. Can you see that? It's too bad. He seems interesting. But I'm just not the 'goody-goody' type." At that her friend upbraided her. "What is the matter with you? Do you believe in heaven?" Yes, my wife responded. "Do you believe in Jesus?" Yes, my wife said again. "Then what is the problem? Just go out with him and see what he is like!" She was completely flabbergasted. Of course, the cultural stereotype of people devoted to God is just the opposite: we are supposed to be inhibited and stultified people barely aware of life's sparks of festivity and light. But that moment of conversion made possible her attraction to me, and therefore also made our marriage.

While I would like to think of myself as good in the image of Christ, I am not a goody-goody. The point is that popular culture is peddling a bill of goods here, and we have been bought and sold as a people. Sexuality and spirituality are connected, not just in some minimal way to meet biological necessities like the conceiving of children. Sexuality and spirituality are further linked in unmatched ways in the depths of our guts and in the loftiest hope for an ardent physicality that renews itself every time it is given away to exhaust itself, over and over again. That is what Paul the Apostle meant in the love chapter of 1 Corinthians 13: "Love never ends." Amen.